MW01070794

PASSING IT ON
THE INHERITANCE AND USE
OF SUMMER HOUSES
& FAMILY COTTAGES

JUDITH HUGGINS BALFE

— INCLUDES THE NEW & REVISED WORKBOOK —
HOW TO PASS IT ON
KEN HUGGINS

PASSING IT ON

THE INHERITANCE AND USE
OF SUMMER HOUSES
& FAMILY COTTAGES

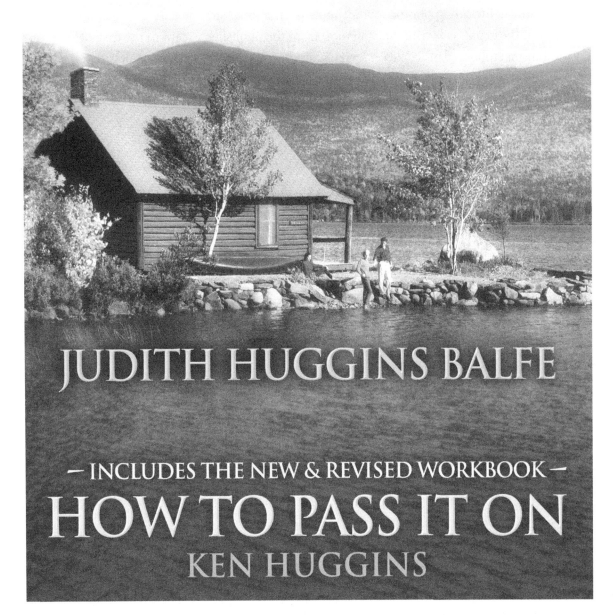

JUDITH HUGGINS BALFE

— INCLUDES THE NEW & REVISED WORKBOOK —
HOW TO PASS IT ON
KEN HUGGINS

Inheritance Publications
an imprint of Rotolo Media
160 37th Street Lindenhurst, New York 11757 (631) 956-0998
www.HowToPassItOn.com
ISBN: 978-1-61010-500-2

©2015 Rotolo Media
All rights reserved under International and Pan-American Copyright Conventions. No part of this book may be reproduced in any form, or by any means, electronic or mechanical, including photocopying, and informational storage and retrieval systems without the expressed written permission from the publisher, except in the case of brief quotations embodied in articles or reviews or promotional/advertising/catalog materials. For additional information or permissions, address all inquiries to the publisher.

Huggins, Judith Huggins Balfe,
Huggins, Ken
Passing It On / by Judith Huggins Balfe & How To Pass It On / by Ken Huggins
p. cm.
An "Inheritance Publications" book
Inheritance Publications an imprint of Rotolo Media
ISBN: 978-1-61010-500-2
Recommended Dewey Decimal Classifications: 346.730, 336.276
Suggested Subject Headings:
1. Estate Planning
2. Inheritance Financial Planning
I. Title

The book and cover design for this title are by Michael Rotolo. It is typeset in the Minion typeface by Adobe Inc. and is quality manufactured in the United States on acid-free paper stock. To discuss the publication of your manuscript or out-of-print book, please contact Michael Rotolo/Rotolo Media at www.michaelrotolo.com.

MANUFACTURED IN THE UNITED STATES OF AMERICA

To my parents, brothers and sister,
husband and children,
nieces and nephews,
and the patient folks who have
been willing to marry into this family—
past, present and future

CONTENTS

PREFACE

Wise was the choice which led our sires
To kindle here their household fires
And share the large content of all
Whose lives in pleasant places fall.

More dear as years and years advance
We prize the old inheritance —
And feel as far and wide we roam
That all we seek we leave at home.

(In a Maine summer house, built in
1896 and still in the same family)

With all the current attention being given to family dissolution, institutions which promote family solidarity over the generations are usually ignored by the media and researchers. A summer house may contribute to either outcome: if the heirs disagree over their inheritance and its use, the fighting may lead them to sell it and never speak to each other again. Thereby they earn the fate to which Dante consigned traitors to kindred in The Inferno: two brothers who killed one another over their inheritance ended up entwined together in an icy eternity of hatred in the lowest, most frozen level of Hell. However, if the founders and their heirs use the summer house wisely, it serves as the sacred hearth for all, to which they return for personal and familial renewal as promised by the poem above. While well aware of the hellish possibility, those who appear in this study fall into the latter, happier situation. How do they manage to do so, when so many others fail?

The question may seem trivial to those concerned with such critical issues as homelessness, domestic violence, and children in poverty, let alone the bitter conflicts found on the international scene, but it is not trivial to the many people who have inherited and share such property, as they deal with the challenges it presents to family solidarity, as well as the means of cementing it. Nor is it trivial in its implications for society, as we shall see in conclusion.

Many of the findings and much of the analysis of this study are applicable to those owning various types of winter vacation homes, such as a ski lodge in Colorado or Vermont, a condo in Florida or a villa in St. Maarten. While the legal issues discussed in Chapter 13 are relevant to all such vacation homes, the major difference with summer houses is in the likely expectations of the heirs. Why?

Only a few of my respondents are new "founders" of a summer house—couples who have only recently built or bought one, whose dynastic purpose or its success is not yet determined. Instead, while some of those whom I interviewed were indeed the founders, their children and grandchildren are on the scene and have spent significant amounts of their childhood and even adult summers enmeshed in a network of extended kin at the summer house. This reflects the primary purpose of the summer house in the eyes of such founders: it is to be used and enjoyed by successive generations to enhance family cohesion through a shared cultural experience, regardless of age or interest.

In contrast, those who have more recently purchased or built winter vacation homes seldom envision them as the location for extended family gatherings over several generations. As the owners of a Florida condo put it to me, while the place was purchased to serve as a winter "escape" for them, their children and grandchildren, they expect the children to see it as a "cash cow" to be rented whenever possible rather than as a "sacred hearth" to return to for emotional warmth. Central air-conditioning does not lend itself to that metaphor. As for winter ski resorts, while the hearth may be blazing, inter-generational activities are likely to be so keyed to athletics that non-athletic family members are likely to have no interests in the place other than financial ones. Thus the emotional, psychological and social complexity of the issues discussed here concerning the sharing and passing-on of use, ownership and responsibility for summer houses among extended family members are far less germane to other types of vacation homes, even as the legal structures for their resolution may be very similar. Accordingly, in the analysis that follows, whenever the term "*summer house*" is used, it is to be considered as inclusive of other vacation homes and jointly owned/used family properties. As that is not usually the case, I will use the term "summer house" throughout while accepting various alternate meanings to include— "vacation home", "family cottage", "weekend home", "family-retreat", etc. I will also clarify the importance of the fact that a "summer house" is not a "home" in the sense of a primary residence, hence my constant use of the term "house" throughout.

My interest in this subject is professional as a sociologist, but even more it is personal: I am a summer house heir. As second born among four siblings, with the other three I have inherited shares in two cottages in Nantucket. They were built by our parents respectively in 1959 and 1969 on adjoining lots. Typical Cape Cod cottages constructed by a local carpenter at my father's direction, they are modest in size, style and decor. However, they are in a prime location that has since been developed by others with much greater wealth, thereby escalating their assessment and the profit we would have if we, as an extended family, decided to sell them. (Were we to do so, the new owner would undoubtedly tear them down and replace them with something much larger. Such "scraping" of the original summer houses with this intent has occurred on several properties near our own.)

Each of the four of us has two children, now all adult, and my older brother has five grandchildren of his own. Our parents always spent the entire summer in the 1969 cottage and until our mother's death in 1997 (our father died in 1985), the four of us and our own families took turns in the other. As our father planned his estate to structure the ownership of the two cottages among the four of us, at our mother's death the oldest brother was granted the right to buy up the shares in the older house which were held by the other three, that money then being used as an "endowment" to support the mainte-nance of the newer one, which we three were thereafter to own with no remaining claim to the first house.

When our father announced this agreement, having reached it independently with my older brother (who after all would be putting up the money), the immediate response was a great deal of quarreling based on sibling rivalry that after childhood had been neither acknowledged nor resolved: Why hadn't the other three supposedly equal siblings been consulted at outset? However, as the four of us began to work through these disagree-ments to our present state of good feeling and cooperation in managing the properties and our use of them, as a sociologist I was sure we were not alone in our difficulties, yet I was also sure that others had similarly resolved them.

Thus in 1994 I began to solicit respondents who would tell me how they have been able to "pass it on" successfully. Through strategic classified ads and a great deal of word of mouth, along with news coverage of the first academic paper I delivered and published on the issues (Akasie 1996; Balfe 1995; Dart 1995; Tyson 1995; Volgenau 1995), 1 have been in touch with some 125 respondents, most of whom 1 have interviewed in person (often in their summer house itself) or by phone, and with all of whom I have had extended correspondence. They presently live in 17 different states; their summer houses are in one or another 18 states and Canada, though disproportionately in New England. These range in size from a tiny cottage worth perhaps $12,000, built on a 25-foot square plot of leased land on the Jersey shore, to a privately-owned island off the New England coast assessed at $8 million. While few of my respondents' properties are of much acreage, given their prime location (however modest may be the summer house itself), their mean assessed value exceeds the current estate probate minimum of $625,000. While this minimum is due to rise to $1,000,000 in 2006, it is not subject to cost-of-living adjustments, and assessments of summer houses have risen at higher rates than inflation in recent years. Given the various state inheritance taxes added to the federal estate taxes, total estate taxes are likely to range from 15% to over 20% on estates of $1,000,000, according to the 1987 tax provisions (Small, 1992). Even if astute estate planning has precluded such a major inheritance tax being passed on to the heirs, higher assessments on summer houses mean higher real-estate taxes needing to be paid to local authorities. Thus the financial burdens of inheriting and maintaining a summer house increase, as do pressures to sell it rather than to pay up.

Where are the necessary financial resources to come from? None of my respondents come from "Old Money," although a few are descended from families of considerable comfort and status. Yet even in these cases, where the summer house typically was built at the turn of the century and endowed with a trust to support its costs, such endowments seldom cover expenses today. Virtually all of my respondents are well educated and most work in a variety of professions, including some skilled trades, and typically their self-acquired "cultural capital" is often greater than their own financial capital. There is often a wide disparity of income among heirs to the summer house, by a factor of ten, in some families. In most cases, however, family members define themselves as equal in their common heritage and their right to use it. Indeed, given the current assessed valued of the house and what a seasonal rental fee would be at market rates, many respondents would not be able to afford to vacation at the summer house at all if it were not such a family right.

Regardless of income, most of my respondents and their extended families lead cosmopolitan lives in large cities or their suburbs. Most have to travel a considerable distance to return to the summer house, the oldest of which were built in the 1890s and are now being shared by heirs in the fourth, fifth and even sixth generation. Other respondents are themselves the founders, intending to pass the house on to their own children and eager to learn how other people have done it. All have shared with me the details of their circumstances, some providing documents of their partnership agreements or annual reports with remarkable trust that I would preserve their anonymity. As I quote them extensively in later chapters, I have disguised them, sometimes by assigning the summer house to a different location or the respondent to a different generation, or otherwise changing details of their family structure. Some quotes are verbatim, taken from my notes made during the interview or from correspondence; others are reconstructions from their questionnaires. All have approved the version that appears here.

I am grateful to all of them, as are the other members of my family: we have learned better ways of managing our own summer houses from their experiences. I am also grateful to my research assistant Jessie Klein of the Graduate Center of the City University of New York, where I am Professor of Sociology at the CUNY College of Staten Island.

Obviously, my greatest and unpayable debt is to my parents, the late E.V. Huggins and Leonora Ornston Huggins; to my brothers Bob and Ken and my sister Janet and their spouses and children; and to my husband Harry and our own children Tom and Jennifer. Our collective experiences in Nantucket have provided the understanding that underlies whatever merit this study may have. My brother Ken has written a "how-to-do-it" style workbook derived from my findings entitled: *How to Pass It On: The Ownership and Use of Summer Houses*, which some may find of more immediate practical use than this sociological analysis. It is now included in this edition as an added bonus.

As for other sources in the field, there are many which give helpful information on how to find, build or buy a vacation home (e.g. GeRue 1996; Scher & Scher 1992) but they don't say much about how to keep it in the family. Attorney Stephen J. Small has written two excellent books (1992; 1997) on tax strategies for preserving family lands, but he too says little about the family dynamics involved. This book, along with Ken's, is intended to fill that gap in the available information on the subject.

In addition to these and the other sources listed in my bibliography, both Ken and I have relied upon attorney Harrison Gardner of Madison, New Jersey (as did our parents in establishing our current formal arrangements) for the overview of the various legal structures through which joint ownership of a summer house can be passed on, discussed in Chapter 13. I have also consulted my own attorney Thomas Loikith of Fairfield, NJ, in that regard. With much gratitude for their counsel, I am fully responsible for any errors in the version presented here. Ken and I have relied as well upon the suggestions of professional mediator Louis R. Matlack of Camden, New Jersey, as to the processes through which families might come to agreement most easily, discussed in Chapter 15.

Readers who are disinterested in sociological analysis of collective identity and the conflicting norms of inheritance may wish to skim through the Introduction and some of Chapter 1— generalized discussions based on the sociological literature which frames the empirical evidence provided by my respondents—and turn directly to Chapter 2. To review briefly here the organizing principles of the book, the first sections focus on the various factors which determine the parameters of summer house inheritance, and their consequences for both families and individuals. Part I (Chapters 1-3) discusses the often conflicting societal norms and practices of inheritance as they contribute to social class differences and to considerable conflict among heirs. Part II (Chapters 4-7) is comparably large-scale in its focus on the distinct cultural values expressed in various summer colonies, which play a significant role in stabilizing a collective social status and identity among the heirs, and thereby in reducing conflict. Part III (Chapters 8-11) sharpens the focus to examine family interaction among individuals of the same or different generations as they deal with issues of power, understood more benignly as legitimate authority over the summer house and the legacy it preserves. The remaining chapters delineate the range of responses, both informal and formal, to the dilemmas which are detailed in the first two-thirds of the book.

As this book goes to press, my family and I are eagerly anticipating our next turn at our summer house, feeling more secure that it will continue to be passed on to succeeding generations than we did when I started on this inquiry. May this book help its readers in the same fashion.

J.H.B.
Montclair, NJ
April 1999

INTRODUCTION

As a sociologist, I inevitably bring the perspectives of my discipline to this inquiry into the inheritance and use of summer houses. The standard definition of sociology is that it is the study of human group interaction. While everyone observes and participates in social interaction, learning at the same time the particular meanings assigned to it by the others comparably involved (and perhaps the grounds for criticizing those meanings), sociology attempts to analyze this interaction systematically. Like all of the social sciences, it builds explanatory theories from the empirical evidence and tests their continuing validity on the basis of new empirical evidence.

In this Introduction, I lay out the broad concepts delineated by the theorists and analysts on whom I most depend. Even if hereafter I seldom refer to them explicitly, they are so much a part of my thinking as a sociologist that their work underlies my own throughout. It is only fair to inform the reader of where I am coming from, not merely in my own experience with a summer house but more consistently in terms of my sociological orientation.

This inquiry focuses on summer houses as factors in the intentional development of a familial and social identity, instituted by individuals who become summer house "founders," among their heirs whose formative years have included summer visits to the house itself. Ideally, anyone who has shared in its ambience incorporates it into his or her "self," his or her core identity both as an individual and as a member of a family as well as of a wider social group. This happens largely because the summer house incorporates them into its identity as welcoming homestead for its family members.

As we will see, the summer house is an important factor in determining the comparative strength of the several "multiple identities" (even "conflicting identities") which contemporary individuals typically carry. For example, as a summer house co-owner, I therefore have particular obligations in its use related to the identities I hold within my nuclear family as wife, mother and mother-in-law. I have other identities in my extended family as sister, sister-in-law and aunt, in which my responsibilities may conflict with the first set, and yet still other identities and their distinct obligations as a professional sociologist and college professor; still more as a summer resident of Nantucket; etc.

At a time when "identity politics" are much practiced, however, the ways in which such multiple identities are constructed and negotiated is seldom examined. What does the sharing of a summer house have to do with such questions? We'll explore this question in greater detail below, hopefully casting some light on the issues that often become divisive because they are not considered important enough to discuss. Summer house owners become well acquainted with divisive issues: just when they think all family members should be enjoying themselves together in use of the place, some major conflict emerges. Why? What might a sociological understanding do to reduce such conflicts?

This study examine these processes and the role that a summer house may play in bringing social identities into harmony or into conflict with others. My theoretical understanding of social identity—the "social self"—is based on the work of American sociologist and philosopher George Herbert Mead, who taught social psychology at the University of Chicago from 1900 until his death in 1930. One of the advantages of using Mead's conceptualization is that it is broad enough to accommodate the concepts of other theorists such as Freud, yet it is metaphorically apt enough to be immediately under-standable.

Mead views the "social self" as being formed through the on-going internal "conversa-tion" of a person's "I" and his "me." The "I" represents the innate qualities of the individ-ual and the "me" is developed through interaction with "significant others," those whose involvement in the individual's life is typically earliest and most profound in effect. The "me," tempered by the personality of the "I," is responsive to the attitudes, gestures and language of those others in mutual and on-going arousal. if the significant others are loving, the "me" affirms that love, not just in response to them but also in the internal dialogue with the "I" that grounds the developing self as positive and loving. However, if the signifi-cant others are punitive or hostile, the "me" responds negatively to those others as well as to her own "I", with comparable and negative effects on the self and its sense of identity.

As the self develops, the attitudes, gestures and the more elaborate roles of the signifi-cant others come to be internalized by children from their earliest years, as evoking the same responses from others that they call out in those who make them. (Consider "peek-a-boo," as a simple example, and with older children, "Say please..." At many summer houses, it is, "Everyone pitches in; come on!")

Children practice such actions and the related attitudes through play, copying and thereby rehearsing the activities of adults, be they parents, teachers, or other "role models" such as siblings or extended family members—or media stars. Thereupon they learn to take part in organized games with particular and increasingly elaborate rules, often built around these sets of reciprocal roles ("cowboys and Indians," "Star Trek," Little League). In such games or other summer house activities,

> ...the individual enters into the perspectives of others, in so far as he is able to take their attitudes, or occupy their points of view. (Mead 1932, 165)

> In the game, there is a set of responses of such others so organized that the attitude of one calls out the appropriate attitudes of the other... The game represents the passage in the life of the child from taking the role of others in play to the organized part that is essential to self-consciousness in the full sense of the term. (Mead 1934, 151-2)

Both the mind and the self, together understood as self-consciousness, are thereby developed in social contexts which they reflect and recreate in turn. Under conditions of great social stability, individuals are likely to have available only a very limited number of roles and their related identities to interact with and to model in turn. These are largely determined by age, gender and status, which have the virtue of security along with the potential defect of rigidity in their interactive structure.

However, under contemporary conditions of rapid social change, any clear understanding of the perspectives of others is undermined by the sheer complexity of the many available roles, activities and related identities, as well as the variety of their interpretations by different players. As a result, the "modern self" is insecurely grounded, as it is apparent that all do not share the same internalized concept of what Mead called the "generalized other," the projection onto society at large of the norms originally internalized through the significant others. "What will grandma say if you don't help out?" has a simple normative answer, based on long experience with her at the summer house. "What will your cousins say if you want to paint the darkened pine paneling of the summer house?" is more likely to have several different responses, based upon less experience with them and less internalization of their points of view. "What will people say if you cut down the trees at the shore line—or sell the property to someone else who will do so?" will have even more potential responses, some in conflict with others.

> We have never been so uncertain as to what will be the common perspective... what are the values which economics undertakes to define, what are the community values of friendship, of passion, of parenthood, of amusement, of beauty, of social solidarity in its unnumbered forms, or of those values which have been gathered under the relations of man to the highest community or to God. (Mead 1932, 167)

For reasons we will explore below, a summer house can become a crucial part of the "self," the primary identity of each individual who shares its use. More importantly, that part is likely to provide a unique sense of stability in an era far more complex and uncertain than that of Mead's day. Such a sense of stability is enhanced by the playfulness built into use of the summer house, designed as it is for leisure use and enjoyed while "on vacation" from the serious routines and emergencies of everyday life. Accordingly, adults who are long past the "play stage" of childhood socialization, as Mead conceptualized it, may rediscover a youthful clarity and singleness

of purpose they have long outgrown elsewhere, and thereby be able to reinforce it to their children.

The importance of such adult play in the very survival of civilization is analyzed by Mead's generation-younger Dutch contemporary, historian Johan Huizinga, best known for his book translated into English as *The Waning of the Middle Ages* (1954 [1924]). Huizinga's more evocative and germane masterpiece, *Homo Ludens: A Study of the Play Element in Culture*, was conceived in 1933, published (in German) in Switzerland in 1944 and first published in English in 1950. 1 mention the timing because of the seriousness of its message in a period when any kind of "playfulness" could scarcely find expression.

Consider what Huizinga notes as the functions of play and their implications for his time, as well as for this inquiry into summer houses (let alone for an understanding of the crucial role of organized sport in modern societies):

> The first main characteristic of play... is that it is in fact freedom. A second characteristic is closely connected with this, namely, that play is not "ordinary" or "real" life. It is rather a stepping out of "real" life into a temporary sphere of activity with a disposition all its own... The consciousness of play being "only a pretend" does not by any means prevent it from proceeding with the utmost seriousness...

> Any game can at any time wholly run away with the players. The contrast between play and seriousness is always fluid. The inferiority of play is continually being offset by the corresponding superiority of its seriousness. Play turns to seriousness and seriousness to play... As a regularly recurring relaxation, it becomes the accompaniment, the complement, in fact an integral part of life in general. It adorns life, amplifies it and is to that extent a necessity both for the individual—as a life function—and for society by reason of the meaning it contains... The expression of it satisfies all kinds of communal ideals. (Huizinga 1955, 8-9)

Huizinga goes on to list other characteristics of play, again with particular relevance to the sharing ownership and use of a summer house:

> [Play is secluded and limited.] It is "played out" within certain limits of time and place... and then plays itself to an end. [But] once played, it endures as a newfound creation of the mind, a treasure to be retained by the memory. It is transmitted, it becomes tradition.... In this faculty of repetition lies one of the most essential qualities of play.

It creates order, it *is* order. Into an imperfect world and into the confusion of life it brings a temporary, a limited perfection... [In so doing, it creates tension and excitement as well as relieving them.]

All play has its rules... The player who trespasses against the rules is a "spoil-sport."... The spoil-sport shatters the play-world itself. By withdrawing from the game he reveals the relativity and fragility of the play-world... He robs play of its *illusion*. (1955, 10-11 [his italics])

We will see below the problems caused by such "spoil sports," heirs who insist on being bought out of the summer house. Thus they demonstrate that its meaning of equality among family members and "pricelessness" for the other heirs is merely an illusion.

Huizinga then notes that the play community tends to become a permanent and distinct group, such as we will see in Part II on summer "colonies". Its distinctive character is based on its members' collective sense of secrecy from others, the "disguises" they put on from the roles of everyday life, and the ritualistic aspect of many activities of play as well as the playful aspects of many rituals. Finally, speaking directly to the Depression and subsequent World War being waged as he wrote, Huizinga says:

Real civilization cannot exist in the absence of a certain play-element, for civilization presupposes limitation and mastery of the self, the ability not to confuse its own tendencies with the ultimate and highest goal, but to understand that it is enclosed within certain bounds freely accepted. Civilization will, in a sense, always be played according to certain rules, and true civilization will always demand fair play... True play knows no propaganda; its aim is in itself, and its familiar spirit is happy inspiration. (1955, 211)

In Part I, we will explore some of the rules governing inheritance and the difficulties summer house owners have in applying them so as to retain the playfulness and the "fair play" that the house is to embody for the extended family. In Parts II and III, we will examine its "civilizing" qualities in its transmission of particular cultural elements which, in turn, come to be experienced in the "self" and the "self-consciousness" of each of its heirs. In the subsequent chapters, we will see how these are set into rituals and organizational forms, both informal and more structured agents of transmission.

Two final "giants" of Sociology must be mentioned at this point: Georg Simmel and Max Weber. German contemporaries a generation older than Mead and thus two generations older than Huizinga, their work was known by both of these younger scholars. Writing in the late 19th and early 20th centuries, Simmel and Weber addressed themes of particular relevance to this inquiry. We will consider Weber's contributions to a much greater extent in Chapters 4 and 5: here I will note some of the specific points of Simmel's work that bear on this study, as well as Weber's confirmation of one of them.

In much of his writing, Simmel explored the forms of social relations: for example, how a "dyad" —a couple—differs from a "triad," or three people: "baby makes three" sets up potential power struggles of two against one that a couple by themselves cannot match. Most important for our purposes are his essays on sociability, which laid the grounds for the more focused analyses of the social formation of the individual self and of the importance of play by both Mead and Huizinga which have already been reviewed. (It is because of the immediate relevance of Mead's and Huizinga's specific inquiries that they have been discussed first, before the chronologically earlier, more general analyses of Simmel's.) Here is Simmel, writing in 1910:

> It is no mere accident of language that all sociability, even the purely spontaneous, if it is to have meaning and stability, lays such great value on form, on good form. For "good form" is mutual self-definition...; since in sociability the concrete motives bound up with life-goals fall away, so must the pure form, the *free-playing interacting inter-dependence* of individuals, stand out so much the more strongly and operate with so much greater effect... (Simmel 1971b [1910], 129 [my italics])

> Sociability is, then, the play-form of association... Since sociability in its pure form has no ulterior end, no content, and no result outside itself, it is oriented completely about personalities... But precisely because all is oriented about them, the personalities must not emphasize themselves too individually... Riches and social position, learning and fame, exceptional capacities and merits of the individual have no role in sociability... Sociability creates, if one will, an ideal sociological world, for in it... the pleasure of the individual is always contingent upon the joy of others; here, by definition, no one can have his satisfaction at the cost of contrary experiences on the part of others. (1971 b [1910], 130, 132 [his italics])

As we will see in detail below, those who share summer houses do so in relations of greater equality and mutual, playful and sociable activities than they usually experience in their everyday lives. Indeed, those are often the principles upon which the founders decide to buy and maintain such a place. If we combine the views just discussed, we might assume that socialization through and into the inheritance and sharing of a summer house is free of conflict, involving as it does the socialization of the various individual "selves" by significant others, in an environment of play and sociability. But Simmel helps us to understand some of the potential conflicts that are also inherent in the situation:

Antagonism on the basis of a common kinship tie is stronger than among strangers... People who have many common features often do one another worse or "wronger" wrong than complete strangers do... They do it because there is only little that is different between them; hence even the slightest antagonism has a relative significance quite other than between strangers, who count with all kinds of mutual differences to begin with. Hence the family conflicts over which people profoundly in agreement sometimes break up.

The deepest hatred grows out of broken love... We cover our secret awareness of our own responsibility for it by hatred which makes it easy for us to pass all responsibility on to the other. (Simmel 1955 [1904], 43-46)

In many cases of inheritance when the property is to be shared, any such conflict, resulting from long-buried sibling or other family rivalry brings about the sale of the property and the dissolution of the heirs' collective bond into mutual and even permanent antagonism. Mead's ideas of the social self show why this is likely to occur: my sibling or close cousin is part of "me," if we disagree it is at risk of tearing our "selves" apart, and I am unwilling to admit my willing participation in this mutual "self"-destruction. To be sure, however common this situation may be, only a few such cases turn up among my respondents—those who have been lucky enough to resolve such conflicts or else they would not be able to "pass it on" successfully. Simmel also notes a major characteristic of contemporary life which contributes to the difficulties that many families have in sustaining an ethos of qualitative experience in the summer house when its carrying costs increase. He calls this the "inconsiderate hardness" that grows from the money economy and the related intellectual development of those who work in it:

Money is concerned only with what is common to all: it asks for the exchange value, it reduces all quality and individuality to the question: How much?...

Punctuality, calculability, exactness are forced upon life by the complexity and extension of metropolitan existence... These traits must also color the contents of life and favor the exclusion of those irrational, instinctive, sovereign traits and impulses which aim at determining the mode of life from within, instead of receiving the general and precisely schematized form of life from without. (Simmel 1971a [1903], 327-329)

While the purpose of the summer house is family "quality time," keeping it going over several generations requires considerable calculation—not just to cover its operating costs and a fair division of the work necessary to keep it up, but also as part of estate planning. These issues will be discussed in greater detail below, but it is worth noting here that for many families, the summer house makes up the largest portion of the estate left by the founders, and given its often considerable worth, without sufficient calculation and planning it would have to be sold to pay the estate taxes. All the more do family members experience what Simmel called "The Conflict in Modern Culture" (1971c (1918]): the qualitative functions of the summer house—its playful character, its enhancement of both a sense of self and of sociability within the family and with visiting friends, its contribution to spontaneity—can be maintained only through attention to exact calculation of both time and money.

Weber would have agreed, having studied at length the "rationalization" that is both cause and effect of the bureaucratic structures of modern Western life and the capitalist economy (1946 [1920], 196-243). Once developed, these structures become an "iron cage" from which there is no escape (1958 [1904], 181). We will hear more of Weber's analyses in Chapters 4 and 5, including some of the less gloomy consequences of their application, as we explore the ways in which the "Protestant Ethic" he described may be taught through the summer house.

In different ways, then, just as these sociologists knew of and responded to each other's work, I build upon their genius in examining how the social forms and interactions they analyze so well are reflected and revealed in summer houses, as the extended families who share them find ways of passing t hem on to succeeding generations.

They do this despite the many conflicts that are built into the situation, for the reasons we will consider in Part I. First we review issues of social mobility in a meritocratic society such as ours. Tensions and stresses result from the frequent denial that there are any real problems combining the principles of a meritocracy with those based on inheritance of both wealth and material property, such as a summer house. This common denial is found even among sociologists who otherwise spend much time analyzing social mobility and social stratification. However, anyone dealing with the inheritance of a summer house is familiar with the conflicts, so it is worth the time to lay the groundwork for their understanding in Chapter 1. The next two chapters explore the basis of such problems in greater detail, focusing first on the inherent conflicts in social norms and expectations based on differences in the inheritance of non-divisible land (such as a summer house occupies) versus that of divisible wealth, and then on even more inherent conflicts based upon discrepant norms of inheritance regarding who is entitled to what, and when.

PART ONE

INHERITANCE AND SOCIAL DISTINCTION

CHAPTER ONE

SOCIOLOGICAL PERSPECTIVES OF INHERITANCE AND SOCIAL CLASS

Obviously, the acquisition and transmission of a summer house to successive generations is a mark of the family's social class, be that house a tiny cottage on a bit of leased land or a grand edifice on hundreds of acres. Yet sociologists, let alone journalists, tend to pay scant attention to the effects of any such inheritance on contemporary families until public scrutiny is attracted by some scandalous behavior on their part. Other implications are also ignored: acquisition of a summer house is almost invariable the result of upward social mobility on the part of the founders, achieving the benefits of higher status and income than their own parents attained. That income is almost inevitably "New Money." But by being able to pass the summer house on to their heirs, founders thereby lay claim to the even higher status of those with "Old Money" to transmit. The social distinction between the two kinds of money is important for our inquiry, as we shall see.

Despite media attention to celebrities with New Money, Few studies have explored the changing implications for class and status of Old Money in contemporary American society. Today, such family endowment is likely to be far less than that or the New Money billionaires, although it may have a wider cultural impact due to the duration of its accumulation and dissemination. The paucity of sociological analysis of Old Money is due in large measure to the willingness of its heirs to permit observation only of their public activities such as marriages, board memberships and philanthropy, denying any outsider entree to Ole private meanings of such activities. One of their own, Nelson W. Aldrich Jr, provides a rare glimpse of the ethos of Old Money:

> The essence of the Old Money project is family continuity. The project seeks to score a generational line through (and slightly above) the turbulence of striving and struggling that is life in a liberal, entrepreneurial society. It seeks to be a triumph of history, the family's history, over time. (Aldrich 1991, 196)

Without question, social class is determined by both the amount or wealth (whether inherited or self-made) and the cultural attitudes and values transmitted with it. Otherwise, the upward social mobility of millions cannot be explained. If that mobility is inherently the result of New Money, the social status it "achieves" is the result of Old Money and the related stability oft he social elites which those with New Money come to emulate. Thus sheer wealth is obviously important, but it is not at the core of social class, as indicated by the terms "classy" or "tacky" applied respectively to any number of goods regardless of cost.

However, the dynamics of class and culture are all too often unexplored by analysts of "elites" such as G. William Domhoff (1971), who sees them as inbred, caste-like in culture and self-perpetuating in membership. Thereby left unexplained is the rise and ultimate acceptance of those with New Money or simply with power, those who are originally unendowed with such a legacy: why else have Horatio Alger, Bill Gates, Ronald Reagan and Bill Clinton captured both the American imagination and positions of wealth and/or authority? Such analysts fail to explain achievement, on the one hand, and decline or bankruptcy on the other.

In contrast to studies of elites which *ignore* individual achievement is the bias built into the general American value system (and much sociological analysis) which emphasizes individual accomplishment and rewards presumably based on merit while it ignores group affiliations and family traditions. Ever since Peter Blau and Otis Dudley Duncan analyzed the American occupational structure in 1967, studies of social mobility or status have tended to be based on occupation rather than the family from whom one might inherit property, and therefore on "achieved" rather than on "ascribed" status. As a result, according to sociologists Stephen J. McNamee and Robert K. Miller Jr,:

> Most stratification research has focused on the individual as the unit of analysis. This is due in part to the methodological individualism characteristic of... most American [sociology]. (McNamee & Miller 1989, 9)

Aware of this problem, these analysts avoid it in their edited anthology of 1998, but as they and their co-authors demonstrate the ways in which inherited wealth and meritocratic principles intersect, their conscious purpose is to provide grounds 1br redressing the patterns of structured inequality that result:

> For the most part... meritocracy is super-imposed on inheritance rather than the other way around—effects produced by merit or luck occur within the context of effects produced [first] by differential inheritance...

> [Therefore] the state could decide to offset the effects of inequality caused by inheri-

tance by decommodification of critical resources, in essence providing collective access to essential resources and services regardless of the ability to pay. (Miller & McNamee 1998, 22-23 [their italics])

One may or may not agree either with the premise or with the advisability of their conclusion, as stated here. In any event, they and their co-authors show scant interest in the dynamics evident in any intersection of meritocracy and inheritance as experienced by individuals as members of families and communities. And it is from such families that *all* cultural inheritance is first acquired and to which it is passed on, whether it be unchanged or considerably transformed. They examine neither any compounding nor any mitigating effects of such inheritance on American society and the innumerable groups of which it is composed.

Their perspective is also an artifact of methodologies using powerful quantitative techniques and computers, which allow national surveys which then categorize individuals as representative of social classes or age groups, for example. Left out of consideration are the particularities of extended family structures and the communities through which social class and generation may be connected through inheritance *or* that connection overcome. These issues are best explored through costly and time-intensive (and perhaps unrepresentative) case studies, which then become dated in terms of the validity of their analysis as circumstances change. Thus an understanding of the role of the inheritance of material property in the perpetuation of social class *and* of cultural patterns— and vice versa—has been lost by the current generation of sociologists, just as it is often denied by the public at large.

Whatever the prevalence of an individualistic and meritocratic ideology, however, it appears to have little real impact on what people actually do as they pass along their acquired class and status to their children, as even these authors regretfully acknowledge:

> There is no evidence... that meritocratic ideology has prevented or even curtailed the practice of estate inheritance... Americans subscribe to contradictory principles for distributing valued rewards, loudly proclaiming the virtues of meritocracy but quietly acknowledging the effects of inheritance, sponsorship and luck. (McNamee & Miller 1989, 12, 14)

If relations with members of the nuclear family are often ignored when justifying one's own achieved place in live, virtually unexamined are the relations among adult siblings, cousins (whether first-, second-, or one-step removed), let alone aunts, uncles, nieces, nephews, and a full panoply of in-laws. Even if not admitted to by those who profit from them, such extended networks are likely to have considerable impact upon their members' social stability or mobility. In sum, unlike novels, most current family studies ignore the full network of kin in which most individuals find themselves, even today when the "decline of the family" is widely discussed. Whether a kinship network is closely embraced or kept as distant as possible, it is *there*, for most Americans—even for the "underclass" and the homeless, who know well the kin and/or foster kin who may have kicked them out of home, and the quasi-kindred with whom they share their "turf" in a subway tunnel or shanty-town. For the enormous majority with enough economic stability that extended kin continue to meet on occasion, in-laws bring their own extended families of origin into some kind of relationship with all of the above. They may see each other only at weddings and funerals, they may love, hate or simply disregard each other, but they know who they are, how they are connected (the popularity of genealogical inquiry is indicative), and what the implications are for both family rituals and inheritance. Even divorces and remarriages do not necessarily sever many of these family ties, as so may queries to "Miss Manners" attest.

This problematic methodological individualism appears even in the work of Remi Clignet, one of the few contemporary sociologists who have examined inheritance patterns. His 1992 book *Death, Deeds and Descendants* is the only sociological monograph on inheritance in print. He is also a contributor to Miller & McNamee's 1998 anthology. (In addition to these sociologists, historians—notably Shammas et al [1987]—have also done extensive analyses on inheritance.) I review Clignet's work here in some detail because I draw upon it later.

In his book, Clignet excoriates the discipline for taking the individual as the sole unit of analysis, but he nevertheless bases his own conclusions on data that have somewhat comparable limitations, at least for the purposes of this present study. Examining federal estate tax returns from 1920 and again from 1944, he delineates such factors as ethnicity which determine what one generation passes on to the next, through what kind of legal instruments with what implications. However, his data are necessarily limited to public testamentary evidence, which by definition precludes revelation of the details of any large estate (including the presence of potential heirs who are not named as beneficiaries) even as it includes the less wealthy who die intestate.

Otherwise omitted in Clignet's study are cases where legal ownership of property is transmitted to heirs *inter vivos*, while the founders are still alive, as is true of most of the families which are the focus of this study. Further, Clignet's data and the analysis he makes of it say nothing about what happens within *extended families* about the wealth the decedents may have inherited from their own parents or acquired from in-laws, and little about what they may share among their grandchildren, siblings or cousins, with what effect upon family cohesion or stability. More specifically, he says nothing about the consequences of the inheritance of *material* property, such as a summer house, that is expected to be held in common by extended kin, let alone whether such a legacy increases solidarity or conflict among them.

To be sure, Clignet's data sets may well have included !sew examples of such legacies, so the issue did not occur to him as a possibility. (Indeed, in private correspondence with me concerning this study, Clignet—now retired to his native France—assumed that the issue I would be addressing was the determination of which individual heir would get the summer house, not how multiple heirs may work out how to share its ownership. In further correspondence, he acknowledged that attempting to share an inherited summer house with his sister had been a disaster for both. Autobiography is a strong determinant of the questions sociologists ask or avoid.)

A further problem in many otherwise useful studies of inheritance and social class is that class is often so broadly categorized as to be useless for my purposes here. What determines membership in the "elite" or the "upper middle class?" Is this to be assessed exclusively on income, or on some other grounds? Most of those with whom we are here concerned don't think of themselves as members of any "elite," (a not infrequent situation [Marcus 1983a]) even if some acknowledge being "upper middle class." As we have seen from Aldrich, income alone is insufficient to designate social class: attitudes and values (i.e. culture) may determine more than does income or wealth. As for these, it matters not only whether the money one has is new or old, achieved by one's own efforts or inherited. Of equal importance in the latter instance whether it permits or requires personal management by the heirs.

> [There is] a most fateful distinction among scions of the Old Money class: the distinction between those who are born to a powerful functional estate in life, in practice most often a business, and those who are born merely to money...

> [For the most part] the Old Money class... lives off the income of inherited capital, or, as Brahmin Bostonians like to have it, the income of the income of the capital. (Aldrich 1991, 195)

Further, if money is acquired or maintained through one's own efforts, it matters for one's class designation *how* one's high income level is attained, even if entirely legally. If it is through the entertainment or sports industries, as is the case of Woody Allen or Michael Jordan—celebrities but not yet part of the "social elite" other than in the fluid New Money havens of Southampton or Aspen—higher social status may then be attained by their children or grandchildren through the latter's attendance at the proper schools and participation in the related cultural events. However, if one has earned one's way to the top through participation in the traditional economic institutions of society, like the Bass Brothers or Malcolm Forbes Jr., one's entree into elite status can be more direct and need not take a generation.

More to the point of this inquiry, what of the vast numbers of people of far more modest wealth, however financially comfortable they may feel? How are they to be categorized in terms of social class? Upper Middle? Professional? Middle? Lower Middle? Working? Many extended families who share summer houses include individuals in each of these class categories as determined by occupation and income, even as they are presumably of the same social class on the basis of their inheritance. Some of those differences are the result of the meritocratic principles which reward some by upward mobility and punish others whose decline is due to their own disinterest in achievement or to mismanagement of their assets.

In any event, while there may be "hidden injuries" to the upwardly mobile (Sennett 1976), their achievement is real enough. Clearly, whether one is motivated by socialization or by sheer ambition, whether one's college tuition is paid by parents, a trust fund, or scholarships, loans or self-earned income, acquisition of professional status and the related income requires considerable personal investment. This may pay off in terms of subsequent ownership of material property, including a summer house, but the wealth necessary to acquire such property may be less important in establishing the status of one's progeny than in the past, given the comparative openness of the American system of higher education and occupational attainment.

Further, while home ownership is the primary mark of middle class status, two-thirds of all American households own their own dwellings today, be they shacks or mansions, compared with 40% in the 1930s. (Many of the rest will own homes once established in careers, or they could readily afford to do so but prefer to rent or lease.) Yet with Social Security and Medicare covering much of the expenses of the increasingly long-lived elderly, usually their homes need not be sold by their children to cover their financial needs. Thus any inheritance of real property tends to go to heirs already in late middle age themselves, when they will have established their lot in life through their own work or luck.

> Housing inheritance is not likely to be passed directly to young, first time buyers, but to people who already have an established housing career. (Munro 1988, 417)

Of course, social inequalities are thereby perpetuated:

> The social distribution of housing inheritance is far from equal, benefitting home

owners and the professional managerial classes... Class position will continue to influence consumption and inheritance for some time to come. (Hamnett 1991, 5095; 535)

As we will examine more closely in Part II below, however, such perpetuation is a major factor in stabilizing the status of those who have put financial capital, inherited or individually achieved, into specific kinds of home ownership. And as we will see in Part III, this has particular ramifications when it is the summer house which is being passed on, rather than the primary dwelling of the parents.

In any event, baby boomers who may presently be suffering from a sense of downward mobility (Newman 1993) are slated collectively to inherit a great deal compared to what heir own parents inherited. However, it will be too late to have much effect on their living standards in the present and immediate future, other than in the luck of some to be able to visit free, or at low cost, a family summer house which they could never afford to rent at market rates.

Further, as estates which include the primary dwelling of the decedent are typically divided among several immediate heirs and assorted charities or other beneficiaries, such a house is unlikely to be occupied by any of the immediate descendants. Presumably, the heirs have by now moved out and established themselves elsewhere, and they (and their spouses) are unlikely to welcome any reversion to childlike emotions and behavior that may happen if they move back to the house they grew up in. Instead, that house is more likely to be sold and the proceeds distributed to a number of people, thereby diluting the effects of its transmission on their social class or status.

While most of the wealthy leave only a tiny portion of their estates to charity, as reported by Shammas et al (1987), most seem to have little intention of establishing a propertied dynasty, preferring instead estate forms such as trusts or corporations which allow for non-familial management by professionals (Marcus 1983b). A standard of living may thereby be preserved for the heirs through allowances or dividends, but any sense of a cohesive family culture is unlikely to survive without some joint enterprise, be it shared property, a business or a trust, to continue to engage the heirs.

The findings of these studies are not particularly remarkable, providing support as they do for the view that social class is essentially inherited and *also* for that which sees individual effort as of primary importance in determining status prior to any material inheritance. Obviously, both perspectives are warranted, with evidence for the latter provided by many examples of both upward and downward mobility and such sayings as "shirt sleeves to shirt sleeves in three generations." But as we shall see, by focusing on social class in terms of presumably liquid forms of wealth such as stocks and bonds, important as these are, such studies typically fail to capture the meanings that certain kinds of material family inheritance are likely to have for both those who pass it on and those who receive it. As a result, the full implications of the findings tend to remain undeveloped.

This study is devoted to such an explication, building upon the strength of the work of all of these theorists and researchers and extending it to reach a more nuanced understanding of the issue: how do contemporary non-elite families manage to sustain enough cohesion to keep a summer house in their ownership over several generations, with what consequences for the stability of their social class, status, and identity?

CHAPTER 2

NORMS OF INHERITANCE OF LAND AND WEALTH

We can increase our understanding by expanding our time frame to include the works of historians and anthropologists who have studied the norms of inheritance of land, the original basis of wealth, which have developed over the centuries in Western Europe and elsewhere. Patterns of inheritance of more fungible wealth will be considered in turn. The often conflicting but coexisting norms for transfers of both land and wealth have become part of the cultural inheritance of most contemporary Americans, reflected in custom as well as in estate law. At the same time, we must recognize that the fluidity of Western inheritance practices resulting from these conflicting norms is not a product of modernity per se, as demonstrated by anthropological studies regarding land ownership and use.

For example, Paula Brown and colleagues studied land tenure and transfer among the Chimbu in Papua-New Guinea. They found that both ownership and transfer patterns varied with particular circumstances, as the grip of colonial authority loosened in the late 1950s:

> Intergroup sharing and mutual accommodation tend to be generally replaced by within-group cooperation and accommodation when land is frequently used. Until very recently, Chimbu have treated their land as the most basic resource in organizing livelihood and status. Where it is scarce and valuable, individuals guard access to a small personal range [of immediate kin]; where it is relatively abundant, they are able to use it entrepreneurially, and both draw on and nourish a wider set of relationships [among non-immediate kin].
>
> Land tenure [is] infinitely varied and flexible according to different and changing circumstances. (Brown et al 1990, 46)

This variability may be an anthropological universal. However, a single type of land tenure and inheritance may also remain relatively stable for generations, as shown by noted historian E. P. Thompson in his classic essay on 16th century English patterns of inheritance of agricultural land-holdings or tenures, "The Grid of Inheritance:"

> In land, what [was] being transmitted through inheritance systems [was] not so much property in the land as property in [its use]... It [was] the tenure—and sometimes the functions and roles attached to the tenure —which was being transmitted...
>
> It depended upon the inherited right but also upon the inherited grid of customs and controls within which that right was exercised. This customary grid was as intrinsic to inheritance of land as the grid of banking or the stock exchange are to the inheritance of money. Indeed one could say that the beneficiary inherited both his right *and* the grid within which it was effectual: hence he must inherit a certain kind of social or communal psychology of ownership; the property not of his family but of his family-within-the-commune.
>
> Yeomen were seeking to transmit down the generations not only 'land' (particularly tenures) but also a social status to *all* their children. (Thompson 1976, 328; 376; 346 [his italics])

If yeomen were doing this in their fashion, using their land not just to earn a living but to place their members within a structure of human relationships, without question the gentry were doing the same. A fellow contributor to the same volume in which Thompson's essay is found grounds these practices even further back, in the 13th century:

> The most fundamental of these [inheritance] principles was that family land belonged to the whole family; every member had a claim to support from it, from generation to generation. Responsibility for its management could lie within a generation-set, or with a single representative, but the position was one of stewardship, not of ownership. (Howell 1976, 113)

However, with population increases and thereby more potential claimants to the use of the land, as in New Guinea, over the centuries the norms of collective family stewardship gave way to others which, while they continued the impartibility of real property, applied the principles of Thompson's "grid" to a much reduced line. The practice of *uni*geniture emerged among the yeomen: the land (along with the obligation to care for the widowed parent who was giving it up) went to whichever single heir (or whose spouse) was the best farmer; the other heirs got equivalents in whatever portable goods were available.

As for the gentry, even without indivisible titles to pass on like the peers and baronets, *primo*geniture became the norm through which all the real property and the income it produced was transmitted to the eldest *son* regardless of his competence to manage it. (The associated problems have become known worldwide through Jane Austen's novels and their recent film versions.)

Yet within a few decades at the end of the 19th century, the British "landed establishment"—those who had the leisure time and the position through which to monopolize government, both at the domestic level among the landed heirs and in foreign affairs among their landless younger brothers—lost control of both land and power, according to historian David Canadine:

> The patrician malaise... had appropriately broad and deep causes. The first was a sudden and dramatic collapse of the agricultural base of the European economy, partly because of the massive influx of cheap foreign goods from North and South American... and partly because of the final and emphatic burgeoning of the full fledged, large-scale, and highly concentrated industrial economy. The result was that the rural sector was simultaneously depressed and marginalized. (Canadine 1990, 26)

With the sudden drop in prices for agricultural products and therefore in rents which the yeomen were able to pay to their gentry landlords, the incomes of the latter became so reduced !hat some had to sell off their property, previously held as a family rust, to the increasing numbers of prosperous industrialists and professionals. The values of the new owners were quite different from those they replaced:

> They regarded the country as a place for rest and repose, where money was spent, not made, and they were fully contented with the amenities of rural living—riding, hunting, shooting and entertaining... They had no interest in building up or administering a large estate. They wanted the recreational aspects of land-ownership without the responsibilities.

> The motor car spelt the end of the traditional county community... by making possible a new and essentially subversive social custom: the weekend house party... Houses that had once been the centres of great estates were now regarded as extensions of metropolitan living rooms. They were places to entertain in rather than to live in.

> [Today] those who hang on to their ancestral homes do so out of a backward-looking and defensive sense of family piety, rather than from feelings of confidence in their order, their purpose or their future. Once such mansions were the springboard for assured and acceptable patrician endeavour; now it is their maintenance and retention that has become a full-time activity... As Lord Montague put it in 1974: "We belong to

our possessions, rather than our possessions belong to us. To us, they are not wealth, but heirlooms, over which we have a sacred trust." (Canadine 1990, 358-9; 693-4)

I have quoted this material at length because it sets so well the themes of this inquiry into the inheritance of summer houses. Paradoxically, some of the values concerning a familial "trust" and responsibility for inherited property are found today in Americans who would be seen by Canadine as the cause of the "patrician malaise" and to whom Thompson would attribute the decline of the stable yeomanly. They are heirs to considerably newer Old Money than that held by British gentry, or may be the self-made who do not consider themselves wealthy at all. While Aldrich's Boston Brahmins are only of third generation,

> The relationship [of owners to property] was not ownership as capitalism understands it and as free markets make possible. It was a relationship... of reciprocal possession. A person was of his property, as the property was of him (and, in many places, her as well). For such a form of property there could be no money value, no market. Alienating such a possession, selling it, was literally inconceivable, like the idea of selling one's name. (Aldrich 1991, 199 [his italics])

Indeed, in a study of fiduciary agents who manage family trusts for wealthy clients, George E. Marcus found that among them, ownership of land may remain the most important factor that keeps such families intact, along with their fortunes:

> I asked [one such fiduciary] what would be an optimum dynastic strategy for a family founder in contemporary America. He answered that one should tie up one's total wealth in a huge tract of undeveloped land, with development potential, but which would lose such potential if fragmented prematurely. This would force a family to stay together more closely and to be more dependent on its patrimonial property than any alternative ownership situation. (Marcus 1983b, 248)

As we will see in greater detail below, such common ownership does not necessarily eliminate conflict among family members who are thereby "forced to stay together more closely." Nonetheless, whether among the wealthy whom Marcus studied or among middle-class families without such "patrician" lineage, the norms of 13th century yeomen as well as those of 19th century gentry and their successors are alive and well. For many with summer houses, these norms come to conscious awareness as the founders of summer houses try to figure out how to pass on their often modest property and its intentionally playful character to their children and grandchildren.

A crucial ingredient in their intended legacy is often the protection of the natural environment which surrounds the summer house from over-development. The fact that

Old Money families may be summer neighbors makes their values more readily emulated on such issues as conservation to preserve the entire area from further development:

> The roots of Old Money environmentalism go back to the most fiercely protected of all the treasures of Old Money, their summer places on the coast of Maine, their "camps" in the Adirondacks, their ranches out West ...Patrician trustees [of such estates] fear for [their treasures] at the hands of the public. Good *God*, here they come!

> [However], Old Money's sense of obligations to its treasures is touched with generosity. The circles that patrician trustees seek to maintain around their treasures are never utterly closed. They cannot be. They are open to the future, to lines of descent and succession, and they are not... individualistic. They are social. (Aldrich 1991, 223-4 [his italics])

Most of my respondents are highly conscious of the social obligations as well as the more lighthearted sociability built into their summer property regardless of the source or the amount of the wealth that supports it. Their attitudes and practices are remarkably similar, whether their summer house is assessed at $25,000 or several million, whether the money to sustain it is inherited or self-earned.

Recent builders of so-called "trophy houses" (those of enormous size and prominence illustrating the "ethic" of conspicuous consumption in contemporary architecture) maybe something else again, as it is doubtful that they will expect their heirs to try to keep it over the generations. By the time such a founder dies, it will have served the purposes for which he built it, and passing on the property intact and undivided for the use of his heirs is not usually one of these. However, if the immediate environment becomes overdeveloped with time-shared condominiums filling the view, his property values will go down, so even *he* may come to share the conservation ethos of the husbandry of natural resources. So too may the more typical and less affluent new owners, even those who buy into time-sharing condos who then discover that they have so driven up the price of land that further development threatens their own lifestyle.

Sociologist Seymour Spillerman (1994) considers aspects of family life, inherited property and wealth that are germane to our analysis at this point. In his formulation, *individuals* who work in most contemporary occupations are units of *production*, contributing to the GNP and earning wages or salaries. In contrast, aside from farm families and those who run family businesses, *families* (be they Aldrich's Brahmins or the middle classes) are essentially units of *consumption*. And as Clignet (1992) reminds us, families are also key units of *transmission*. The decisions that families make about what they consume or transmit determine much about the present and future status of their members. For example, does money above basic expenses go into transitory experience (travel, restaurants, clothes, jewelry, media equipment) or into college tuition or charity? Does it go into wealth-building investments to provide for a secure retirement, into mortgage assistance for adult children, or into maintaining a summer house? Is it immediately divisible by all heirs, as fungible wealth, or is it inherently much more indivisible as material property, such as land?

Whether extra capital goes into real property or instruments of liquid wealth such as stocks and bonds, there are ramifications for both those who presently own these assets and those who anticipate inheriting them in the future. Their behavior is altered by their possessions and the way in which they use them, just as Lord Montague is quoted above. As Spillerman notes, some material property can be transmitted and enjoyed without being consumed: given sufficient attention to conservation and repair, a Renoir is not "used up" by being hung on the wall, nor is a summer house by being occupied. At the same time, such material property produces no income, although it surely contributes to *cultural* capital in ways we will explore in Part II.

To be sure, a summer house may have a *kind* of fungibility, expressed in terms of shared or sequential occupancy among its several owners. Further, it can be rented or, in a crisis, sold—in which case it passes into the hands of others who may regard it as the seat of their own dynasty, to be passed on down the line. But if it is to be used and enjoyed by the family, in playful sociability, both the summer house and its immediate environment must be preserved, involving its owners in serious practices of rationalized conservation that they may not need to follow in their respective year-round dwellings.

Independent of any inherited material property, inherited liquid wealth obviously influences behavior, but in somewhat different ways. Of course wealth does not always accompany inherited real property. Thus most of the summer house heirs in this study are, in some respects, "house poor." However, in Spillerman's analysis, those who expect to inherit wealth don't have to sacrifice their own time to earn it, nor do they need to accumulate savings. Like Aldrich's Boston Brahmins, the "income from their income" that is necessary to maintain any property will not stop upon their retirement. At the same time, whether the money is old or of more recent origin, such wealth may come "entailed" with particular obligations as to its use. Viviana Zelizer points out the social characteristics of "special monies," particularly "domestic money:"

> While money does indeed transform items, values, and sentiments into numerical cash equivalents, money itself is shaped in the process. Culture and social structure mark the quality of money by institutionalizing controls, restrictions, and distinctions in the sources, uses, modes of allocation, and even the quantity of money.

Extra-economic factors systematically constrain and shape (a) the uses of money, earmarking, for instance, certain monies for specified uses; (b) the users of money, designating different people to handle specified monies; (c) the allocation system of each particular money; (d) the control of different monies; and (e) the sources of money, linking different sources to specified uses. (Zelizer 1989, 342; 351 [her italics])

The intentions of its original earners affect the liquidity of money in the hands of those who inherit it. Is this wealth to be spent as they please, or is it capital which must not be touched, with only the interest used for some specific purpose such as college tuition or the maintenance of a summer house? Is it legally tied up in trust, or only emotionally so? The situation is compounded by the fact that, as Zelizer notes,—

Questions about how [inherited] money is divided between family members are seldom even asked. Once money enters the family, it is assumed to be somehow equitably distributed among family members, serving to maximize their collective welfare...[Yet] the distribution of money among family members is often as lopsided and arbitrary as the distribution of national income among families. (Zelizer 1989, 353 [my italics])

Fellow sociologist Marcia Millman agrees that love and money can become so mixed up that individuals in extended families are frequently confused about their own motives and desires.

Our society provides few explicit conventions or guidelines for dealing with family money, so many people wind up feeling cheated... [But] even if we lack explicit rules about family money, we still have deep expectations, and when these expectations are disappointed, people are devastated.

Perhaps the one principle widely accepted in the middle class is that children should be given equal amounts... [But] because the middle class emphasizes individual mobility and personal autonomy above all else, it has few shared values and customs concerned with money in the family. When money is based on individual achievement rather than membership in a family, there is little need to impose collective rules and norms on family finances. (Millman 1991, 1-2)

The situations analyzed by Zelizer, Millman and other analysts (e.g. Sweeney 1997) in which family members do not talk about family money are compounded by media coverage about presumed conflicts over inter-generational equity, with seniors on Social Security anticipating the resentment of younger generations who assume they will find much lower public financial support in their own old age. Certainly such conflicts exist, as we will see in detail below. But both intra-family silence and media exaggeration inhibit an accurate assessment by family members of how much they may actually agree on the appropriate level and timing of support, financial or otherwise, to be contributed inter-generationally.

> Unfortunately, Americans do not usually express normative expectations of elderly parents or adult children; perhaps this failure to communicate familial expectations is why there is more perceived tension than actually found in families regarding obligations and expectations. (Bengston & Parrott 1995, 14)

This lack of expression is partly because, as Zelizer demonstrates, rational discussion of the equity of the assigned use and distribution of family money becomes more difficult as different family members give varying and usually unexpressed symbolic meanings to it, beyond its cash value. Whose money is it, for whom is it being held in trust, with what obligations expected of the potential heirs in the meantime?

> In the end, money doesn't corrupt love or families as much as it illuminates them... Money always threatens to uncover what families go to such trouble to disguise. (Millman 1991, 15)

A major issue appears when there is not enough money to go around to cover the obligations presumed of all family members. Obviously, the founders of the summer houses under discussion here have had enough money to finance their daily lives and some to spare to invest in the summer house. Frequently that extra capital was not large, which partly accounts for the modest size and simplicity—even primitiveness—of the amenities and decor of the typical summer house. However, a virtue is usually made of the implicit necessity of the summer house: there are enough resources and commitment to support it *only if everyone* pitches in to help.

Typically, family members expect that they are not to be divided by their inheritance and use of the place but rather to be brought together in mutual and synergystic cooperation. The summer house is to become the family's emotional "sea anchor," steadying the direction of related individuals by linking them to their shared past and pointing them toward the future with the kind of collective identity analyzed by Mead and aspired to by so many "identity" politicians, one made up of interlocked networks of present and potentially future extended kin. In this case it can be maintained only by following the principles set out by Thompson and Aldrich, whereby the property and the related set of roles are both to be conserved and passed along intact to the generations yet to come, together functioning as a unit of consumption and transmission equivalent to the family farm as a unit of production. Indeed, as Part II will reveal, such property is often a unit of cultural production in very important ways.

In turn, the moral boundaries of the family and its extensions through distant kin and in-laws are delineated. In her comparative analysis of French and American upper-middle class culture, Michele Lamont concludes that moral character, centered around such qualities as honesty, the work ethic, personal integrity and consideration for others, is more important to Americans than is social position or high education, manners and taste or even money, which matter more to the French. For Americans,

> Respecting one's moral obligations, particularly vis-a-vis one's family and friends, is often valued as a goal in itself... In keeping with the populist tradition, drawing boundaries [on the basis of knowledge of high culture or money] can be seen by Americans as undemocratic, the way selecting on the basis of religion or ethnicity is perceived by many as illegitimately bigoted. (Lamont 1992, 184-6)

This emphasis on moral worth is expressed by American "patricians" as well as the upper middle class, and surely colors heir relations with their summer neighbors or employees:

> Old Money's breeding in the courtesies and graces and the toughening realities of its ordeals are supposed to lift its beneficiaries above the moral and aesthetic ugliness of the marketplace, but at the same time to discipline their freedom, giving it shape and vigor and the moral content of "character." (Aldrich 1991, 195)

Accordingly, regardless of their own financial standing and whether the wealth that permitted the purchase of the summer house was inherited or self-made, most of the families in this study deny that its economic value has *anything* to do with its symbolic, emotional or moral value to the family. (Of course, those to whom its financial worth *was* the determining value have usually sold the place and aren't in my sample.) Similarly, echoing Simmel's views on the inherent equality built into sociability, they deny that the comparative income or the occupational status of family members, let alone of their summer neighbors, have anything to do with their own decisions about using the place. Instead, the summer house is seen to embody the family's moral worth in its own eyes as well as in the eyes of their similarly concerned neighbors, not so much those in the summer colony but rather those in their communities of year-round residence.

CHAPTER 3

NORMS OF INHERITANCE
AMONG THE MIDDLE CLASSES

For all that middle class Americans may be uncomfortable Milking about the inheritance and distribution of family assets, here are general norms about inheritance which are followed by most. The first is to disregard the inevitable financial inequities among the individuals who make up their extended kindred: equally distanced kin, such as all second-generation children in the direct line, are to inherit equally. The norm conflicts with others, such as that specific bequests should go to the neediest or to the one who most valued a particular item, as well as with principles written into American intestate succession statutes. Thus norms and law may express contradictory principles which Families struggle to resolve, particularly when it comes to such questions as who is entitled to inherit shares in a summer house...

If a will is made, the testator is legally entitled to ignore any such norms, disinheriting some heirs, distributing the estate unevenly among others or putting all kinds of restrictions on its eventual acquisition. As this may contradict the heirs' expectations of fairness or equality, it will surely leave a legacy of family antagonism that becomes the stuff of novels. If no will is made, the commonly accepted legal principle in most intestate statutes is that the surviving spouse inherits a third to half of the estate, the rest being divided equally among the children. The spouse's portion is passed to the next generation only at his or her own death and thereby, perhaps, to members of a second family contracted after the estate was settled rather than to the heirs in the direct line of the decedent, and regardless of the respective contributions or needs of the other kin.

However, in their study of public attitudes toward inheritance, Rita Simon and colleagues (1980) found serious discrepancies between attitudes and current intestate statutes. In the public mind, a far greater proportion of the inheritance should go to the surviving spouse, with a majority believing that *all* of it should do so. Shammas et al (1987) find further evidence for this pattern in the changing history of estate law, which they see being based on assumptions of greater importance in the conjugal bond than in the linear descent.

When there is no surviving spouse, however, rather than an estate being divided equally among the children Simon's respondents thought it should be distributed equally among the direct heirs *regardless of generation*, allowing grandchildren to share the estate with children immediately, instead of only after the children have died in turn. This is based on the belief that similarly distanced heirs should inherit equally, and only if they are included at this point are grandchildren likely to get comparable shares.

> So long as there is a living child, his or her children cannot inherit. This is a general legal principle in Anglo-Saxon law and it is incorporated into the intestate provisions in all 50 states. But it received practically no popular support [from the respondents to our study]. Moreover, contrary to intestate succession statutes, the public did not treat the families of the children equally, but rather treated all grandchildren equally regardless of their parent. (Simon et al 1980, 1270)

Aside from being based on the principle of equality among the grandchildren, there is sound sociological reasoning behind the principle of directly passing on some of the inheritance in equal shares to the third generation. (We will consider the role such a practice plays in estate planning in due course.) There is considerable evidence about the negative reactions of adult siblings to an inheritance that is equally and totally shared by them with no consideration for their own children, the third generation, however that may be based on the norm just described. For example, in a study of partible inheritance in mid-20th century Brittany where the principle of equality among siblings was followed without allowance for any other factors, Martine Segalen found that problems emerged primarily *after* the estate was passed down:

> Deep feelings... only came to the surface amongst siblings and not between parents and children or between husband and wife. Affective relationships between siblings, whether of love or hatred, were rooted in earliest childhood and were brought into the open by the competitiveness that the partible inheritance system imposed. The egalitarian system of transmitting goods thus produced constant and lasting competition between siblings... In such a system, nothing was ever finally settled... Tensions, rivalries and speculation on the future still go on shaping relationships within sibling groups year after year. (Segalen 1984, 142-3)

Granted the differences between French and American culture and legal traditions, the emotional pattern described here is perhaps universal. Such frequent sibling rivalry, perpetuated or re-emergent in adulthood, is used to support the rationale for unigeniture in France, at least so far as material property is concerned. However, the practice of unigeniture finds very little support in America. Instead, the assumption is that problems resulting from equal inheritance among the second generation will be mitigated when some of it is transmitted directly to the third. Cousins have not usually grown up in the same household and therefore have fewer childhood rivalries to overcome.

Accordingly, as they also don't expect to inherit from their parents for some time, any grandparental legacy distributed equally among them is comparatively untainted by any inequalities they might anticipate from their parental legacies. Thus they may be less likely to fight over any inheritance that is passed on to them immediately, and that fact may help to temper the disagreements of their parents, aunts and uncles. Such an outcome is not guaranteed, of course, and the cousins may have additional problems, as we will see in Part III.

One factor that helps to diminish conflict within or across he generations is the degree to which rules of inheritance are sufficiently stable that they are generally followed and can therefore be anticipated as being both just and fair. However, especially in America, while such norms governing inheritance do exist, that does not mean that testators go along with them. As we have observed above, these practices vary even among pre-modern peoples such as the Chimbu or 13th century yeomen, according to circumstance. Such circumstances obviously include variance in the number of potential heirs as well as in their needs, as these are perceived both outside the family and within it.

> There is evidence that patterns of inheritance correspond with power and status in families, and that wills are rewritten as these social arrangements change. There are also indications that satisfaction with one's legacy is a function of how the beneficiaries perceive their status relative to one another. (Rosenfeld 1980, 330)

Perception of relative status involves more than the principle of equality among similarly distanced heirs (among siblings; among cousins). It also involves and frequently conflicts with the principle of fairness. Some heirs are obviously more needy or more devoted to the family than others.

> If all beneficiaries want fair treatment and a will attempts fair treatment, conflict may occur because beneficiaries have different perceptions of what is fair. Fairness can mean that something is divided equally; but fairness also takes into account various

principles of deservingness or right; a division of an estate can be fair without being equal.

> [This is derived from the fact that] there is an inherent conflict between treating children equally and treating them appropriately as they grow up. (Titus et al 1979, 337; 343)

In subsequent chapters we will explore how different families deal with these issues in greater detail. The point is that in the absence of a principle like unigeniture, adhered to by custom and/or written into estate law, Americans have no generally accepted way to resolve disputes among siblings over their inheritance, let alone among cousins or between generations, whether in regard to divisible wealth or indivisible real property. In turn, a family member who acts "dishonestly" to siblings or cousins so as to maximize his or her own share of the estate at their expense may see nothing wrong with those actions.

> As perceived by others, the person at issue is involved in a value crisis. However, in most instances the person at issue sees his actions as consonant with his own system of values and tends to ignore the perceptions of others which are at variance with his own.

> With the realignment of the family power structure [caused by the death of a parent], the behavior of the person at issue could be designed to define, consolidate, or establish a new position in the power structure. (Otto 1977, 16)

Consider what happens when these conflicting principles and their practice or violation are confounded by family structures that include step-relations. From the perspective of the children in the direct line, should a surviving stepmother inherit half of the entire estate or hold lifetime tenancy, or should it come directly to them, assuming they are adults? How might real estate be regarded differently than financial wealth, in this regard? Should step-siblings inherit anything, especially if they have been part of the family for decades? What about half-siblings when the original inheritance has come down through the marital (step-parental) rather than the immediate parental line?

> The ambiguity in [step] relations is part of the American kinship system. Should one consider the several spouses of a decedent or the "children" of several marriages of the decedent as equally distant from [him] and equally deserving, or should one attend to recency of relationship, length of time in relationship, affect level of the most recent relationship, "blood" relationship with the deceased, or most recent co-residence with the deceased? (Titus et al 1979, 344)

Such factors contribute to what family members may think of as "fair," definitions of which are more likely to vary than their definitions of equality. However, whatever their motives and actions, these are experienced in response to both the actual testament and the *process* by which its form and contents are determined. Thus we must consider as well a final set of variables that affect the timing and the procedures through which the inheritance comes to be structured (to be discussed in greater detail in Part V). The motives and values of the testator contribute to the amicable or conflicted relationships of the heirs, regardless of the estate's fair and/or equal distribution.

In Clignet's 1995 analysis of inheritance, the motives of testators were largely derived from their occupational experience, regardless of their social class. He describes three typical patterns. Those who have been self-employed or otherwise entrepreneurial in their occupations (almost entirely men in Clignet's sample) have tended to operate from motives emphasizing efficiency, which in the absence of norms of unigeniture leads toward a simple division of the estate into equal shares with no further fuss, as well as toward an emphasis upon preserving the value of the estate once it has been passed on.

> [The purpose of efficiency] is to maximize familial wealth. Both the actions taken before death (transfers inter vivos) and the dispositions of the will are said to facilitate the same desire to perpetuate the estate... [This] induces many Americans to see the major purpose of estate planning as consisting in reducing federal or state estate taxes. Heirship strategies are evaluated [primarily] in terms of their fiscal implications. (Clignet 1995, 282-3)

In contrast, those more accustomed to cooperative activities typically follow a norm of reciprocity in drawing up their wills, based on the past behavior of the specific heirs and that anticipated of them in the future. It is likely to lead to informal or contingent arrangements which could be easily restructured at a later time. When testators were so motivated,

> There are greater variations in the size and form of the bequests made in favor of daughters than of sons since again parents expect more from the former than from the latter.

> Reciprocity displays time orientations that are reversible since testators and beneficiaries are all influenced by the memory of the deeds performed in their favor and by the anticipation of the benefits they expect to enjoy in the future. (Clignet 1995, 292; 297)

Finally, there is a norm of *ascriptive equality* which is oriented toward the past and is based upon precedents in which those of equivalent status in the family are given *analogous* but not identical rewards. It is typically followed by those in the second or later generations regarding wealth or property they had inherited themselves:

> The greater the diversity of assets accumulated, the easier it is to provide each heir with bequests that are symbolically equivalent to one another, but are nevertheless tailored to specific needs.

> As this [norm] implies the search for the right thing to do, it is influenced by the practices of preceding generations that are seen as exemplary. (Clignet 1995, 295; 297)

As we will see in greater detail below, my respondents vary in their use of these norms according to sex and generation. Founding patriarchs typically value efficiency. Accustomed to dealing with lawyers and accountants, many set up a formal legal structure such as a partnership or corporation for the perpetuation of their property in the family if only as a matter of sensible estate planning. Following a norm of efficiency that they have used in their business careers, such founders of estates are then likely to make "top-down" decisions about the structure of the inheritance, without much consultation with the intended heirs.

If estate planning has not been completed when the patriarch dies, his widow is likely to operate from the contrasting norm of reciprocity, assuming that members of the second generation will work things out informally on a basis of contingency and fairness rather than equality. This pattern among widows has a long history. In a study of women in a town in Virginia in the late 18th and early 19th centuries, historian Suzanne Lebsock notes:

> When we compare what women and men did with what they had, we find the outlines of a distinctive women's value system or culture. At the center of this culture was personalism, a tendency to respond to the particular needs and merits of individuals. When women wrote wills, for example, they tended to pick and choose among their potential heirs, rewarding personal loyalty and taking note of special economic need. (Lebsock 1984, xix)

Thus in transmitting the legal ownership of s summer house, a widowed matriarch may simply add her children's names to the deed to the property: so long as she is alive, she expects it be sure that they treat each other fairly—at least in her eyes. Once they inherit, however, unless they are particularly compatible, the members of the second generation are likely to find implementation of such unstructured arrangements unworkable. Instead (and often with great difficulty but potential success in reaching agreement, as we shall see), they set up an association or partnership which determines the formal obligations and privileges of their use of the property. If they succeed in doing so, they are likely to follow the norm of ascriptive equality, building on the precedents set by both of their parents and thereby incorporating "patriarchal" principles of efficiency and equality as well as "matriarchal" principles of particularity and fairness by finding alternative portions of the inheritance for any heirs who do not want to participate in maintaining of the summer house. The ramifications of all such arrangements will be explored especially in Parts IV and V below.

Obviously inheritance rules are simplified if there is only one direct heir, or at most two. Those born during the 1930s were far more likely to be "only" children or have only one sibling than those born during the 1950s and '60s, the fabled baby boomers. (The 1930s fertility rate of 2.0 children born per woman between 15 and 45 soared to 3.8 in 1957, dropping to the earlier rate by 1965. It is now at 1.8.) Members of these birth cohorts, now respectively in their late 60s and 40s, make up the preponderance of my sample of founders of summer houses and their immediate heirs, with many in the third generation already adult. Many others born in the 1930s are second generation, the place having been founded by their parents, but as many of them are also likely to being sole heirs, as only children or through a buyout, they are in a comparable situation to founders as they prepare to pass on the property to their children.

The principles of sharing the estate equally among the second generation and also settling equal shares upon the third generation at the same time appears all the more sound under these circumstances. All of the cousins have grown up knowing their grandparents, the summer house founders, and have presumably been treated equally by them, typically having visited them every summer. If these cousins—usually born in unequal numbers to the members of the second generation—are denied equality in their inheritance from their grandparents because it has gone totally to their parents, how are they to get along in supporting and sharing the house in their turn?

In the meantime, however, what is equity or fairness for the second generation members if the one with fewer children must relinquish some of her own share of time at the summer house to the siblings with more? In Parts III and IV we will explore how families manage these issues.

We will also examine what happens when the second generation has not yet inherited, even by late middle-age, with at least one of their parents not just alive but also still in charge. Four-generation families are increasingly common, with second or third generation members becoming "status equals" to their aging parents and aged grandparents in the world outside the family, yet remaining distinctly unequal in status within it. The longer such unequal relations among extended kin, both in the direct line and among siblings, cousins and in-laws continue, with all remaining in some state of "child-like" dependence upon the seniors, they less happy they are likely to become. Indeed, even during the mid-1960s, when researchers were proclaiming the functionality of extended kinship in the terms of systems theory, caveats were still registered as to the supposed emotional closeness that was involved:

> Fairly strong forces of social change may limit the experience shared by different generations and may even serve to alienate them from one another. Under these conditions, the strains of emotional distance may develop which ritual observance could serve to ease or control. Thus symbolic behavior—ritualistic visitation (the Sunday visit to grandma [or, for our purposes, a week spent with her at the summer house]) or ceremonial observance (attendance at births, graduations, anniversaries, illness)—can adumbrate the forces which separate people. Thereby it becomes possible to meet obligations and maintain appearances with or without strong emotional attachments, so that different emotional meanings may inhere in similar participation patterns. (Rosow 1964, 375 [my italics])

The larger the number of siblings or cousins and the more they are expected to stay in some contact with each other, the more inevitable and visible are "different emotional attachments" underlying common family rituals and the inherited property in which they may take place. At the same time, these variances may contribute to the strength and richness of assets and affect of the extended family rather than dividing it:

> The larger the family becomes, the more internal organization develops... The large family typically involves greater specialization and multiplicity of roles and functions —greater complexity. (Irish 1964, 284)

Thus in large families, the absence of a temporarily estranged family member may be scarcely noticed and the more readily overlooked if she returns to the fold. If she does not, she is likely to be the subject of much intra-family gossip, all the more to keep the others "in line and to pressure the prodigal to come back. Indeed, one ofher"specialized functions" becomes that of "bad example." Meanwhile, solidarity offered by other engaged family members and the in-laws they bring with them compensates for the emotional distance of any direct kin. Mutually enhancing each others' esteem, those who willingly participate in the extended family typically share their expertise in collaborative family enterprises, especially when it comes to maintaining a summer house:

> Among our generation, considering the direct line and the in-laws, we have a lawyer, an accountant, a doctor, a couple of teachers, an engineer, a carpenter and a painter/paper-hanger, and everyone contributes what they do best. One of has to marry a

plumber and another become an electrician, if we're going to keep this place going with less money than the previous generation had. (Fifth generation in New Hampshire)

Of course, the birth cohorts who make up "Generation X" following the baby boomers are smaller. Numbers of siblings are reduced, as are numbers of first cousins. At the same time, the chances for enjoyment of the summer house are reduced among the third generation, as at least one of the founding pair may still be alive as are all of the enlarged second generation, and with allocation of use of the summer house usually determined by generation with the oldest given first choice. Non-use may diminish their potential attachment to it, whether or not they could have taken the time to visit it if a slot had been offered. Yet families work out means of equitable scheduling, and attachment among the younger generations can remain strong, as we will see below.

One factor in the continued attachment of extended kin to a family summer house is the rise in the number of individuals living alone since the late 1980s. With later or non-marriage, divorce, extended widowhood, to say nothing of increased geographic mobility among young people, for long periods of time single family members may have no kin to "be family with" other than members of their family of origin or procreation. All the more may individual family members need to return to the nest for even brief periods to reconstitute the primary family unit, the *Gemeinschaft*, as distinct from the wider society, the *Gesellschaft*, in which they live.

> I have spent parts of almost every summer since 1948 on the pond—it has been a constant for an academic family that has lived in four different states over the last 34 years. Both of our daughters have likewise gone to the pond most summers of their lives and both were proposed to on the pond.

> Our friends there are the children of my parents' friends, and…we all have a continuing interest in preserving the quality of life we remember as children. (Second generation in New Hampshire)

The perspectives of Mead, Huizinga and Simmel, reviewed in the Introduction, would support these sentiments. All the more may such heirs react negatively to any perceived unfairness in their inheritance, however it may be divided among their kin, if only for the lack of common norms in this regard, as we have seen. It is especially complicated if they are expected to share a place that each may regard as "sacred" in somewhat different ways, regardless of the motives and practices of the founders in making the bequest.

> There are no established norms for a shared household once residence does not conform to the one nuclear family form, when the shared household is the "sacred

hearth" for all family members as the heart of whatever nuclear household they once occupied. (Koburn 1978, 70)

In the absence of norms about shared households and the existence of conflicting norms about inheritance, those trying to keep their summer house in the family are bound to experience difficulties. For all that family members may deny that social class issues affect their decisions and practices in its regard, especially in recent years it is usually true that for the founders, acquisition of the summer house was part of their own upward mobility as they established a higher status than their parents occupied, with considerably more income. Spending summers in what becomes a summer colony of similarly situated people, in the sociability among equals that it affords, confirms t heir new status to themselves. For the second generation, the summer house affirms the higher status to which they were born, as it may for the third.

However, some in the third or fourth generation may deny it out of greed for "their share" of its assessed value, like I Huizinga's "spoil-sports", or renounce it out of guilt or simply embarrassment at being heir to such unearned assets, following Lamont's analysis of the values of Americans as different from the French. Instead, with either motivation to express their own moral worth through achievement, such heirs are likely to assert their own place in the social order through forms of self-acquired material property or experience, even if it takes a sell-off of their inherited material property to finance that achievement. They may thereby set up new tensions and rivalries with their siblings or cousins through their unwillingness to share their inheritance as status equals. Indeed, among my respondents, it is typically the richer heir who insists on being bought out rather than the poorer, those with least means to do so.

Whether or not such a buyout is desired by one heir, members of all generations will find themselves renegotiating their relative positions as they work to keep the summer house in the family. These dynamics will be explored in Part III. In the process they contribute not just to socio-economic change but also to the class stability of family members. In turn, they contribute to change as well as stability in their status and prestige in the system of stratification in the wider society, independent of any economic ranking of social class. We turn to these questions in the next chapter, considering the transmission of cultural identity and the status it provides through the summer house.

PART TWO

CULTURAL TRANSMISSION THROUGH SUMMER HOUSES

THE TRANSMISSION OF RELIGIOUS VALUES

> Cultural conservation is inseparable from the conservation of place... Place links local identity and its specificity with the globalization and inter-dependency of the modern world. Without place conservation, the contexts for culturally meaningful behaviors and processes of place-making disappear, cutting us off from our past, disrupting the present and limiting the possibilities for the future. It is hard to imagine cultural behavior without its culturally appropriate place. (Low 1994, 66)

Independent of the ramifications for social class that the inheritance of summer houses helps to establish and perpetuate, such a house is among the mechanisms for transmitting the specifics of a family's culture to the next generation, providing some of the "glue" that gives meaning and cohesion to its collective identity just as does its "mother tongue" or its religious rituals. Yet maintaining a summer house is more self-determined and hence less taken-for-granted than either language or religion are likely to be. As heirs freely elect to keep the summer house in the family, developing both informal and formal/legal mechanisms of doing so, it becomes part of their conscious identity.

Still, while maintaining the summer house is a serious and even "sacred" business, what goes on there is not primarily a matter of class assertion. Rather, it is intended as "serious play," following the analyses of Georg Simmel and Johan Huizinga discussed in the Introduction. By definition, use of the summer house is limited in both time and space, even if it has been winterized and used as home base for cross-country skiing in January. As a non-divisible asset for families who are able to pass it on to extended kin, it is to be enjoyed for its own sake, ritualistically. Regardless of other purposes to be explored here, the major function of the summer house is sociability, which as we have seen for Simmel is the necessary "play form" of the constituent elements of society itself. Only if the summer house provides opportunities for play and leisure will the younger generations come to value it accordingly; only then will they go on to choose the cultural identity it establishes, at least in this aspect of their lives.

This identity provides a very particular status for those who share it in a collective "we" of mutually "significant others," as George Herbert Mead would have it. This is a state of essential equality within the family, despite the inherent differences of generation, birth order, gender, or any additional inequalities among their "external" statuses based on income and its effect on social class. Following Simmel, we understand how this sense of equality contributes to how family members perceive themselves, as part of a larger kindred. We have also seen how strongly this norm determines American estate planning, especially by men, despite any resultant conflict with the concurrent principle of fairness more frequently attributed to women.

In addition, the assumption of equality within the family affects how its members may be perceived as "unequal" and indeed, as superior by their everyday associates. To own or be an heir to a summer house is usually to be seen as privileged, even by those of greater wealth or occupational status. This may be especially true for owners who do not fit the stereotypes of a local "gentry:"

> Because my last name isn't "WASPy," people are surprised WI mention that I have a summer house in New England, and if I then mention that it was designed by a well-known architect (before he was well known, which only shows my discerning taste!), they suddenly treat me with more respect. (Founder on an island in New Hampshire)

What does it say about one's virtue or that of one's immediate ancestors to have such a second homestead as a matter of right? Without inherited money to provide an endowment, the founders must have been talented and ambitious to earn enough new money to acquire such a place when it was affordable. To keep it going, they must have been possessed of thrift and business acumen and they must have been endowed with generosity of spirit to provide love and security to their descendants if the latter want to keep it in turn, as evidence of the inherited "virtues" it embodies.

No wonder so many founders of summer houses, whose status is a mark of their achievements which enabled the purchase or construction of the house in the first place, want to pass the house and that status on to their descendants. In turn, it comes to be a mark of their ascribed status in the eyes of those without such property, whether these are deemed merely less fortunate or less virtuous. No wonder they want to be sure that their summer neighbors have similar status and virtues, whether achieved or ascribed: one does not want to find "vice" in the same vicinity.

I rented a cottage on a small lake for a secluded summer of thinking and writing. One day I swam out from the beach to a nearby float, on which sat a woman who immediately asked me who I was. I explained my academic and professional background. The woman turned toward the dock, on which sat another woman (her sister), and called: "She'll pass!" Thereafter I was taken in almost as a member of the family. (Friend of a multi-generational family in Vermont)

What attracted this respondent to this location to begin with, and why was it important to her houseowning as opposed to renting neighbors that she "pass"? What subcultural values may be enforced in the wider community of the summer colony even if its residents may deny, as do many of my respondents, that there is such any such community ethos that affects their own individual family decisions, such as whom to befriend? How do they demonstrate Simmel's point that the egalitarian nature of sociability almost requires a prior assessment of equality for its "play" to be engaged?

Given the American emphasis upon individualism and self-reliance and the importance of thinking for oneself, being held morally and legally responsible for one's actions, it is paradoxical that the founders of summer houses so often intend them to become the seat of family through reinforcement of an identity not just within a family, but also in a *community* whose relevance the heirs frequently deny. Of course, in the process of becoming part of a summer colony, organized as such or not, founders and their heirs develop a symbiotic relationship with the "native" residents, who typically make their living servicing the needs of the summer people. While these may be cultivated as "family retainers" over the generations and the younger generation even regard them as social peers, they are not—at least not at first—usually part of the intended audience for the assertion of a particular cultural identity or status which the summer house affords. (This point will be expanded below.) Rather, the "message" of the summer house is directed at family members themselves and at friends who are treated "like family" in their expected allegiance to the sacred character it holds in the eyes of their hosts, as Huizinga would predict.

Founders may build or buy as individuals, but they are also likely to be attracted to incipient or already developed summer colonies where neighbors will be those with similar social and cultural characteristics which they wish to enjoy without a constant wariness over being potentially "different," and which they value enough to want to affirm in their children, their children-in-law, and their grandchildren. Indeed, typically the founders have located the summer house in consultation with friends who may have preceded them to that area or who buy into it at the same time. Historically, such friends have often shared religious or other ethnic or racial identities which the summer house and its adjoining neighbors are expected to affirm, however contested these identities may be in the outside cosmopolitan and polyglot everyday world.

More recently, affirmation of professional sub-cultural identities may be more important than religion. One respondent, an academic and his wife, joined a partnership of eleven other academics and their spouses to buy and renovate what had been a set of camp cabins on Lake Michigan, east of Chicago, to develop a cooperative summer colony.

> In the beginning, we had frequent and often formal meetings every week to agree about such things as the common sewer line or controlling roaming dogs or individual rights to decide about changing the external appearance of our individually-owned cottages. Unfortunately, these meetings often took on all the characteristics of faculty or department meetings at our respective institutions. But we've all been there so long now that we've finally realized that we're like tenured full professors and departmental colleagues passing it on to the junior faculty, and we've relaxed. Now the younger generation does the work or we hire out. (Founder on Lake Michigan)

Establishing and/or maintaining a summer colony of like-minded families, even among secularists like this academic, is a practice that has deeply religious roots in North America. In the absence of pre-existing religious structures like cathedrals and monasteries staffed by professional clergy, any continuity of religious site and practice has depended upon the investment of like-minded laymen who come to take a proprietary interest in both. In many mainstream denominations, as well as evangelical churches, institutional authority is local, with each congregation hiring and sometimes even ordaining its own clergy rather than having them assigned by some higher level of the church. If this is characteristic of many permanently sited religious organizations, it is even more true of occasional rituals of religious retreat and revival.

Unlike all-season pilgrimages to European sacred sites (be they formally religious like the Vatican or Lourdes, or secular like the Pantheon in Paris), from the beginning American religious retreats have been more limited in terms of time and more temporary in terms of place. Typically, such retreats have been held in late summer, out of town and after harvest, when travel was easiest and short-term rental of now-harvested fields or groves cheapest. Once given a successful start, supporters of such retreats returned to the same camp grounds year after year, leading to the establishment of religiously-based summer colonies. The development of Methodist Camp Meetings into summer cottage colonies shows the pattern clearly.

The Wesleyan Great Awakening in the early 19th century led to the practice of holding "revival" meetings of about a week, usually in August, at secluded sites in the countryside untainted by secular activities, where the primarily "townie" devotees could get in touch with the natural and transcendental aspects of their religious traditions. At such camp meetings, with tents pitched a few inches from each other and with shared kitchen and sanitary facilities, the faithful would be reinforced in their devotion, backsliders reclaimed and newcomers converted. Repeated visits to the same leased sites led in short order to the purchase of the acreage and the permanent establishment of Camp Meeting Associations, which in turn leased tenting sites to those who returned year after year.

As their "Protestant Ethic" virtues led to sufficient affluence to afford a longer vacation, the faithful came to spend increasing amounts of the summer at the site, arriving well before and staying after the actual Annual Revival Meeting itself. Before long, they built permanent cottages, typically owned by themselves with the land itself leased from the Camp Meeting Association. Accordingly, all had to agree to comply with a long list of rules governing day-to-day behavior, construction and rental agreements. In many such places these remain in force today and set the basis for any individual family's decisions about the use and inheritance of its summer house.

At Oak Bluffs on Martha's Vineyard, the origins of the Camp Meeting go back to 1835. Within a decade, over 500 tents were being set up by those attracted to the annual Revival Meeting. Permanent ownership of the site was acquired by the Camp Meeting Association in 1857; several hundred cottages were built there between 1860 and 1880. They are now much admired for their fanciful Victorian decoration and the architectural cohesion of the entire community. Like the tents they replaced, in terms of living space the cottages are very small and only a few inches away from the neighbors on all sides. They surround the central park and the Tabernacle in which daily services are held along with Vacation Bible School classes and community hymn sings. The Tabernacle also houses the major revivalist events which continue to attract thousands of outsiders today.

Within the walled limits of the Campground, general rules and regulations include: quiet after 11:00 p.m., a 10-mile an hour speed limit for cars with no overnight parking on the streets, no motorcycles, skateboards or roller skates, no unleashed dogs, maintenance of the cottages to conform to specific standards of appearance, no Sunday repair work even by owners during July and August, and no noisy power tools at any time. All such rules apply to tenants as well as to the cottage owners, who are responsible for enforcing them upon the tenants if they do rent the place.

Since 1931, the Camp Meeting Association of Martha's Vineyard has ceased to require adherence to Methodism among its lease-holders, and indeed, cottage-owners need not even be Protestant. However, transfer of cottage ownership, whether through direct sale to outsiders or through inheritance in the family, requires prior approval of the Camp

Meeting Lease Committee, as noted in the 1992 rules of ownership. The application to transfer ownership must be accompanied by:

> Three letters of recommendation, one from a clergyman in the church in which the applicant is active, and two from persons by whom the prospective transferee is well known. At least one of the latter two should be from a Campground person, if possible....

> In the event of disapproval, proper arrangements must he made for further transfer of ownership to owners acceptable to the Lease Committee (within two years). (1992 Cottage Ownership Transfer Rules, Martha's Vineyard Camp-Meeting Association)

All of this means that any cottage heirs who want a more secular or glamorous summer lifestyle will choose to go elsewhere. To be sure, lively, loud and tawdry activities of particular interest to adolescents and young adults are available just outside the Campground walls in downtown Oak Bluffs itself, but when the young thrill-seekers come home to the cottage to sleep, the traditional rules apply. One does not return to the Campground in a state of boisterous exuberance. Senior members of the community remember their own youth, when gates were locked at 10:00 p.m., and are inclined to disapprove of any noise thereafter.

To those brought up to these rules, conformity seems to be easy even for those whose lives include divorce and all the other problems of contemporary society. Indeed, especially for such people, regardless of religious conviction a stay at the summer house is revivalist in the deepest sense, providing a sense of order that may otherwise be absent in their everyday lives. The summer neighbors understand each other better than they are likely to know people elsewhere; voices raised in ecstasy or anger would immediately be heard by outsiders to the immediate family, and most have spent their summertime lives in such intimate relations with these same neighbors, across generations. In Ocean Grove, NJ, where the Camp Meeting Association still leases several hundred tent platforms, typically held by the same families for generations alongside the permanent cottages, the norms are explicitly taught:

> You are trained to keep your voice low while you are in the tent. You can be louder in the attached shed, where the kitchen and bathroom are, but still not really loud. (Second generation in Ocean Grove)

While the Camp Meeting Association controls only the Campgrounds, its values are perpetuated as well by the Ocean Grove Homeowners' Association, which works to reduce the influx of former mental patients into group homes in the neighborhood as well as to limit access between Ocean Grove and impoverished and crime-ridden Asbury Park, the municipality next door (Schmelzkopf 1997). Only like minded people are to be welcomed, subscribing to Methodist values of temperance and hard work even if not to the tenets of the faith. Clearly, anyone marrying into such a family must be ready to join in the prevailing ethos, if only for a few summer weeks, if the marriage itself is to survive without enormous tension.

> The sense of community and family is consciously valued: neighbors remind each other of the rules and talk about any infractions. The sense of security is palpable: there is nowhere else I feel so safe! (Third generation at Oak Bluffs)

Such values are sought by many families who haven't been able to purchase a summer house in one of these colonies. They frequent such family camps as Rockywold and Deephaven, established by Methodists on Squam Lake in New Hampshire at the turn of the century. Such camps continue to attract the same families who have rented cabins for a week or two for several generations, during the same weeks year after year so that neighboring families see each other every time. Having such long-term summer neighbors contributes to every camper's acceptance of and respect for decorum and a public display of temperance, consistent with the religious origins of these camps. 'Mat sense ofcommunity is increased as well by a common dining room for those housed in the camps' 60 or more cottages on the Squam Lake shore:

> Eventually all the arteries lead to the dining room. Rockywold's wooden refectory overlooks the lake and its loons, dispatching meals by the hundreds, cafeteria-style. The camp becomes the Great Mother, feeding everyone and taking care of all chores: each cottage receives daily housekeeping, wood for the fireplace and ice from the icehouse.

> Perhaps this recognition—that a summer vacation should include freedom from domestic routine—is left over from the days when servants were the norm, or perhaps it's because women founded the camps. Whatever its origins, with all the food, ice, wood and maintenance taken care of everyone can get down to the business of a family vacation. (Cross 1992, 120-121)

Obviously summer colonies based on religious principles, be they Methodist at Oak Bluffs or Ocean Grove, Jewish in the Catskills, or Irish Catholic during the early development of Spring Lake, New Jersey, reaffirm and perpetuate core values that are articulated in liturgical practices during the year for the vast majority of the summer residents. For them, the summer culture is a reflection and enhancement of a specific and consciously promoted "year-round" identity. Indeed, it may be the major location for that promotion among like-minded friends:

> My grandparents and ten other couples—all Jewish and in the same congregation—
> bought consecutive lakefront lots... As immigrants or the children of immigrants, they
> were now successful in their adopted country. In building summer homes for their
> families, they were celebrating their success and their ability to provide a place for
> the family to escape the heat of the city. We were there every summer for the joy of
> it. We were not guided by anything resembling the Protestant Ethic. Judaism is a very
> demanding religion for those who follow it closely, but it is not like that stern Puritan-
> influenced religion that dominated New England. Summer is so short and we were
> encouraged to enjoy every moment of it...
>
> In Detroit, we did not live in a "Jewish" neighborhood [but] my parents constantly
> reminded us of the importance of having Jewish "contacts"... At the Beach [however],
> we were surrounded by our own kind... I never felt as comfortable with my school
> friends as I did with my Beach friends. (Third generation on Lake Michigan)

What of cultural communities where such lines are not so obvious, let alone so articulated? Consider those families whose cultural values are so consistent with those of the
wider secular culture that many heirs deny that the summer house plays any role in their
cultural identity. The founders may have held strong religious values, but the basic ethos
of the site and the practice of its perpetuation in the family have few creedal strictures. To
be sure, in many summer lake colonies, an interdenominational chapel with "low church"
Protestant liturgy has long been maintained on a small island, to which summer residents
come by boat on Sunday mornings. Historically, such a lake-community chapel has often
laid the ground for the more recent establishment of lake associations of property owners,
as from outset the chapels' volunteer clergy affirmed values about land use and property
rights consistent with a conservation ethic.

Given the alternatives of vacation possibilities, the continued participation of heirs
to such secular summer houses is even more voluntary than among the Methodists at
the Campgrounds. For many historical reasons, New England, with the most "Anglo-
Saxon" demographic profile in the country, is full of such houses with sustaining extended
families. Yet if American national culture is generally based on "WASP" values, these are
thus presumably available anywhere. Nonetheless, family members return to their New
England summer houses from great distances. In the next chapter, we explore the reasons
why they do so.

CHAPTER 5

SUMMER HOUSES AS SHRINES TO THE "PROTESTANT ETHIC"

The great German sociologist Max Weber was noted in the Introduction for his analysis of the "iron cage" effects of the rationalization and quantification which are built into bureaucracies. However, he is better known to laymen for his analysis of the "Protestant work ethic" and its unintended consequences for the development of capitalism. The ethic requires work to be done for its own sake, as a "religious calling" and as the means to possible salvation, not as the means to the end of greater wealth and the leisure it may thereafter afford.

> What is preached is not simply a means of making one's way in the world, but a peculiar ethic. The infraction of its rules is treated not as foolishness but as forgetfulness of duty.

> The real moral objection is to relaxation in the security of possession, the enjoyment of wealth with the consequence of idleness and the temptations of the flesh... It is only because possession involves this danger of relaxation that it is objectionable at all... Waste of time is thus the first and in principle the deadliest of sins. (Weber 1958, 51; 157)

Unlike the robber barons who took their leisure and their possessions seriously, building enormous "cottages" at Newport or "camps" in the Adirondacks staffed by servants and with guests arriving by private railroad cars, as we have seen the founders of the summer houses of concern here were hardly wealthy. Typically, they were educated professionals, bankers, lawyers and businessmen, and particularly clergy and teachers whose occupations were scheduled to include a long summer holiday though with little salary left over to enjoy it. Most of those originally attracted to New England for the summer were and are of Protestant stock, like the Methodists we have just considered, including a surprising number of Quakers, but their heirs are a remarkably "multi-faith" lot, through conversion and intermarriage. Protestant Ethic values, rather than any specific creed like Methodism, have been expected of those marrying into such families.

Such summer people intentionally participate in what they want to believe is the ethos of the native Yankees, unchanged since visiting French aristocrat J. Hector St. John de Crevecoeur described Nantucketers in his 1772 *Letters of an American Farmer*:

> Idleness is the most heinous sin that can be committed in Nantucket: an idle man would soon be pointed out as an object of compassion, for idleness is considered as another word for want and hunger. This principle is so thoroughly well understood and is become so universal, so prevailing a prejudice, that literally speaking, they are never idle. (Crevecoeur 1989 [1772], 16)

Certainly the founders of New England summer houses already subscribed to the Protestant Ethic, through which their hard work and thrift led to enough capital to invest in a summer house to begin with. But notably, they were here investing in land for family leisure use, not in property designed to appreciate for profit-taking, nor for crude status-assertion. Still, like the wealthy, such people wanted to get their families out of the heat of urban centers such as Boston, Hartford, New York, Philadelphia and Washington. They wanted to give their children the invigoration of fresh air, fresh milk and produce, along with a certain amount of hard work to maintain the necessary disciplines of mind and spirit without liturgical enhancement.

Whether their summer house was modest in scale or not, they were all skilled in teaching by example as well as by precept and determined to pass along their cultural values to their children. Comfortable enough not to have to rely on the labor of their children at home, they wanted some sphere in which to teach those children how to learn to work through play during the ostensible leisure of the summer vacation, so that work could be enjoyed to become an inherent part of their cultural identity, "for their own good." This was to be "serious play," indeed, as Simmel and Huizinga understood it.

> Labor must... be performed as if it were an absolute end in itself, a calling... Such an attitude is by no means a product of nature... but can only be the product of a long and arduous process of education. (Weber 1958, 62)

At the turn of the century, property ideal for such quasi-didactic purposes became available with the increasing declines in family farms in New England. Among other efforts to develop summer tourism, the New Hampshire Department of Agriculture allied itself with the Boston and Maine Railroad, the former to sell off small parcels of now-vacant farmland for summer colony development, the latter to advertise the ease of rail access to such communities. Together they published a brochure detailing how to build a summer house, from $250 up. There were many takers, and summer colonies grew rapidly on inland lakes and in the mountains as they did along the coast.

These houses teach that family identity and individual morality require hard work; one can enjoy sailing or hiking only after having put in a stint clearing dead brush or staining the deck, whether alone or with children or cousins, thereby fostering both self-reliance and cooperation with the group. Writer Susan Cheever, a fourth generation heir to "Treetops," a family compound of several cottages in New Hampshire, describes its ethos when her mother was there as a child:

> It was to be a family place with organized activities and the discipline of manual chores—the children even wore informal uniforms, middy blouses for the girls and sailor shirts for the boys... Treetops was a pastoral paradise, but it was run more like a work camp than a resort. Vegetables had to be picked, cleaned, and washed before children went to the lake. The chickens and turkeys had to be fed, their houses cleaned and eggs gathered. Jobs [were] assigned to each child according to age. Work Is Pleasure was Grandma Watson's favorite motto. (Cheever 1991, 20-21)

Indeed, cooperation and collective identification is crucial if there is to be agreement about the use and maintenance of the house at all (to be explored further below), regardless of the size of the house or its surrounding property. Like subscription to Methodist values of temperance, the Protestant Ethic becomes "second nature" (as Mead would have understood it) to those who have learned it as part of the summer "leisure" activities at the family's summer house. So ingrained does it become that those of my senior respondents who have retired and spend the winter in Florida, returning to the summer house when the weather is warm enough, still speak about "working" at their golf or tennis, rather than simply "playing" at it. For Protestant Ethic types, one's duty is to constantly strive toward self-improvement, leaving little time for the sense of leisure that permits "play" in Johan Huizinga's sense.

Family members must agree on these values if the property is to be kept in the family despite its undoubtedly escalating value. Regardless of their comparative wealth and whether or not it is relatively new or old, their Protestant Ethic "calling" is to be exclusively and irrationally devoted to family and the conservation of the land, not to profit. Despite the fact that the summer house may well be the largest portion of the estate provided for the heirs so that selling it off to "new money" people or to developers may be tempting indeed, these respondents find such a response unthinkable, even as they are likely to need more financial capital for such expensive items as college tuition and mortgages. (Of course, those who find such an option thinkable tend to take advantage of it and do not become one of my respondents.) Indeed, so firmly has the summer house instilled a "non-profit" ethic among my respondents that many of them earn less in their professional occupations than do the local contractors upon whom they sometimes depend!

In any case, the very appearance of profit is to be avoided, even when family finances would no longer require a hard-scrabble appearance, there is an ethic of "conspicuous non-consumption," individual and collective self-expression through conscious and visible self-denial. For many members of the younger generations, somewhat embarrassed about being heirs to a summer house which they have not "earned" themselves, the only way it can be enjoyed without guilt is that it is "primitive." Friends are invited to bear witness to one's ability to endure deprivation, as a mark of classless self-reliance, of which we will see examples below.

Whether one would prefer a more leisurely vacation or not, to stay in such a New England summer house is to learn that there is always work to be done and then one must go on to learn the skills to do it: to fix the dock or the plumbing, to keep the boats in working order, to fire up the wood stove when he electricity goes off in a storm, to repair the winter damage ices or shore, to tend the garden and chickens, as Susan Chever described activities at Treetops. Local contractors are expensive and consulted rarely, but they are vital for the major projects the family can't do. Thus they are cultivated as family friends, who will come out and lend a hand in an emergency.

> We always take my elderly mother up to the family place and help to get her set in her cottage next door to the one the rest of us share. Last year, I went over the morning after we had arrived, and there she was serving freshly-baked cookies and coffee to the plumber. We didn't have any plumbing problems just then—this seemed to have been just a social call—but a few weeks later when the hot water heater died on Saturday afternoon, he was there in 20 minutes. (Second generation in Martha's Vineyard)

As a result, many traditional status rivalries between "'Townies" and "Summer people" have been erased; if anything, it is the younger members of the latter who strive to emulate the former, again as part of the guiltless and "classless" identity they often wish to convey both to other family members and to visiting friends. In many communities within ready driving distance of big cities, where increasing numbers of people come for weekends only, long-term summer residents have come to side with the "natives" against these new arrivals, to protect the simplicity and lack of pretension (if also their presumably higher status position within its structure) that drew them to the place years ago, as analyzed by Roberta Satow (1993a and 1993b). All the more do they participate in summer activities with the largely working class natives, acquiring a greater sense of classlessness and a new cultural identification in the process.

Granted— there is often a degree of "colonialist" condescension, as well as a touch of "going native," in such an identification on their part. However, from the point of view of the natives, having allies among the summer people is often critical to the survival of their year-long community and their chances to live there after weekenders drive up property values. Joining together in activities supporting a local historical society, for example, both groups benefit:

> By working for the [local] historical society, newcomers show their willingness to participate in and value [the summer colony's] history, and implicitly show that they do not desire to transform [its] society nor to condescend to it, but only to be engaged in it. For their part, the natives welcome the historical society for the opportunity it gives them to establish social ties to the urban business and political networks. (Greenhouse 1983, 128-9)

The symbiotic relationship of natives and longtime summer patron families is obvious. And as the quotes above indicate, such patronage takes attention and work.

For summer house owners with Protestant Ethic values, then, it is clear that one does not go to the summer house to relax, even for a week or two, but rather to undertake a different kind of work. Whether of WASP ancestry or not and whether the summer house is located in New England or not, inner-worldly ascetics (those who were defined by Weber as the "carriers" of the Protestant ethic) are nourished in these summer communities. If one did not arrive with the learned appreciation or an elective affinity for such discipline, one would not want to return.

> My wife and I would be sunning on the deck and suddenly my mother-in-law, in her 70's, would come out with her stepladder and squeegee and start to wash the windows, and my father-in-law would announce a trip to haul trash to the dump and bring back compost for the garden. It's very hard to relax when the older generation is working all the time. (Second generation in-law on Nantucket) I laving married into this family, my husband sometimes takes a dim view of the work that is expected of every one. Friends who visited us there once remarked how wonderful it would be to own a house like this. He said: "No, what's wonderful is to have friends who own a house like this." (Second generation in the Smoky Mountains)

My parents's view was that you weren't put on this earth t o make money but to work, and with 200 acres to be limed under the pretense that this was a place for summer leisure, we worked. In our case, it was the Zionist work ethic, and while I have great admiration for Zionism, that is one aspect of it that I have *not* passed on to my children. (Second generation in the Catskills)

My grandmother insisted that even the youngest child should help around the place, and then we would get a reward. When I was about eight years old, I had spend a hot and stupid hour pulling up grass from the driveway (even then I knew it would just come up again). My reward was a trip to town to get a beachball from the Five & Ten. Gramma and I then took it to the beach to play catch, and of course the wind caught it and blew it out into the lake. I was in shorts, not my bathing suit, and hesitated before going in after it. Gramma urged me on, but of course I couldn't stop it before it was well on its way across the lake. "Never mind," said Gramma, "It will blow up on the other side. Let's just go over and post a notice at the hotel." So over we drove, with me still dripping wet in my shorts, where I then suffered the mortification of having to walk into the elegant hotel lobby to ask that a sign be posted about a missing beachball.

Of course, no one ever turned it in, Gramma never replaced it for me, and I learned lessons about Gramma and her rules at the place that I have never been able to forget: I've done everything possible not to follow them with my own kids. (Third generation in New Hampshire)

Obviously, some heirs or their spouses agree with Weber's sense that the Protestant Ethic can become an "iron cage" from which escape is difficult. That may be true for many in terms of their occupational lives, but given the other opportunities for summer vacations now available to middle class people, let alone to the heirs of summer houses, why do they come back? Wouldn't they rather rent or sell out and go to Paris or Antigua? Indeed, some do, especially if another heir is affluent enough to buy out the defector before he becomes the "spoil sport," in Simmel's terms, and brings about the selling off of the whole place. What of the others? How does the summer house institutionalize their identity, despite or, perhaps, because of its costs, so that there is no sense of being caged but rather of being liberated to be themselves (as Mead would see it)?

We come back to keep in touch with who we are.
(Fourth generation in New Hampshire)

The underlying text is keeping the tribe together. The Lares and the Penates are there: it's the family hearth. (Third generation on Lake Champlain)

This is where we *are* and *do* family. (Third generation in Maine)

As family members maintain such sacred traditions and sites through participation in the planning necessary to determine the use and maintenance of the summer house over the generations, they reaffirm the original Protestant Ethic values it has taught. Today, for the founders or their heirs, the bottom line is not the financial capital that accrues through any "iron cage" of hard work; of greater value is the cultural capital based on free choice of thrift and the conservation of resources, which allows for a rich fulfilment of self and kindred rather than mere acquisition or display of wealth or status.

To be sure, outside New England, the ethic of work for its own sake is less evident among summer houses owners, Protestant or not. Elsewhere in the country, the whole purpose of the place is more likely to be to get together with extended family members and to relax. The necessary work gets done without formal scheduling, whatever informal mechanisms are used to be sure it is taken on evenly.

For example, at Mackinac Island, Michigan, where no cars are permitted and many summer residents keep horses, getting around by buggy if not by bicycle, the necessary mucking out the stable is regarded as play! Susan Cheever's great-grandmother would have understood that definition, but as Cheever's memoir demonstrates, she was totally consistent in making sure that the lesson to be learned was that of disciplined work, not of *fun*.

Such consistency of discipline is far more relaxed elsewhere in the country: one need not get up by 8:00 a.m. for a mandatory breakfast of Grandma's blueberry pancakes prior to spending a full morning at chores before one is allowed to go swimming, and rather than work being defined as pleasure, it is defined as fun, as play. For children, that is a major distinction, just as it is for the adults who must enforce and themselves live by whatever discipline is to be applied.

If you don't make your bed, that's OK. My grandmother would say, "We get up at the crack of noon." (Third generation on Lake Michigan)

My father would get out all the tools and equipment when we arrived, and taught everyone, both adults and children, how to use them. From childhood the kids were driving the tractor and mowing the thistles and thinking it was all great fun. And because there was no shower, if we washed off the sweat at all, it was in the creek. More fun! (Sixth generation in North Carolina)

We get up, eat, go back and lie down, get up, eat, lie down again. We do only enough work to get the food on the table. It's very relaxing. (Second generation in Wisconsin)

We have absolutely no rules. I wouldn't know what rules to make.
(Founder in Oregon)

Among such families, opening and closing weekends are understood as times to pitch in to get the tasks done, in an atmosphere of mutual enjoyment of grandparents, siblings, in-laws and cousins with no accounting as to who does how much of the work. Such families frequently encourage overlaps and casual "dropping in" by kinfolk, operating to some degree without a formal schedule detailing anyone's exclusive rights of use at any one time.

We think the summer is a time for getting together with kinfolk, not to travel as a tourist to someplace you don't know anyone. So if one of the more distant cousins comes in, we all arrive for a "lake weekend," everyone bringing food and drink to share. If we outnumber the beds, we just put sleeping bags on the floor. (Third generation in Missouri)

It has been really important to have the cousins get to know each other and for my parents to spend some extended time with their grandchildren... More than giving us the house, they gave us each other. It is important for a sense of yourself as being part of a larger family. (Second generation in Michigan)

Such sharing in the Midwest is facilitated by the fact that family members are more likely to live within driving distance of the summer house (and/or be more accustomed to long hours of driving to get anywhere) than is the case for owners of New England cottages, which were typically established a generation or two earlier than elsewhere in the country. Accordingly, New England summer house heirs, driven by the Protestant ethic that mandates individual achievement more than the maintenance of close family ties, tend to be more geographically widespread in their current residences. Not living nearby the family summer house, they find it harder to come in for a weekend dedicated to collective house tasks or simply to enjoy the place and their kin.

However, some New Englanders of Protestant stock do not share the work ethic I have just described. These are the oldtime Yankees whose summer cottages were built as fishing shacks on isolated necks of coastal land by their grandfathers at the turn of the century. The original squatters' rights became formalized years later, as property lines were drawn up to permit tax assessment. Some of these tiny cottages still have no electricity or running water, and can be reached, as in the old days, most easily by boat. Composting toilets may have replaced the old privies and propane gas may be used instead of the old Franklin stove for cooking, but water is still hand-pumped and solar heating is the only source available for hot showers.

If the original attraction to such fishing or duck-hunting shacks was for working-class men to get away from townfolk who wanted them to behave according to middle-class standards, the often still working-class heirs to these cottages experience the same "funky" pleasures. They go to the cottage to relax and do only enough maintenance work to keep the place from falling down rather than insisting on keeping idle hands busy at "make-work" activities. Those whose occupation requires physical labor, as is so often the case in these families still today, do not have "hobbies" such as painting or quiltmaking in their leisure time. The *choice* of "conspicuous non-consumption" made by more affluent people in their use of a summer house does not exist for those with lower incomes and less education.

At the same time, the latter usually have less geographic and social mobility, so they are more likely to marry someone local, brought up to the same cultural values, and settle nearby. In turn, casual visits to the cottage of only a few days duration are more possible, and therefore living temporarily without standard amenities is less onerous for in-laws and extended kin. To be sure, even in such cases those thinking of marrying into such a family may not find it easy:

> My daughter brought her first serious boyfriend to spend a weekend at the cottage. He could handle most of it, but using the privy really turned him off He was constipated the entire time. That was the end of that romance. (Second generation on Cape Cod)

The New Jersey shore has a number of neighborhoods of similarly tiny and primitive cottages built originally as fishing shacks like those on Cape Cod. While owned by individuals, many of these are on leased land of plots as small as 25 feet square, a fact which precludes the owners from investing very heavily in improving them. Simplicity is the rule, but the landlord determines the terms of cultural exchange.

> When I first bought this cottage 30 years ago, all the neighbors hung out together; we had collective July 4th barbeques and also on Labor Day, and we all felt a sense of ownership in the whole place. Then the lease-owners died, and their heir is only after money and control, so he has put in all kinds of new regulations and fancy lease agreements as if we didn't always get along and respect the whole property and each other. His need to control has killed the sense of community that made this special. I'm still here, and my husband loves it as a getaway place, but I no longer feel I belong or want to pass it on to our children. (Founder in New Jersey)

Clearly, a sense of cultural identity—religious or not—can be fostered by a summer house if the family's own rules for its shared use are in accord with the norms of the surrounding community. As we have seen, many come to such summer colonies so that their own standards of manners and behavior can be reinforced by their neighbors, as is seldom the case in the urban and suburban communities where they pass their everyday lives. As the children are taught, so are the adults persuaded of the importance of the traditional values they sometimes find difficult to keep "at home"—just as others come to find release from those same values of hard work and moral rectitude which are enforced by their hometown neighbors, in a more relaxed and carefree code of behavior at their summer house.

CHAPTER 6

SUMMER HOUSES AND ETHNIC OR RACIAL EXCLUSIVITY

Some summer colonies have been ethnically or racially exclusive from outset, not simply exclusionary on the grounds of class or cultural values. However, covenants excluding Jews and blacks, in effect when some of these colonies were first settled, are now illegal and in the eyes of many heirs, immoral on their face, even as they may affirm them unintentionally, given community traditions and not wanting to give offense to the summer neighbors. This is clearly true in WASP New England and elsewhere. However, when the summer community has been *founded by* such previously excluded groups, there are even stronger community pressures to restrict ownership and use to members of the same "tribe."

For one example, the particular ethnic exclusivity in the summer lake and river colonies in Michigan's Upper Peninsula was determined by the large number of laboring-class Finns who settled the area at the turn of the century, working first in lumber camps and iron mines and then moving into the developing towns and middle class occupations. Cabins next to the water, with separate buildings for saunas, were a mainstay of Finnish immigrant life, brought with them from home. Even after they have lived in town for several generations, most still keep the tradition of having saunas every Wednesday and Saturday. Thus the necessary saunas at the summer "camps" have been maintained, sometimes just a half-hour drive from home. (In their central role in the solidarity of family and neighbors, these camps differ from other hunting and fishing camps which are almost entirely masculine preserves, sometimes owned by the same families.)

Given the work needed to get the sauna heated up, once it is ready the whole family may occupy it and the neighbors may be invited to join in as well. Men and women may sauna sequentially (the women first, who then cook dinner while the men take their turn); other times friends and family members sauna in mixed groups. In the words of a third-generation Finnish-American historian:

> Saunas are crucial in Finnish-American cultural survival. Total open exposure among all who join in the sauna, with socializing before and after in the changing room as well as over dinner, contributes to a sense of trust in each other that nothing else does, over generations.

> You go out there to relax, to be free from small town conventions. There were only a few public saunas in town, anyway, which were not as personal and family-centered. So even as some in the later generations have married out and moved across the country, they come back.

> Ancestral spirits mingle with our own here as at no other place. It's where culture and nature arc united in a single landscape. (Saari 1996)

However, time has brought changes: the largest such lake colony is no longer "Finn Lake" because changes in ownership have opened the ethnic exclusivity, and some summer camps have been converted for full-time residency by retirees, who spend the winter in Florida. Some of the ethnic flavor has been lost, but without these camps, Finnish-American culture would likely have been more diluted as a distinct entity.

Racial exclusivity is something else, being more deeply rooted in American culture than is that concerning ethnicity. Here too, summer colonies have played a role in confirming the identity of African-Americans. The oldest of these is Highland Beach, Maryland, founded by the son of ex-slave and abolitionist hero Frederick Douglass over 100 years ago as a place where Washington's "black bourgeoisie" could experience the same water-front leisure activities as their white counterparts. Summer residents or visitors have included Langston Hughes, Paul Laurence Dunbar, Booker T. Washington, E. Franklin Frazier and Paul Robeson. Similar long-standing black summer colonies are found at Sag Harbor on Long Island's North Fork, and at Oak Bluffs on Martha's Vineyard, not far from the Methodist Campground. In such racially-distinctive summer colonies, integration would undermine the community's cultural history and the identity it provides for the summer residents. Thus any sales of the 80 or so houses which make up Highland Beach have, until very recently, been only to family friends or other "insiders." Indeed, the notion of "passing" as a community insider has the opposite connotation here. One Highland Beach respondent reported that two uncles were able to "pass" as white during the Depression; as work for educated blacks was scarce, no one blamed them, but having done so they could hardly lay claim to their inheritance at a black resort. This, in turn, reduced the number of family members who wanted to use it, a further reason for casting no blame.

But even here, racial integration is coming, as family members many interracially and some white family friends buy into the community. Indeed, the original Douglass summer house was bought and restored by a white architect who was responsible for the historic preservation projects of nearby Annapolis before being acquired by the Highland Beach Association as a community center. As more Highland Beach houseowners take up full-time residency (improved highways make a daily commute from Washington quite possible), they and their children increasingly socialize with people from the racially-integrated communities next door, who then start to feel proprietary about the waterfront.

Some of the historical character of the community is lost, but one is unlikely to get much "black flight" from a community that is *home* to so many, and any whites affiliating with its residents are unlikely to determine its future by themselves.

Indeed, the traditional and friendly rivalry is between Highland Beach, an incorporated community, and Venice Beach, an unincorporated black community immediately next door. Residents of the former pay higher taxes but do not have to rely on the county for services or permits; at the same time, they do not have a sheltered inlet for boats that Venice Beach has.

Still, the bigger threat to both is development in the county just outside these two small communities, driving up property values and taxes on beach lots to the point that some heirs of old-time summer residents have no choice but to sell out. They may value it less if only because fewer of the younger Highland Beach residents can spend the whole summer there, while others live there year-round, leaving the original summer residents are caught between the two extremes. They may also have fewer extended kin sharing the costs: these summer houses have typically been left to the one or two heirs who valued the community more than did their siblings. This has led to tensions in some families with "disenfranchised" heirs, but is readily accepted in others. Any unigeniture may be determined for other reasons than those of sustaining community values:

> I have three daughters and so did my late brother. I just can't see six women sharing one kitchen. I'll leave it to just one of them, whoever wants it most. (Second generation in Highland Beach)

As change comes to Highland Beach and some heirs seldom return or sell out to newcomers, stability is provided by others who have become full-time residents, either in retirement or as commuters to work in Washington or Annapolis:

I want to join with those of my generation to preserve the quality of life and the history of this community. It's up to us now. I've known this place all my life. (Third generation in Highland Beach)

The Highland Beach Centennial celebration helped to bring the community together, including those in Venice Beach. It also helped the newcomers to understand what our traditions are. We've had typical difficulties between old-timers and the newcomers, as in: "Who are these people who just got here yesterday?" They'll learn and become old-timers themselves. (Third generation in Highland Beach)

There is also a very strong Highland Beach Association of home owners, which has real power to regulate this incorporated community.

Sometimes I think we have ordinances about when to brush one's teeth. (Third generation in Highland Beach)

In comparable racially-determined summer colonies, stability is also provided by the continuing relationships among younger heirs, whether or not "on site."

This has been a very strong community across generations, the kind of community that doesn't exist much any more. This is home, wherever else I or my daughters live. My kids see their summer friends throughout the year in the city, and even if they can't come down much during the summer, they identify with it. (Second generation in Oak Bluffs)

My grandmother bought this property in the 1930's. We now have four houses, two owned by my mother's siblings, one by my brother (he converted the barn) and the other by my sisters and me. We have 8 children together, and I have 4 step-children who have been here for ages, and we're trying to keep all of it in the extended family. It's where we feel we all belong. (Third generation in Sag Harbor)

Such restrictive racial or religious identities help summer house owners, as well as native year-round residents, to resist selling out to developers attracted to the same amenities of the site that attracted the summer people in the first place. Given the long-standing cultural ties, those who might "sell out" against the values of the neighbors will be less able to disappear into oblivion, regardless of wherever else they settle. Accordingly, they are less likely to abandon their house in the summer colony to the mercy of purely market forces, and more likely to sell, if they must, to friends of summer neighbors.

Further, Highland Beach, like other summer colonies newly protected by historical preservation restrictions, requires that any new house built on a lot following the demolition of the previous dwelling must use the same "footprint:" it must conform to the original foundation. In addition, minimal acreage for any single house has been enlarged, so few second homes can be built on the same property. Even with all of the *social* reasons for keeping Highland Beach "within the tribe" of a racially-defined group of "insiders" and their friends, legal regulation has become necessary to preserve community values.

CHAPTER SEVEN

MATERIAL CULTURE IN THE SITES AND STYLES OF SUMMER HOUSES

The discussion so far has focused on what might be called the "ideal culture" or the owners' values which are embodied in the summer house. What of the "material culture," built into the site and the very design of the house? If Highland Beach residents don't have access to a safe anchorage for their boats as do their neighbors, both the importance and the problematics of site differences become immediately and constantly apparent as they change little over the years.

Most of the summer houses under discussion here are within easy reach of water, be it that of lake, river or ocean, or they are situated up a dirt road somewhere in the mountains. A large number are on islands, whether located among the Thousand Islands in the St. Lawrence River, in small or large lakes or off the coast. One of their attractions to their owners is the typical difficulty of getting there at all, with ferry reservations booked months in advance or boats maintained personally with considerable effort. If an island airport makes it possible to fly in, it is taken as a mark of personal strength of character I hat one can deal with the resulting disruption of plans occasioned liar both island host and guest when frequent fog prevents arrivals and departures. At small islands which may be totally owned by the family, all provisions and other necessities must be brought in by boat, and a run to the drug store for some forgotten item will take hours. Medical emergencies can become horrendous:

> They didn't put in a phone line until after my wife was born, when my mother-in-law got a bit nervous about the isolation. As it was, both my grandfather-in-law and my father-in-law died of heart attacks on the island before doctors could get there: as I see it symbolically, that island has killed its men, and after I turned 50 I have not gone back. (Third generation in-law in the Thousand Islands)

Those who can drive directly to their summer house may still treat it as if it were an island, defining the drive either as part of the Protestant Ethic sense of work which the cottage may embody or as the road to carefree escape which may otherwise be part of its ethos. (How any of the latter regard such a long drive as "play" is beyond me, having been brought up to the recognition of the hard work involved in getting four children, two dogs, and two weeks worth of gear and provisions from New Jersey to and from Nantucket before the days of vans, interstate highways and rapid ferries.) For workaholics, however, the drive itself is often part of the process:

> We always drove straight through from Chicago to New Hampshire, 18 hours in the car. It was the only way to convince my father that he was so far away from his work that he could relax. I still live in the Midwest and we still do the same thing: it's part of the family tradition, I guess—both the hard work and the way of escaping from it. (Second generation in New Hampshire)

Why work so hard to get there, when surely vacation sites are available nearby? Most summer houses are at sites of considerable natural beauty, which attracted the founding summer residents to begin with. Once they have incorporated that beauty into their sense of personal identity, as an entitlement, heirs usually seek to maintain that environment through local Historical and Conservation Associations, as noted above. Only then can they justify to themselves their sense of privilege, whether or not they are of the Old Money families analyzed by Nelson Aldrich. To fully understand this thrust, we must consider other sometimes ignored aspects of the Protestant Ethic as Weber has ideal-typified it.

> Man is only a trustee of the goods which have come to him through God's grace... The greater the possessions the heavier... the feeling of responsibility for them, for holding them undiminished for the glory of God... (Weber 1958, 170)

As interpreted through generations of New England thought (and through Thoreau and others, spread elsewhere), transcendental spirituality involves some closeness to and respect for the natural world. Accordingly, aside from learning about sea, lake and woodland through sailing, swimming and hiking, one is to practice an ethic of conservation. This is likely to involve small matters such as using only environmentally-approved shampoo when washing hair in the lake, as well as considerably larger ones such as setting aside large portions of the acreage for permanent conservation rather than for sell-off to developers. While some such practices are motivated by estate planning to reduce inheritance and property taxes, as we shall see, such economic considerations usually come after those based on Weber's perception of the Protestant's responsibility for any "God-given" possessions.

Such a conservation ethic is particularly strong among New England lake and island summer residents, at places such as Squam Lake in New Hampshire or Nantucket or the many Maine islands, where the beautiful landscape has such a fragile ecology that it would be destroyed by much further development. These values are clearly visible elsewhere in the country such as at Mackinac Island in Lake Michigan, much of which is now administered as a state park, preventing any further development.

In many locations, nearby summer colonies which have become developed beyond the carrying capacity of the water are readily identifiable. Their summer residents struggle to combat what has been called "China Lake Syndrome" from the Maine lake where polluting run-off from the cottages that rim the shore has made the previously crystalline waters quite opaque with the microorganisms and seaweed that flourish in what is now the "soup" of the lake.

Others resist the possibility of "visual pollution", especially those in mountain regions such as the Berkshires in Western Massachusetts, who do not want to see rows of condominiums suddenly occupying their views. All the more do those in still pristine locations contribute to local conservation efforts beyond the limits of their own property. Some summer house owners become so engaged in these causes that they establish legal residence at the summer house in order to vote in local elections for candidates who support limited development, often against the wishes of others among the locals.

Granted their obvious self-interest, cosmopolitan summer people have worked at both the state and federal level to develop and get passed legislation allowing for what are variously called "conservation," "original use," "farming" or "historical preservation" easements of the assessed value of the property (Small 1992). These are sometimes acquired with the help of local non-profit Land Councils, which may even take over the administration of the portions of the property so designated. Through such an easement, owners of property assessed at several million dollars—an island off the Maine coast, for example, or several hundred acres in the Sierras—can restrict *all* future development of the land around the small parcel containing the summer house itself (and perhaps a lot or two set aside for heirs to build upon). A designation of "forever wild" or "forever agricultural" allows ownership to be maintained in the family by precluding heirs from selling off to those who would build trophy houses, condos or country clubs, thereby greatly reducing its assessed value. It stays in the family not only because on-going property taxes are much reduced, but so too is the size of the estate on which members of the next generation will need to pay inheritance taxes. Among several of my respondents, the reduction in assessed value through such easements is as high as 80%.

One such founder who has taken this option with his wife, with the full support from their nine children, has given "forever wild" easements over most of their 100 acre island in Maine in trust to the Audubon Society. Remaining under direct family control is only the old house along with its immediate surroundings and access to the waterfront and the dock. Exemplifying the conservation ethos of the Protestant Ethic, following Weber, he describes their motives and values as an intrinsic part of the legacy of stewardship that they are passing on to their children along with the property:

> "Do you mean you own the whole island?"— I answered feebly: "Legally." And that is the truth but not the whole truth. Legally the island is ours, but it's too precious to be owned by anybody and is meant to be shared by [many birds and animals] and the fishermen who have been coming to the island for generations—each feeling that he has island rights.
>
> What we do own is the responsibility for keeping up the old stone house, for pointing and painting and roofing. We spend days each summer repairing the old stone dock... and there are fields to keep from the encroaching forest. And friends and family to share our joys in island living. There are times when we feel that island living is the least private existence one could choose.
>
> When the next awed visitor blurts, "Do you mean you own the whole island?" I'll probably reply, "Well, yes and no. We're *honed* by *it*." (Davis 1974, 41)

As his oldest son is co-trustee on the family trust that was set up to partially fund the place and the other children and grandchildren return whenever possible and happily do the work, those values of conservation and spiritual renewal through hard work appear to have been successfully passed on.

Another form of easement concerns the summer house structure itself historic district designation typically means that no additions can be made at all and that any reconstruction must maintain the "original footprint" of the summer house unless given express permission by the Historic District Commission or its equivalent (as we have noted above in Highland Beach, MD.). Such designations may affect entire summer communities like the Methodist Campgrounds or the "funky" fishing shacks described above, and add an additional reason for keeping the house in the family or, if not, restricting its sale to insiders who appreciate the community's values.

More restrictive still is a facade easement, which means that no changes can be made t the exterior *appearance* of the summer house, even to a change of color from the original. Such easements are available only for houses that are themselves designated as architecturally or historically significant. Altogether, to the degree they are applicable, such easements may be the only way the summer house and its adjoining property can be kept in the family by reducing its assessed value and thereby the estate, even as they contribute to the general conservation ethic that its preservation teaches.

At the same time, truly historic properties such as lighthouses, sold off since the 1930s by the federal government to private owners who have kept them as summer cottages every since, cause special problems. Given their inherent prominence, they tend to bring out any latent "trophy-hunter" or "spoil-sport" characteristics of younger family members who may wish to exploit the site.

> While this place is historically designated, that hasn't done much to reduce its current market value, however primitive it is by current standards. One of the next generation is insisting that we develop it, ignoring how expensive it would be to lay on water and electricity, let alone fully restore it. Otherwise he insists on being bought out. We're really sick about his sense of disloyalty, as he is willing to force a sheriff's sale if we don't pay him voluntarily. It won't be easy but we'll do it. Once this gets settled, we'll try to revise the trust and partnership to prevent anyone else from pressuring the rest of the family. If we could agree on a "no buy-out" provision, like some neighbors have, that would take care of it. Then the family can concentrate on preserving it as it is. (Second generation in Maine)

To the degree it may preclude development, an historic district designation is not always welcomed by some family members, and may happen against their expressed wishes. At the same time, it is facilitated by the fact that as summer colonies developed from the turn of the century, the cottages that make them up were very similar, whether or not they were built according to standardized plans. Later houses in the same area have tended to be based on the same general designs, following the now-established conventions of local contractors as well as those of community taste. The similarity of design and decor becomes part of the aesthetic appeal and community character of such summer colonies, enhancing the likelihood of their historic designation.

In Nantucket, for example, the entire island is included in the historic district. In practice, this means that you can build almost anything as long as the general design is reasonably traditional, the house is covered by cedar shingles destined to turn grey in two years rather than being painted pink, and plate glass windows are restricted to the facade away from the road. Unfortunately, architectural good taste and a respect for an appropriate scale of building is not otherwise required for approval by Nantucket's Historic District Commission.

Similar conventions are followed elsewhere, with or without legal enforcement. This is partly due to the fact that many such cottages were built by their owners themselves or with the help of a local carpenter, drawing up the plans together on a piece of shelf-paper. The design and materials are common: standard two-by-four framing, unpainted shingles which turn grey in salt air, brown in the pine woods by lakes, and are cheap and easy to replace, minimal painted trim, interior pine or oak paneling which darkens with age; no sound or heat insulation.

At some of the oldest houses I have visited while interviewing respondents, wiring for electricity and telephones was installed less than 20 years ago, and some have not yet brought showers indoors (what else is the lake for?). At one Maine house on a small lot with neighbors in very close proximity, there was only an outdoor privy until 15 years ago. A house built in 1815 in a Rhode Island shore community, with only a bit more acreage, is still lighted primarily by kerosene lamps. Among the third generation, using its privy is regarded as "more correct" than use of the indoor bathroom installed for the senior generation 20 years ago; the connection of a telephone line at the same time was regarded as sacrilege; electricity is used only for the refrigerator and hot water heater and the shed from which family members operate power tools for the extensive maintenance this place needs. When these modern improvements were installed, one third-generation member responded with the following poem:

The Bull Frog's Dying

Have you heard, or should I tell
of dial tones and ringing bells
that now compete with croaking frogs
who sang along from floating logs?

At Smithtown now, there's been installed
with wires run (you now are called
from anywhere) the telephones
which end charades with stabbing tones.

Until today, for all the years
emergencies, both joys and tears,
were managed fine without Ma Bell;
we sought the peace of wishing wells.

It was because no outside call
could interrupt and cast a pall
with distant news, both good and bad.
We came for quiet, but now I'm sad.

But soon comes radio, then T.V.
What's to stop the re-runs nightly?
Then the only place I knew
where we would often talk 'til 2:00
will fade into the thousands more
like condos on the Jersey shore.

So now the bull frogs croak no more:
"Why should I sing; whatever for?
Why croak out loud, when I can dial
and send my song a thousand miles?"

This summer house heir is not alone in his sentiments. At a 19th-Century farmhouse in Virginia, the modern bathroom was deliberately installed in the garage, further away from the house than is the privy; the telephone is out there too. Sometimes guests are not informed of the on-site presence of either.

Elsewhere, even when there is modern plumbing, it may not be adequate:

We have to interact: if someone is working at the kitchen sink, it may use all the water, and the toilet won't flush. And of course, there is no television up here, so we have to amuse each other if we are to amuse ourselves. (Third generation in Michigan)

The absence of television is sometimes due to poor reception in these remote areas, but more often it is a deliberate decision by owners of summer houses, just as is continued use of the privy. Two weeks of wet weather can then seem interminable to families with young children or teenagers who are unaccustomed to a video-free existence, but the trade-offs in family togetherness are seen to be worth it.

In other ways, the summer house brings family members into closer proximity than they experience at home. Bedrooms on the second floor may give visual but not aural privacy: the dividing walls may extend up only seven feet, with a single open loft above to help in ventilation. Even if the walls do go to the ceiling, they are likely to be only one board thick. Accordingly, grandma's snores, babies' cries, and squeaking springs are heard by everyone: the institutions of informal social- and self-control arc built into the very design of the house. (As we have seen, at Methodist camp grounds neighbor and neighbor are the ones who are only a few inches away, not just members of the same immediate family.)

Given such structures, if they come to identify with them at all it is no wonder that family members regard them as sacred. Quilts handmade by elder aunts cover the beds;

ashes of deceased family members are often scattered on the property. One family I visited has a specified "Memorial Garden" for this purpose, where weddings and family reunions are also held. As the summer house is the one single family homestead across generations, it is where family archives of photos are kept for all to enjoy. One family has calendars made, both for the summer house itself and for distribution to all family members, with the monthly illustrations taken from photos of the family reunions of the previous year. Successive generations mark increasing heights of growing children and grandchildren on an upright in the garage. Any change in exterior planting or interior decor is usually regarded as sacrilege. Indeed, in many cases it is the youngest generation (now the fourth or fifth) who insist that nothing be changed, as *The Frog's Lament* above indicates.

At the same time, some replacements must occur and even these are not always made easily or accepted readily.

> The mildest suggestions for changes in decor or lighting are met with resistance, even by the next generation, so I don't try. The blood-heirs have all their childhood memories at stake there. When burglars once destroyed some of the furniture, Aunt Jane bought identical little spindly chairs and tottery floor lamps, and placed them just as her mother had furnished the house. No thought was given to improving the seating capacity or adjusting chairs to the size of later descendants' bottoms. It was as if a Ming shrine was being perpetuated. (Third generation in-law in North Carolina)

> I think I have, finally been forgiven for having new slip covers made in 1960, after 30 years of wear on the originals. (Second generation in-law on Cape Cod)

> This house was Grandma's. She was the guiding light, but when the guiding light gets passed on, it loses some of its primary colors. I'm finally learning to value a little more diversity in taste. (Third generation on Nantucket)

> My daughter-in-law has pots of flowers all over the place, even on the dock! She is turning this into Ralph Lauren country, and it's not "mine" any more. (Third generation on Lake George)

Even when the founders were affluent enough to build a summer house of sufficient size to require a live-in servant or two (typically an Irish cook and a housemaid), living was intentionally "familial" and collective, with little opportunity for privacy. This is recognized by the heirs to these larger houses today, who can no longer afford servants at all: whether or not they intentionally subscribe to the Protestant ethic, these extended families must do even more work of maintenance, themselves, than do those with smaller cottages, and their expenses multiply far beyond the ability of any single family to pay.

Last year, one such extended family briefly rented its summer house for use as interior background for the L.L. Bean catalogue. The proceeds paid for the previously unaffordable modernization of the kitchen.

Yet even at such larger houses, the overwhelming pattern is one of greater simplicity than is experienced "at home," in terms of both the material property itself and in terms of what is required to maintain it. As no family members live there all year round, no one's material possessions accumulate and fill the closets. Pots and pans and tableware tend to be sturdy rather than elegant, if the pieces are to survive frequent changes of family members relegated to cook, serve and wash up. Some breakage is inevitable, and no one wants to feel too possessive about objects held in common that may disappear before the next visit. This pattern may seem contradictory to that discussed above concerning the sacred character of summer house furnishings that must remain exactly the same: they can remain the same because they are so common in design that they can be readily replaced with nearly identical pieces.

Replacement is one thing: throwing things away is something else. Despite intended simplicity, some foul weather gear and a great deal of outdoor equipment typically remain at the summer house for all to use during their visits. Those who arrive for several days or weeks can then travel "light," expecting to spend their leisure time in a few changes of casual clothes. They may discover that a long-counted on piece of equipment has been chucked by someone else who took on the annual chore of cleaning out the garage.

Book shelves may keep the same volumes year after year, as demonstration that leisure means the opportunity to re-read the same mystery for the fifth time, or they may burgeon with the gleanings from local library book sales. Summer reading is, well, summer reading and therefore books left in the house are also typically "light" if they are not devoted to local geography, history or nature. For all the seriousness of the latter, a sense of lightness is to prevail in at least some summer pursuits. One may become seriously engaged in racing model boats in the cove or real ones in the harbor, but if the sense of play is lost by too much seriousness, the whole purpose of the summer house is diminished as well, as Simmel and Huizinga be sure to remind us.

At the same time, some common leisure activities are frequently prohibited, such as television viewing as noted above. One family even elected to remove a record player that had been donated by one member, and they have no radio either: any music or other entertainment is to be "home made." If cabin fever and family togetherness become too intense, a trip to town for ice cream or a movie is regarded as a treat. Otherwise, in the evening adults and children tell stories, play cards and do picture puzzles together, just as during the long days they pick berries and make jam or mess about with the boats or build sand castles.

Those who have grown up as children and grandchildren at such summer houses, seeing in turn the next generation enjoying the same spot, experience a sense of timelessness. Even a few summer weeks become miraculously endless as they connect the present and the anticipated future to the past. The very simplicity of material possessions provides for a greater richness and complexity in the family's sense of its own identity, one which is both inclusive as in-laws and newborns are brought into the fold and exclusive in the distinctive sense of "who we are". And it is where already socialized members of the family can recover that sense, as if in a golden age of timeless childhood and innocence.

> Treetops has always been a place where the past is very much alive. The old ways are sometimes inadvertently, sometimes desperately, preserved. When my mother and her siblings visit it now, they occasionally revert to what they were as children. They pick and clean vegetables. They take marathon swims and mountain climbs. They tell stories. They sit around and talk nostalgically about their father's human Rototiller—five children crawling through the dirt with their noses to the ground. Their voices change, becoming higher and lighter. Sometimes, as they clean a cottage or mow the lawns or work in the kitchen, you can hear them talking to themselves —they seem to be talking to the dead.

> We were all children at Treetops. Even our parents were children. (Cheever 1991, 25; 183)

Simmel and Weber, Mead and Huzinga would nod in recognition. In the summer house, the past and its cultural legacy live in the present, transmitted concurrently to those of all generations who are in residence. The elders are reminded of those who came before them and the younger generations made aware of what it will be their turn to embody and to pass on to the next. How they manage to get along in the process is the subject of Part III.

PART THREE

FAMILY STRUCTURE AND INTER-RELATIONS IN SUMMER HOUSES

CHAPTER 8

RELATIONSHIPS BETWEEN THE GENERATIONS: THE FOUNDERS LOOKING AHEAD

We have seen that some elements at the broad level of society—norms emphasizing individual achievement in determining social class, for example—may be modified in their implementation concerning summerhouses by other such elements which emphasize equality or fairness, based on affiliation with the culture in which the family locates itself. These contribute to, as well as derive from, the norm of sociability which is taken by family members as inherent in their use of the summer house, following Georg Simmel's analysis (discussed in the Introduction).

We now turn to factors at the level of individual families that contribute to how their members negotiate their roles and relationships with each other. For all the importance of the social norms and cultural values discussed so far, it is the family members themselves who, as distinct individuals, will determine their success in passing on the ownership and use of its summer house through the generations.

Obviously, the size of the family and the number of heirs in each generation contributes much to the dynamics of the result. The crucial issues to be resolved concern authority over the place, and the rights and obligations of any individual family member in its use and financial support. Who has this authority, how many share it with what degree of autonomy? Most critically (as shown in Shakespeare's *King Lear*), by what process is this authority transferred? We shall hear from my respondents at more length in this chapter than up until now: their individual stories reveal more than any summary analysis.

Without question, the present relationships among the various family members are reflected in, and their future determined by, the structuring of authority over the summer house and the processes by which it is transmitted. As we will see, the varied motives of the founders, as analyzed by Remi Clignet (1995) and discussed in Chapter 3, are particularly important to the outcome when the inheritance can't be divided and must be shared. Such motives are influenced by the complex and often contradictory norms of inheritance in contemporary America, as we have seen.

With each of my respondents, the process through which authority has been and is expected to be transmitted is a nearly always a direct expression of how it has been exercised by the founders, a pattern passed on to later generations. The greater the sharing by the founders with their children, in both informal ways of getting the necessary work done and in formal ways of structuring financial support, the easier is the transition and the better are their on-going relations with each other as they continue to share its use. We will consider both informal routines and formal legal structuring in Part IV: here we consider some of the problems which such routines are designed to overcome.

In this chapter, we look at the *inter*-generational relationships from the perspectives of successive generations of inherent inequality, with elders always superior to juniors in their exercise of authority. 'How do they deal with such differences in power? To begin with, we shall hear from the founders or their heirs in sole possession, with the voices of their children and children-in-law response. In the next chapter, we listen to those of the second or later generations who are sharing authority with at least one other kin member and who must consider as well the interests of the successive generation of cousins. We also pay attention to those of the third or fourth generation of cousins as they deal with their elders.

In the subsequent chapters in Part III, we shall examine *intra*-generational issues of inherently greater equality, focusing on how members of the same generation see themselves as sharing the summer house, whether as siblings, cousins or the in-laws of both. Then we shall look at "life course" variables: issues raised for inter-generational relationships as a result of the birth of new family members, divorce and re-marriage of some, the aging and retirement of others. We will also consider the stabilizing effect of family friends upon the inter-generational dynamics. How may any of these factors set limits to change in the role that each member plays and the authority he or she is allowed to exercise, be that person a founder or one of a later generation?

> Family members each play a role, which is sometimes so inalterable that they seem to be reading from a script. In the world outside the family, they have the freedom to change and to establish who they are through actions. At home, they will always be the character they were as a child within the family context. No matter what their successes, members of their family will forever see them reliving the failures of their youth. (Cheever 1991, 115)

About a tenth of my respondents are founders, married couples and a few widows who retain sole ownership of the property they acquired with the intention of passing it on in to the next generations. Another quarter of my respondents who represent later generations are presently in sole possession because of direct gift, a buyout of siblings, or simply because they were only children. They are in the same structural position as founders in that they need not share decisions with any siblings. However, they also have the advantage of lesser ego investment in the perpetuation of the place *exactly* as the founders established further, they have themselves experienced its inheritance from their parents, usually over an extended period of time as one Parent pre-deceased the other, so they have some pre-existing structure to work from as they enjoy its use and prepare to pass it on in turn.

In most cases, the founding partner who has been more prominent in determining the acquisition of the property, as well as in the initial stages of planning for its subsequent inheritance structure, is the "patriarch," the husband/father. This is consisted with the general pattern of family roles as practiced among pre-baby boom cohorts, those among my respondents who are of the generation to be in the role of founders, among whom the "matriarch," the wife/mother, typically did not have a career outside the home and community. To be sure, such matriarchs have all been full partners in every sense of the word, contributing greatly to the informal arrangements that facilitate sharing or the summer house with their children. However, having made less of an economic contribution to it, the female founders in this sample have tended to go along with whatever legal strategies their husbands have made for the property's disposition, both in terms of structure and timing, and sometimes to their cost.

> While my husband did careful estate planning, we had only just started to turn over shares of ownership of the summer house to our children when he died, so I was the primary co-owner on the tax rolls. It's in Massachusetts, and this was at a time when that state taxed the inheritance of a second house by a surviving spouse to the degree that he or she who could not show financial contributions to its costs (sweat-equity was not counted, as if I hadn't painted and planted and pruned for years to make it worth its assessed value!). Given its prime location, as modest a house as it is, I had to pay an enormous inheritance tax, and if I had died soon after, my children would have had to pay it all over again, and probably would have had to sell the house to do so.

> I immediately increased the gifting to include our grandchildren directly as well as the children, and fortunately I've lived long enough so that together they now own all of it. (Founding widow in Massachusetts)

Such changes in estate strategy, including setting up conservation easements with the local Land Trust, are typical of founding widows who may have a broader understanding of family needs and issues of inheritance than did their late husbands. Such an understanding on the part of widows is not always present, as we shall see—and of course, it is present in many patriarchs, instances of which have been noted above.

Of my respondents, one of the nineteen founding patriarchs and three of the subsequent sole owners of later generations, all male, intend that just one of their several children will get the place. (Everyone else intends that all of their children will inherit equal shares in it, sometimes with shares directly intended to the grandchildren as well.) In each case, their wives were in full agreement with these intentions, at least as stated to me. However, at the time I interviewed them, *only two of those intending just one heir had followed through on the legal arrangements for that transmission*, with the rest of their estate to go to their other children. In the course of the interviews, it was obvious how difficult it is for them to "let go" and start such legal disposition of their property, and the authority that goes with it, while they are still alive—as regretfully experienced by the founding widow above. Regardless of the matter of paying any estate taxes, a number of heirs told me about the problems that had resulted from the lack of any structured provision for transfer of authority and use made by the only people with the power to make such practices stick: the founders, patriarch and/or the (widowed) matriarch as well.

If there is only one heir, there is of course no problem about this aspect of the inheritance. For those with multiple direct heirs, presumably in whose collective interest the founders have kept the place, why do some intend to keep its ownership in a single line when their other children may scream about unfairness? Listen to an elderly founder, his wife still alive and both very much in charge of a property in Vermont of several hundred acres. Its timber has long been culled for commercial purposes and its fields farmed for blueberries over the last 50 years, so it is economically self-supporting. With long-standing farming easements regarding its use, its assessed value is comparatively small, and it is not the major portion of what is otherwise a sizeable estate. Thus any burdens of its ownership are more managerial than financial, so presumably his four now middle-aged children, all professionals, could handle it with no other costs to themselves, and there is plenty of room for additional houses. Even so:

> In my years as an estate lawyer in Boston, I saw so much acrimony over shared inheritances that in my own will only one of my children will get this place. They are all established in their careers; my grandchildren are through college; none of them need it to enjoy life. So in six months after I die, when my estate is probated, the four children will "duke it out" in lottery-fashion as to which one gets all of it. That may seem

unfair, but it was the way we always used when dividing scarce desirables when there wasn't enough to go around among the children, whether it was a single piece of candy or use of the family car on Friday night. They'll accept it as fair...

I had my doubts about such an acceptance. Then, with a twinkle in his still sharp blue eyes, he said:

> Now of course, nothing need prevent them from getting together before the "duking" to make some other arrangement among themselves, so that all can use it in some fashion if they want, but legal ownership and responsibility will be with only one—the one who shows up to "duke!"

In contrast, consider the way another founding patriarch tried to get a sense of how his heirs respectively valued his property, both the summer house and other assets, so that he could will the property appropriately. In Clignet's terms, his motivation has many elements of *reciprocity* rather than the *efficiency* which was demonstrated by the patriarch above. However, one might say that in this second case the underlying purpose was the same: being fair, as well as being just, meant that every item in the estate should go to the heir who wanted it most, who would then be most likely to care for it as the founder had done. However, this method of determining equity was different than that of the patriarch expecting his heirs to "duke it out," if comparably idiosyncratic:

> At Christmas, when the whole family was assembled, my grandfather distributed Monopoly money to everyone for a mock auction to get an idea of how to divide the estate in his will, according to what people valued most. He gave a quarter million dollars to each adult child and also to each of their spouses, and ten thousand to each grandchild. Everyone could bid on any piece of property listed on the itemized estate: presumably, spouses and their children could combine their money to bid on the same thing if they wanted to, which is the only way that just one family could get the summer house.

> Well, no family got together for such a bid so no single family was marked as sole heirs to it, the largest single item in the estate—maybe because no one wanted to exclude their siblings and cousins from sharing it. So in one way the mock auction was inconclusive, even if it was great fun. It was also very instructive: Grandfather's view was that you can only keep this going with creativity, not with law, and that legacy is going to help us settle the issues now that the younger generations are in charge. (Third generation in Missouri)

When I mentioned this story to the wife of the old lawyer with the place in Vermont, she remarked:

> If I had a mock auction like that, I might know which of the children wanted what, but then nothing would seem to be mine anymore. Let them work it out after I'm gone: I want to enjoy what I have while I have it. (Founding matriarch in Vermont)

The notion of "letting them work it out after I'm gone" is typically held by women (a few male respondents voiced it as well), often those who had not been engaged professionally as had their husbands, and who are less comfortable with the idea of relying upon legal structures to resolve internal family matters. Following Remi Clignet's analysis of the motive of reciprocity, such women trust that their adult children will cooperate with each other just as they have done with their mother. But by avoiding decisions about the transfer of responsibility (if not that of legal ownership), they also avoid being confronted with the possibility that their children may have quite varied ideas of fairness in the sharing of their inheritance. Saving themselves trouble, they may compound it for their children.

> My mother is 85, and she can't deal with the rivalry my sister and I feel over the place, even though each of us has her own house on it. She just says, "Can't you just love each other?" We do, of course, but that doesn't settle anything about different standards of maintenance or improvements and all that. (Second generation in New Mexico)

Top-down decisions by founding patriarchs are usually based on the motive of efficiency, again following Clignet. However, such self-determined arrangements, like those of the lawyer with the Vermont property quoted above, may also contribute to more conflict than to less as the once beloved patriarch comes to be seen, by his heirs, to be dictating from the grave.

Of course, no one intends to cause problems for his or her children: rather, founders see themselves as merely exercising power on behalf of their children, not in their own self interest. All of my founding respondents have welcomed their children mid grandchildren to the place over the years: indeed, it was with such an intention that they acquired it, whether in early maturity or middle age. All realize that the pattern of sharing which they establish, involving both responsibility and pleasure, will determine much about how the heirs will administer the place in turn and how they will get along with each other more generally.

Indeed, they readily accept and include their children's spouses, knowing that this is vital to the on-going relations their children will have with each other in the next generation, when they will be in control. The frequency with which potential marriage partners are "tested" by a week or more with the family at the summer house, as we have seen examples of above, shows its importance to the "extension of the family line" through the sons- and daughters-in-law. *Their* families of origin present alternative lines of affiliation which may attract the children, thus diminishing their loyalty to the summer house and the family culture which it inculcates.

As with so much else, however, there are typical gender differences here. Given our society's patrimonial system of kinship in which the male line carries the name and, usually, pride of place, women seem more willing to identify with their husband's family than the reverse, "marrying in" to his family and thus to some degree "marrying out" of their own family of origin. If the reverse happens, they pull their husbands into potential rivalry with their own fathers (or brothers.) We have seen occasional examples of the younger men's resentment above. While some very secure sons-in-law readily fit in, generally it's easier to be a daughter-in-law to an entrepreneurial founder. This is especially the case if his own daughters have "married out," which is a reminder of how valuable are the daughters-in-law in cementing the loyalty of his sons. Sensing this, many founders try to prevent the disaffiliation of their children by special attention and accommodation to their children-in-law—especially their sons-in-law.

> My husband is a computer expert, and my father, an engineer, so respected him that he was the only person whom Dad allowed to sit and relax when all the rest of us would be getting dirty and sweaty working at some project or other. (Second generation in Virginia)

Others, especially the siblings of those who disaffiliate and thus reduce claimants to the family summer house, may welcome their departure.

> My father was a strong character, and everyone in our summer community knew "Mr. Doe." As part of my widowed mother's estate planning, my oldest brother bought us out of our parents' place and I and my other brother each acquired his own cottage in the vicinity. All of our wives have gotten along just fine. But neither of my sisters came back: each married a man who refused to be another "Mr. Doe, Jr." in the summer community when he was rightly "Mr. Jones" in his own name somewhere else. And by marrying men who intended to be patriarchs in their own right, like my father, each could become a matriarch such as my mother was without any rivalry from her sister on the same turf Actually, the fact that they're not here has cleared some of the air for me, as their younger brother. I'm not sure I'd like to meet a sisterly stand-in for my mother every time I tried to do something in town. (Second generation in Massachusetts)

If there is any continued rivalry between father and sons (perhaps exacerbated by the sons' resentment of their dependency on their parents if they are not given some autonomous authority over the summer house until the parents die), the daughters-in-law play a key role in easing it or making it worse. So is it true in reverse for the matriarch vis-a-vis her daughters and sons-in-law (Verdon 1979).

> My first wife never got along with my parents, which made it harder for me when we were their guests at the summer house. I had enough trouble establishing myself as worthy in my father's eyes and my mother found it hard to think of me as adult anyway, maybe because I'm the youngest. So even though my wife thought she was just standing up for me against them, every time we were there we fought with each other. When we finally divorced, it was much easier—and of course I was older and more secure in my work by then. My second wife gets along very well with my folks, especially my mother, and now so do I. (Second generation in Maine)

Not surprisingly, from the point of view of a daughter-in-law herself, it is more likely to be the matriarch rather than the patriarch who presents problems, especially if her husband has married her partly because she is different from his mother. (Again, a son-in-law may find himself in a comparable position with his wife's father if it was their differences which led to the attraction. We have heard from such sons-in-law above.)

> My mother-in-law has very strict standards of behavior and appearance. I'm much more relaxed in both ways, which is one reason I think my husband was attracted to me. But when we go to visit them at the summer place, not only do I have to meet her standards but I have to make sure that our kids do too. It's not easy being their guests, but the place is so wonderful that I'm trying to take the difficulties in stride. (Second generation in-law in Nantucket)

Still, however easy may be the founders' relations with their sons- and daughters-in-law, perhaps inviting members of the latter's families of origin to the summer house, founders seldom see their generosity and sharing as being based on equality between themselves and their heirs. Typically, founders retain moral authority over the place as long as they live, keeping even late-middle-aged children in a state of quasi-dependency rather than full autonomy even when their estate planning may have turned over its legal ownership. In this, they repeat an old American pattern, as analyzed by historian Philip J. Greven in his study of 17th century Andover:

> This distinctive form of family structure is best described as a modified extended family, defined as a kinship group of two or more generations living within a single community in which *the dependence of the children upon their parents continues after the children have married and are living under a separate roof.* (Greven 1978, 33 [my italics])

That pattern of parental support continues today in many areas of family life. According to sociologist Elmer Spreitzer and colleagues, three quarters of the "transfers" of time and money among "living" households (as different from estate transfers) flow from parents to their adult children and are "relatively rare among siblings (and) other relatives," regardless of race, ethnicity and income level (1995: 10). John R. Logan and Glenna D. Spitze (1996) agree, with particular relevance to this inquiry regarding co-residence of aging parent(s) and adult children. Living under the same roof is far more often due to the needs of the adult child than to those of the aging parent. Further, it is the parent who continues to do most of the household work, even when the co-resident adult child is a daughter, the presumed caretaker and kin-keeper.

However, as they focus primarily on the generosity of the senior generation, Logan and Spitze pay less attention to the situation of the beneficiaries, the "in-between" adult children, who usually have children of their own. Such middle-generation members are the subject of a longitudinal study by Reuben Hill (1970) of relationships and decision-making in three-generational families. In contrast to the studies just noted (perhaps because he used different measures of support), Hill found that the second generation plays a crucial role in kin keeping, providing more support for the first and third than they received reciprocally. Thereby those in the middle generation enhance their authority as brokers in the multi-generational continuity.

Both sets of findings are confirmed in the most recent and extensive analysis of these issues by Vern L. Bengston and Robert A. Harootyan (1994). They reiterate the importance of the way founders deal with transmission of authority to their children so that the latter may be willing to serve as "the linear bridge across the generations" (Hill 1970, 330). They conclude:

> The middle generation is the "pivot" in grandchild-grandparent relationships. Moreover, the greater the presence that grandparents had when one was a child, the greater the emotional closeness felt with one's parents. Thus, one "hidden connection" at the family level is found in the bonds that transfer across multiple generations and relationships. (Bengston and Harootyan 1994, 213-4)

It is worth emphasizing that these patterns of extended kinship support exist among middle class whites, comparable to those among poor African-Americans and Hispanics, minorities whose reliance upon extended family has been much documented (Blaydon & Stack 1977; Hays & Mindel 1973; Sena-Rivera 1979).

Obviously, continuing support of adult children by parents exists despite the middle class ideology of individual achievement hat usually precludes *even acknowledging* the dependence of the younger generation upon the older one, even in sharing a summer house the elders have founded and continue to occupy. Rut without acknowledgment, it is harder for both generations to deal with the continued dependence.

Financial differences have much to do with the nature and direction of kinship support in extended families, of course. Respondents for my study (and also in those of Spreitzer et al, and Logan and Spitze) are usually more economically-privileged than were Hill's, which may contribute to the fact that the senior generation remains in charge of the summer house so long as physical health permits, both in terms of covering costs and asserting responsibility for maintenance. Thereby they support their children and grand-children, not the reverse, nor do they rely upon the second generation as "the bridge" or "the pivot" until they are quite infirm. However, most feel only benevolence in their continued exercise of parental authority and the dependence of their children:

> As a teenager and college student, I did a lot of work on the place, including the initial clearing of land for the cottage. As a young husband and father, though, I found that my parents (my mother especially) so much wanted us to "enjoy the lake" that they would take on jobs we had expected to do. This pattern has carried into the next generation in the approach my wife and I take toward visits from our daughters, in that we continue to do most of the work. (Second generation in New Hampshire)

As sole heir, this man may have just as hard a time "letting go" as did his parents: "doing most of the work" maintains a sense of possession that is hard to share when the work is not delegated as well.

Some founders try to mitigate this tendency and reduce possible conflicts among the heirs over use of the place by dividing the property itself while they are still alive. If there is sufficient acreage for other houses, the founders may split it among the children; alter-nately they may help them finance a place of their own on the property next door. Thus are family compounds created, with multiple houses held either in common or individually, but usually with some common land (especially any waterfront) for use by all. There is a concomitant increase in the complexity of its management, which in turn almost requires greater and earlier sharing of authority by the founders with their children (Shammas et al 1987). Such formal arrangements may not be enough to resolve the issue of who is truly "in charge:"

> My mother, in her early 90s, always wants to come and visit when all of us are there. What with two houses, one for my family and one for my sister's, you'd think there would be plenty of room for her with one of us. But she always wants to stay in the separate "little house" (it's really just a bedroom and bath) which she and Dad put up

so they would have more privacy once we all returned with our families. But then, as she is "next door" alone rather than in the same house with either of our families, if she fell it would take us longer to get to her even if she agreed to wear and use an alarm button—which of course she won't do either. She is going to continue to be in charge just as she always was! So of course she has to supervise my cooking, too, as if I haven't been cooking there for years now! (Second generation in the Adirondacks)

However, most of my respondents would not be able to subdivide the summer house property into separate lots. Others have deliberately precluded any such division by establishing the conservation easements described in the last chapter, reducing the assessed value of the land for both property and estate tax purposes, on the one hand, and on the other obliging the heirs to cooperate in the preservation of what is left. As noted, widowed matriarchs often make such determinations, readily taking the role of conservator rather than that of entrepreneur, the one so frequently held by their late husbands. To be sure, such decisions are frequently made jointly by the founders, while both are still alive. We have already heard from such a couple, those with the island which "hones" them still.

Other inter-generational problems abound concerning the exercise of authority over the summer house. If the founding matriarch becomes widowed, she is likely to remain so, given the sex ratio among the elderly. However, if she dies first, the patriarch may well remarry. Such a man, if motivated by efficiency and making provision for his second wife in keeping with the norm that the surviving spouse should inherit the bulk of the estate, may will her the right to lifetime occupancy of the summer house rather than have it come directly under the legal ownership and authority of his children. However cordial may be the relations of step-mother and possible step-siblings and the children, they are likely to change over time—and for the worse.

There is plenty of space at the summer house for us to share with my stepmother and her son in separate quarters during her lifetime tenure, and the trust my father set up still pays for the bulk of its costs. But over the years, despite provision in his will that she and we would share ratably in the expenses, as these have gone up she has become less willing, and things are now so acrimonious between us that we are in court over the matter. It has much to do just with her getting old, possessive and crotchety, but the situation has become impossible.

If there had been a prenuptial agreement settling the summer house directly on my brother and me, we would have been able to avoid this problem. But people like us didn't think about prenuptial agreements at the time my father remarried, and in any case, he didn't discuss this issue with us when he made his will. (Second generation in the Poconos)

Even when prenuptial agreements are thought of and carried out by the founder, there may be discrepancies that cause conflict in the relationship of the stepmother and his children.

> The prenuptial agreement leaves the summer house to be shared by my stepmother and me. However, my father's will provides that it be sold and the money put into a trust for her. He has severe Alzheimer's disease so he is not in a position to settle these legal contradictions. She has no interest in the place other than as a source of money, yet she knows how important it is to me. Now it is my lawyer talking to her lawyer, and I have no idea how this will be resolved. (Second generation in Rhode Island)

Those with stepfathers are not immune to such problems, especially when the summer house comes down in the maternal line:

> My mother willed the two small cottages directly to my brothers and me with no other formal instructions, assuming that "we would work things out." She also left my stepfather the income from her securities as well as her half of their house (they'd been married nearly 20 years when she died). We have had to sell some of her stock to pay the inheritance taxes, thus diminishing his income, but if we are to maintain the summer houses at all—none of us has any cash to spare, what with medical bills and college tuition to pay—then we'll need to go into her capital even more. My stepfather is in his mid-80's and sometimes feels generous and sometimes very definitely not, so we feel we don't really inherit her estate and comfortably manage to keep the cottages going until he dies. That's a terrible bequest to deal with. (Second generation on Cape Cod)

However, such relations are not always conflicted:

> My stepfather was married to my mother for over 30 years, and *his* children by his first marriage and his grandchildren were always welcome at the place she and my father had originally bought together. One of those grandsons loved the place so much, and had contributed so much to it, that when both stepfather and mother were gone, we included him as a voting member of the trust along with my own children and my brother's children with whom he has spent so many summers. His trust membership stops with him and can't be passed on to his heirs, but for the meantime this keeps us all together, as the whole family we think we are. (Second generation in the Massachusetts)

CHAPTER 9

LATER GENERATIONS: LOOKING BACKWARD AND LOOKING AHEAD

Obviously, the varied motives of the founders contribute t o how well members of the second generation will get along with each other once ownership is passed on: the original family roles are often hard to break, as Susan Cheever has ruefully reminded us. While the deaths of both parents may remove the primary audience for any sibling rivalry, the sibling relations established in childhood and maintained through middle adulthood may resist change, even without the presence of the parents to mediate or exacerbate that rivalry. In the words of one psychologist who has studied sibling relationships, "they can't find a solution because they've forgotten the original causes w the problem" (Kutner 1992). Whether or not the cause had anything to do with their shared childhood in the summer house, it is likely to become the site where they continue to relive—or work to relieve—those problems. First, hear some responses of second generation heirs to the legacy left by both patriarchs and matriarchs with respective motives and expectations of efficiency and reciprocity, (following Clignet's analysis discussed in Chapter 3) indicating that neither perspective is without difficulties:

> As the only son, even though I am the youngest, I was the one to whom my father turned over routine management for the whole family compound where each of us owns our own cottage in addition to sharing the common property. He wasn't being chauvinist: my mother, two sisters, and an aunt were trustees, but because my two sisters weren't brought up to do the outside chores as I was (and my professional career has been in business, as theirs has not), it made sense. As a result, over the years there has been a good deal of disagreement over tasks done or not done according to whose standards, just as we used to disagree as kids. With our children it's different: the daughters are just as competent as the sons in every respect. It will be another matter when they're in charge. (Second generation in the Berkshires)

My father was a classic Type A personality, who made decisions first and then told us what was to happen. The way he divided and structured our inheritance of the family compound made sense financially, but the way he went about it made the older two of us feel disinherited emotionally as the youngest seemed to be favored. There was a lot of screaming— it was as though we were adolescents again rather than being our mature middle-aged selves. It was a real surprise, too, because we always seemed to get along as adults, each leading his or her own life independently. We've worked through it now and communication among us is just fine. But there would have been a lot less resentment—even if maybe no less argument —if all of us had been consulted originally. We'll try to apply that lesson with our own kids. (Second generation on Cape Cod)

My mother always preferred one of my brothers and when she was in residence, he could arrive at any time, without notice, and virtually take over the place with his family and friends, even when I was there doing all the cooking and cleaning as she grew more infirm. When she died, she just left it jointly to the three of us, with no provision for how we were to maintain it. I refused to indulge that brother the way she had, and he made so much trouble that my husband and I finally sold our own house, bought out both brothers out, and moved in permanently as sole owners. We'll deal with our own children more equally, for sure. (Second generation in Delaware)

My mother gave the summer house to me when she went into a nursing home, giving my brother in Oregon a comparable share of the rest of her estate as he had little interest in the house. Well, his three kids now want to come back, and she insists that I let them, rent free, even though I and my kids are otherwise paying all the bills. And their use of it reduces our time there. We all resent this. Mother can no longer get there at all, but her authority still prevails over mine. (Second generation in North Carolina)

We're a large family, so there is much variation among the third generation. Some are Phi Beta Kappa and others have been in jail or are simply flaky. Maybe in ten years they'll all have gotten their acts together, but that is not the case now. I can't see why they all deserve equal shares at present, and I can't see how they are ever going to manage it if they do become equal partners in the future. So my siblings and I have put off including any of them in our discussions about a partnership, even though we know we ought to do so. We just haven't figured out any criteria for inclusion or exclusion that we all think is fair. (Second generation in the Poconos)

Having seen some of the difficulties that the second generation may go through in the course of inheriting the place and managing it with the intention of passing it on to the third, let us see positive examples in cases where the founders have operated from the motive that Clignet calls *ascriptive equality*, also discussed in Chapter 3. Here the inheritance process and structure emulate the models established by admired patriarchal as well as matriarchal predecessors, within the family or outside it, which facilitate equality and dignity among all heirs in the same status, i.e. those of the second, third or later generation:

> My father dealt in real estate for a living, and that determined the way he managed the summer house. My brother and I grew up learning to handle it as a family business, and that's how I administer it now, after buying him out in an amicable business-like way. My sons are junior partners in my corporation, and we deal with issues concerning the house just as we run the business.

> The single major change from my parents' time is that my wife and I refuse to "run a hotel" all summer long the way my mother did, which makes business-like management and scheduling of the place even more imperative—and also more possible. (Second generation in Delaware)

> The house had been built by three siblings, one of whom was my grandmother. She and then her daughter (my mother) did all of the scheduling for its use for the extended family of cousins, and my father handled the maintenance. The maternal principle was carried on when I agreed to take over, with both my husband and my brother taking over the tasks my father did. With the next generation, though, there seems to be a greater mixing of activities among the female and male cousins. The main point is that it was always a shared operation, and continues that way. (Third generation in Vermont)

Clearly, some founders have found ways to ease the transition of both authority and autonomy as the summer house is passed on. Without question, they build upon, even as they contribute to, the positive feelings that members of the second generation have toward each other and pass along to their own successors, as Reuben Hill's respondents show us:

> The modified extended family would seem to require an active "kin-keeping" middle generation in order to function in three generation depth. Who needs such an extended family network? Apparently all three generations do for they turn predominantly first to immediate kin when trouble strikes... Less than a fifth (of my respondents) utilized non-kin only for help during the year of the study. (Hill 1970, 78-9)

Perhaps fortunately, a summer house provides both the occasion and the necessity for such mutual help among extended kin, even when family members are independent and affluent enough that there is less need for reliance upon each other "when trouble strikes." Indeed, given the importance that a summer house plays in cementing family solidarity across generations, under conditions of summertime leisure and play, it surely contributes to the willingness of extended kin to step in to help other family members in need, and of the latter to accept that help.

While unconcerned with the sharing of property such as a summer house by multi-generational kindred, Hill's as well as Bengston and Harootyan's findings also support the view that the smooth transmission of property from first to second generation determines the success of the whole enterprise. However, average life expectancy has risen since Hill's study of nearly a generation ago, thereby extending the period during which the second generation is dependent on the founders so far as the latter remain in control of the summer house, to the point that they have grandchildren of their own. The degree to which they are *allowed* by their parents to serve as mediating kin keepers may depend upon the wisdom, as well as the health, of their parents.

> My daughters were married and had started to have children before my father died, and I now have five grandchildren, the oldest in third grade. My widowed mother was willing to depend upon me when we were at the summer house far more than Dad would have been willing to do, even more so during her last summer when her health was beginning to fail, so by the time she died this Spring I had in effect been running the place for several years, as well as handling the family relations with my siblings and their families so far as the place is concerned. Dad had gifted it to us, sure, but he never gave up a bit of authority. At least Mother did that, letting us all (finally!) act like the responsible adults we are. (Second generation in the Adirondacks)

Such a transition to administration by the second generation may not be an easy one for the recipients, regardless of the motivation and wisdom of the founders:

> My parents involved my brothers and me in their discussions of the best possible legal structure and the process for transmitting ownership of the summer house to us. But we weren't really in charge until they had both died. Much as we get along well, we've learned how hard it is to go from their rather authoritarian regime to a participatory democracy. I now have more understanding of what the Russians have been going through in the last few years! (Second generation in Maryland)

An additional factor is the degree to which the founders were able to "assimilate" their children-in-law into the family. If these have fully "married in," thereby contributing to the perpetuation of at least some aspects of the husband-wife roles of the founders, the second generation siblings and in-laws may find themselves slipping into the personal roles taken by the same-sex founders, typically divided along traditional divisions of labor by gender. So sisters and sisters-in-law share "feminine" domestic tasks and brothers and brothers-in-law share "masculine" business aspects of the summer house management.

While we have seen a number of positive examples of this pattern, it may also set off new rivalries among any *same* sex siblings ("Listen, brother, *I* am the one to take over Dad's role here, not you!") as well as contributing to the perpetuation of old ones between cross-sex siblings. Fortunately, this tendency is mitigated by the fact that the inheritance almost always comes down only in the direct line rather than being legally shared with in-laws. As a result, so far as his or her own spouse and children are concerned, each second generation sibling is heir to *both* of the parental roles enshrined in the summer house, with the spouse serving as supportive partner rather than as stand-in for the cross-sex parent, a point to which we return shortly.

> Whenever my brothers and sister and I had our "annual meeting" to discuss summer house issues, as our parents' health declined and we took over more and more of its operation, we found ourselves playing the old games of sibling rivalry based on the traditional sex roles our parents had embodied. My brothers dealt with external maintenance and legal issues and my sister and I talked about things like replacing the washing machine or the bedspreads. But since our parents died, we've come to make administrative decisions on the basis of convenience (for example, whoever lives near-est or has the time oversees any work) and competency (for example, my sister is better at keeping the books than either businessman brother so she now does it). We're finally acting like colleagues, including the in-laws, regardless of gender. What a pleasure it is now to get together, as mature adults! (Second generation on Martha's Vineyard)

As the numbers of extended family members increase, given increased longevity in every generation, first or second cousins may have little opportunity for autonomous use of the summer house and therefore little reason to invest in it emotionally and to incorporate it as part of their adult "selves," as understood by George Herbert Mead and reviewed in the Introduction. On the other hand, if the second generation has remained involved, adding their weight to the enhancement of a specific family identity initiated by the founders, any greater scarcity of autonomous use by the third generation may make t heir attachment to it, and any attendant rivalry, all the greater.

In Chapter 3, we considered the norm that has says that all grandchildren should be treated equally in inheritance, regardless of how many are born to any individual child of the decedent. not built into the structure of inheritance, that norm may take moral prece-dence over legal ownership, leading to continued quarreling among extended kin as we have already noted from the perspective of second generation heirs, above.

I thought I would inherit the house from my mother, but my aunt thought she should get it, as surviving sister: after all, it was her own parents who built it and she had spent summers there even though she expressed no interest in it when they died. Now she has sued me, as my mother died intestate, and at the moment all we do is deal with lawyers and no one uses the place at all. We'll have to sell it to pay the legal fees! (Third generation in Maryland)

My aunt and uncle lived much closer to the place than my family did, so they did most of the work and used it much more. There's only my sister and me on our side, but I have seven first cousins there, and they were upset that we have inherited half of it, especially when their parents were still alive and wanted to keep using it themselves. I finally sold my quarter to my sister so that I don't have to deal with the hassles. (Third generation in Rhode Island)

I'm an only child, so I inherited my mother's half, sharing ownership with my aunt. She has five kids with whom I get along pretty well, but we're not equal in present or future authority or inheritance shares. If my aunt insists that the bathroom tile has to be replaced in the same awful shade of green and my cousins all side with her, morally it's six against one regardless of legal ownership. (Third generation in Connecticut)

When my grandparents died, only a few months apart, my seven cousins and I were all adults and launched (if not really established) on our careers. Grandma and Gramps willed the summer house equally to all of us, skipping the middle generation altogeth-er: as cousins, we had all loved going there but both of my aunts had fought with my grandmother so they wanted nothing to do with it. However well we cousins get along, my aunts so hassle their children about taking part in its use and management at all that those five cousins want the other three of us to buy them out, and none of us can afford to do so without selling off the whole place. (Third generation in Maryland)

These examples illustrate the problems that all too frequently result from the found-ers dealing inadequately with the inherently contradictory principles of equal shares to the second generation *and* equal shares to the third. If basic guidelines of managerial authority have been established when the summer house was transferred to the second generation, whether they are administered informally or are detailed in a legal partner-ship or other formal arrangement, the third and later generations are far more likely to work things out despite differences in style and "deservedness."

When my grandfather and his brother inherited the summer house, they started the principle of sharing it between the two lines, identified still as the "Vermont Smiths" and the "Kansas Smiths" from where the brothers respectively settled. Each line gets one summer month in the main house, alternating by years, with the other being able to occupy the small house. Each line pays half of the basic expenses, and there is a small daily users' fee to cover the rest. Right now it's all being administered, in terms of scheduling as well as bills etc, by the wives of the oldest cousins on each side. They've been trying to pass the jobs on to the fourth generation, and they are insisting that we talk among ourselves to decide who will take over.

We always overlapped with cousins, as I was growing up, with both those in the third generation and those in my own, and in both lines. I've grown up knowing all these extended kin so I'm sure we'll find a way to keep it going. (Fourth generation in Vermont)

The rules of the trust that my great-grandmother established provided for priority use by generation, at least during July and August, as well as for the two managing trustees to come from different generations. Right now, the "business manager" is from the third and I, the "social manager," am from the fourth. Even though there are about 100 living heirs, the scheduling isn't much of a problem, as everyone knows and accepts the priorities by generation, and is happy to take turns accordingly. It's big enough that the senior members usually invite their own children and grandchildren to share it with them during their week or two, so that members of younger generations are included even without autonomous reservations. And since those who use it pay rental fees, if you don't get there for a few years you're not resentful on financial grounds. (Fourth generation in Maine)

There are four lines in the family from the siblings who set up the trust to administer the family compound they inherited from my grandmother. Each line provides one trustee, each of whom helps fund it during his or her three-year term. Altogether there are over 40 family members of three generations who use the houses in some way in any given year, with time-share by rotation, by line, in four-year cycles. On the whole it all works remarkably smoothly, and the youngest adult generation remains involved: there are three weddings scheduled for next summer among the fourth generation, and all will take place in the field by the lake. (Third generation in New Hampshire)

These examples show the importance of inter-generational communication and cooperation, as with increased numbers of extended kin, both informal mechanisms and some formal legal structure detailing both financial obligations and privileges of use become necessary if the inequalities built into the multi-generational structure are to be resolved. We will consider the available alternatives in time. In the next chapter, we turn to *intra*-generational relationships— among siblings, their immediate in-laws, and among cousins—where greater basic equality can lead either to cooperation or to open discord.

CHAPTER 10

RELATIONS WITHIN THE SAME GENERATION: SIBLINGS, IN-LAWS AND COUSINS

Despite the inequalities built into adult sibling relationships, reflecting original family status in terms of birth order and gender and adult status in terms of professional accomplishments and income, as we have seen siblings tend to regard themselves as entitled to equal rights of inheritance. In Chapter 3 we considered the fact that equality and fairness may be differently understood. For the most part, the siblings among my respondents share equally in the ownership of the summer house (or may have bought one another out at market rates), even as they sometimes divide up its use and expenses in terms on principles of fairness based on such factors as the respective numbers of their own children, amount of maintenance work they do, etc.

And that is not always easy:

I have only two kids and my brother has six. He's strapped for money, understandably, so he insists that the place be rented sufficiently to cover most of its expenses. Well, that means very little time for us to use it, to begin with, and because I have fewer family responsibilities and also live closer, I'm the one to go down at change-over day every couple of weeks to make sure that the departing tenants have left it in good order. That isn't always the case, so I have to deal with the mess, and then, even though I have come to resent the tenants, I also have to deal with realtors to promote its rental as much as possible. Much as I love my brother, this business is driving us apart, as it makes me feel like I'm pimping the family property. (Second generation on Cape Cod)

Most of the founders in my sample were raised before feminism and the sexual revolution altered traditional gender roles in which women, not men, are the "kin-keepers" regardless of generation, and they have to some extent passed this role on to their daughters. That may contribute to the fact that their children who get along with fewest difficulties are usually sisters only, or brothers only (itself pointing up the key role of sisters-in-law in helping brothers stay close to their family of origin.) Among my respondents, those who have the greatest difficulty over rules of sharing the summer house are cross-sex siblings, who can't respectively assume the roles taken by their father and mother, traditional or not, if only to avoid any implication of the sexual bond which united their parents, and where cross-sex in-laws may conflict with each other on the same grounds.

Certainly many sets of cross-sex siblings get along very well, especially if their mother has fostered the cross-sibling bond (Goody 1970). However, some have such difficulties that they are relieved only by the sister(s) buying out their brother(s) —more common than the reverse among my respondents—or by a total sell-off with neither keeping the place and continuing unpleasantness between them as a result. These patterns are consistent with the findings of Francine Klagsbrun, whose 1992 study of adult sibling relationships provides much evidence for the greater closeness of sisters than of brothers, with cross-sexed siblings being least close of all. Degrees of closeness among adult siblings, regardless of sex, obviously continue the patterns set in their childhood, both positively and negatively.

> My older sisters bought me out. It wasn't the demands of the house that drove me away: it was the smothering relationships that got to me. I am the youngest and my sisters have always tried to "mother" me, even now when we are in our 50s! I have seen my sisters several times in recent years, but I prefer keeping some distance between us. (Third generation in Virginia)

Despite this example and others we have seen above, sisters are thought to be able to cooperate more than do brothers:

> [Traditionally] sisters learn to help one another and rotate leadership positions at home... and they carry those skills [to other situations. Instead,] brothers learn more about competition with each other...

> Sibling relations do not lend themselves easily to change. With parents, our roles, of necessity, reverse over time. As they grow older they become more dependent... But as members of the same generation, siblings travel together across life's time lines, and nothing in the natural course of events forces them to uproot their deep-seated ways of behaving and assuming new roles or new responsibilities.

> That we do modify our behaviors toward each other at all is testament to the flexibility of human nature and the process of growth and maturation. But change is not

built into sibling relationships, as it is with parents, and new situations often parallel earlier ones. (Klagsbrun 1992, 334, 328)

As we have seen above, extended families with summer houses in the Northeast tend to have less spontaneous sharing in the use of the place than do those elsewhere in the country, perhaps because having been founded earlier, there are typically a greater numbers of heirs which necessitates greater formality in the scheduling of visits. However loosely or tightly scheduled are any joint visits, any opportunity for siblings to overlap with each other allows their own children, the first cousins, not just to become close to each other: it allows them to connect with perhaps more congenial aunts and uncles, thereby deflecting any difficulty that members of the third generation may have with their own parents and that which the sibs may have with each other. Further, as they are likely to have more choice among cousins with whom to affiliate than siblings have with each other, members of the third generation may be in closer touch with at least some of their "horizontal" kin than are members of the second, a pattern supported by Hill's findings (1970, 66).

As noted in the previous chapter regarding relations between generations, critical to the successful relationship of siblings sharing a summer house are their respective spouses who have "married into" this family and who must feel comfortable spending their vacations at a location where they seldom grew up themselves. At the same time, the relations of second generation in-laws to each other (as well as to the siblings they have respectively married) will determine much of the success of their management of the summer house.

[A majority of my respondents said that] husbands and wives improved relations between siblings rather than hindered them, and sisters-in-law—so often maligned— were the most helpful... Along with sisters, sisters-in-law can be the glue for family togetherness. (Klagsbrun 1992, 312-3)

Again we see the importance of a woman having a sense of "marrying into" her husband's family, accepting and being accepted by his siblings as well as by his parents. Among my respondents, the fact that sisters usually bought out brothers rather than the reverse indicates how critical is the role of a disaffected sister-in-law, who may pull the brother out of the family inheritance despite patrilineal traditions (Verdon 1979). But it also shows the critical role of the in-marrying son- or brother-in-law who must overcome any rivalry with the patriarch and his wife's brothers if he is to support her in this buy-out, if not just to simply to enjoy visiting his in-laws.

Regardless of the gender constellation of the siblings, if there are only two heirs, the relationship of each with the other's spouse is particularly important, as there is no one to break any deadlock between them:

My brother and I would get along very well in making decisions about the house, except that my husband can't stand his wife and possibly due to guilt by association, she isn't too fond of me, either. It has taken some time to work out an arrangement where my brother and I discuss house issues only on the phone, and our spouses don't have to run into each other in person. (Second generation in Maine)

Even with more siblings sharing the inheritance equally, the in-laws are often perceived as being the cause of any disagreements between brothers and sisters, or with neighbors:

You see how long it takes to get out to our place from town. Well, when my brother and his wife had finished with their slot of time before turning it over to me or my sister, his wife would take home everything they had brought, including the toilet paper, rather than leaving anything for those who followed her. Relations with her got so bad we finally agreed to buy him out. (Second generation in the Adirondacks)

We got along fine until my parents died and my sister and brother and I inherited the place. My brother-in-law immediately started to get very domineering, which he hadn't been when my father was alive, and my sister of course sides with him. Now we have disagreements all the time, even over such things as using pesticides on the bugs or DeCon on the mice. He's a rabid environmentalist while my brother and 1 just want to zap the vermin as quickly as possible. (Second generation on Cape Cod)

The wife of one of my nephews didn't realize that we always let the neighbors swim in the pond: after all, they made up the construction crew who helped us build the house. So when she saw them there, she chased them off. We didn't hear about it for some time, by which point they were full of resentment at this uppity family member. It took awhile to straighten it all out. (Second generation in Oregon)

Such acrimony lies behind most of the buyouts among my respondents, with any troublemaker being paid off, if the others can afford it, so that they can enjoy the place in peace. Such a "spoil-sport" who refuses to play "the summer house game" according to its rules (following Huizinga's analysis in the Introduction) causes even more trouble if the others can't afford a buy-out to meet his demands. If the place must be sold, the break is likely to be life-long. Whoever gets blamed, supposedly-forgotten sibling rivalries surely fuel any disagreements that break out after the founders have died (as the work of Simmel and Mead, also noted in the Introduction, help us to understand). This is especially true if the founders have not arranged for the orderly transmission of their authority to their children while they are still alive. All the more important, then, are the sisters- and brothers-in-law who usually have no legal standing in the house ownership but who are relied upon as silent partners, at very least.

We have seen enough positive examples along the way that discord should not be taken as inevitable. Indeed, those who have given such testimony above (and more to come, below) take it for granted that they can work out any difficulties with other family members, and even those with problems have found ways of dealing with them in order to keep the place in the family. One often overlooked strength that in-laws provide is the easing of any sense of structured inequality and rivalry among siblings based on birth order or gender: their presence strengthens the adult roles that the siblings play, supporting their maturity in the face of the tendency to "become children again," as Susan Cheever describes her mother and aunts.

As for the cousins in the third or fourth generation, in most cases they have not grown up in the same household, so they have been spared the sibling rivalries that may appear, still unresolved, when fully mature sisters and brothers share a summer house. At the same time, they are likely to have fewer common understandings and standards, which often leads to tension. However, the summer house itself can be a source for resolving the stresses it engenders:

> The host of group routines required by the primitive technological existence at our house turned out to be one of the primary origins of our close family identity. When you have to pump water, boil it and hand wash dishes for 30 with four other cousins you didn't really know well, or spend an hour filling kerosene lamps with an uncle or cousin who live across the country from your home, or gather a group of initially disinterested cousins to travel up to the house in the winter to shovel out the outhouse so it will be ready for summer use, group identity is both created and reenforced. Putting a load of dishes in a dishwasher provides no such opportunity. (Third generation in New Hampshire)

Whether or not cousins overlap and join together in routine tasks, if a structure has been established to assign shares of use and responsibility of the summer house by the time they come to adulthood, their relations are likely to remain cordial, even if some of them do not get to the house very often.

However, if such a structure is not in place, because no normative pattern of hierarchy exists among cousins it is more difficult for any one of them to assert the necessary authority to lead the rest into closure on some formal partnership or corporate structure.

We are 11 cousins, children of two sisters, one now dead and the other who turned her half ownership over to a bank for administration. Members of my line are thorough

New Englanders who believe in protocols; the other cousins are laid-back Californians, who don't. For five years now, we've been circulating drafts of a proposal as to how to arrange for maintenance and equal use of the summer place, but we can't agree and no one is willing to insist that we at least decide what people can do without prior consultation and approval. Last year my husband and I arrived for our slotted week to find that someone had painted the pine paneled living room white, including the full stone fireplace! I don't know what we're going to do—our kids are becoming adults, and some of them want to use it too, and we have absolutely no guidelines about that possibility. (Third generation on Lake Champlain)

That it is difficult does not mean it can't be done:

> Of the ten cousins, four were disinterested in the place. The other six formed a "buying group" and we used the remaining inheritance from our grandmother to buy out the rest of the heirs. We're working on a formal governance structure now. (Third generation in Nantucket)

> My grandmother set up a trust to keep the place going, and since most of us live within two hours of it and there is room for some overlap in use, the first cousins were pretty relaxed about the whole operation. It was the second cousins, members of the fourth generation, who insisted that we get together and set up a formal structure so that the increasing costs could be met on some equitable basis and they wouldn't be left with the job of trying to figure it out. (Third generation on Puget Sound)

While many of these successful arrangements were rather "ad hoc" in origin, they are made easier if a number of alternatives can be considered. In Part V , we will consider guidelines for others to follow intentionally, rather than just by luck, in reaching agreement on some formal structure.

CHAPTER 11

LIFE COURSE EVENTS: MARRIAGE, BIRTH, DIVORCE, REMARRIAGE, & RETIREMENT

Family continuity in owning the summer house through several generations assumes that "life course" events—marriage, birth, divorce and remarriage, aging and retirement—will alter the family structure through the appearance of new members and the disappearance of older ones. We've seen above how prominently the summer house appears in the family rituals that surround all such changes in life course, with weddings and honeymoons frequently taking place there.

> Most of the cousins want to have their weddings at the place. If all the family members come, which they almost always do, there are 43 people to be put up just on our side. Fortunately we have a compound of several houses! Planning for weddings there helps to connect the new in-laws and their families to our family. (Fourth generation in Maine)

> Since we built it 35 years ago, there have been 13 honeymoons in that house, counting both family members and friends. The young couple have to arrange the wedding according to the schedule of rotation of its use, but that brings both into an understanding of what, they're in for if they want to visit it later. (Founder in Nantucket)

As members of the second generation give birth to the third, cribs, highchairs and other baby equipment accumulate on the site, to be replaced by floats and life preservers as the cousins get older, to be replaced in turn by outboards and windsurfers. Whoever cleans out the garage or shed where the layover equipment is stored for the winter must take into account the ages of all in the youngest generation as to whether something will be used again.

If the second generation has always shared residence with the founders, their bringing babies along presents both enchantment for the new grandparents and attendant problems.

My father retired and my parents now spend the whole summer there, which was fine until I and my brothers started to bring grandchildren with us when we visited. The walls are only one pine board thick and you can hear everything from one end of the house to the other. Crying babies were not what Dad wanted, and of course then my wife got more on edge too. Dad solved the problem by remodeling the garage into a bedroom, happily at the other end of the house, so he and Mom don't hear us when they want to sleep. (Second generation in Vermont)

My husband gets along wonderfully with my folks and has always enjoyed being their guest at the summer house when it was their turn to have it (they share its ownership with my aunt and my uncle, and always included us at some point). But now we have three kids of our own, and it would be neat if my family could have it all to ourselves once in awhile! But I can't tell my parents that my husband wants to be "head of the family" when we're there, just as he is at home. He only gets a couple of weeks off a year, so vacation time as family time is real important, and it's impossible to meet simultaneously the desires of my parents that we be there with them and those of my husband that I and the kids be somewhere alone with him. (Third generation in Rhode Island)

Some families try to resolve such problems by putting up tents or simply having sleeping bags on the floor, solutions which work with older children if less so with babies. In one family, the "kids only" tent sprung a leak and was then found to be permeable by spiders (horrors!); the solution was to put the tent up inside the garage rather than outside. The garage walls also muffled, to those inside, the noise coming from fights over Monopoly when wet weather kept all confined.

For all of the problems that increasing numbers of children may bring to daily living at the summer house and/or to passing on its succession in both a fair and equal fashion, the rewards are seen as being worth the difficulties, for all concerned. And if the summer house is large enough that siblings can share its use simultaneously, cousins get to know each other as they seldom can at a few family gatherings at holidays, as we have seen, as can sisters- and brothers-in-law. Siblings may then discover that as adults, without their parents to serve as audience, they have indeed gotten over whatever rivalries divided them as children as they rejoice in a new-found sociability as equal kin.

Just as new in-laws bring new personalities and talents into the family, to be appreciated (or not) by those already there, so too do adopted children, who are less likely to "take after" any of their siblings, aunts, uncles or cousins.

> My siblings and I have four adoptees out of the 11 children in the next generation. Talk about personality differences! Among other things, it means we have even more stuff around than most people because none of the cousins have the same tastes or interests. But my parents made no distinctions between their adopted and homemade grandchildren, and it has really helped to incorporate these kids into the family. At the same time, as they are all so different, I can see trouble ahead as to how they will get along when it is all in their hands. (Second generation in Connecticut)

Many of the families in my sample have members who have experienced divorce and remarriage. In one case of divorce involving the founders, they had more problems agreeing on custody of the summer house than they did on custody of the children, finally settling on joint custody of both. In another, remarriage of one family member and divorce of another had equally happy outcomes:

> My father was very much a "nature boy" and he thought we should leave all the cobwebs intact, as part of the atmosphere of the place. One of my sisters-in-law was a real neatnik and it drove her crazy. But she died, and my brother remarried someone who loves it just the way it is. A nephew's wife so loved the place that when they divorced, she insisted that she get one week of his allotted time at the house. We still get along with her just fine. (Second generation in Vermont)

Remarriage may bring a disaffected family member back into the fold, as the second spouse may get along better with the family than the first. The obverse may also be true: second or third generation members who had always gotten along may resent the new-comer.

> When my older brother divorced his wife after 18 years, I felt as if! had lost a sister. We had shared so much at the summer house where we often overlapped! I'll never be able to relate to his new wife the same way: we haven't gone through early motherhood together. Her taste is fancier, too, and now being married to the oldest male in the family, she thinks she can play the role at the house that my mother did. Not in my lifetime, she won't. (Second generation in the Adirondacks)

Remarriage also brings with it the likelihood of step-and/or half-siblings and cousins. We have seen in Chapter 3 that there are no norms governing their inheritance, although most families who settle on formal agreements for joint ownership of the summer house deliberately exclude anyone who is not in the direct line and thus in-laws and step-children do not have any legal share of the property. This is the case even when the second marriage and the step-relations have lasted for a long time, as was the case in Susan Cheever's mother's family. Cheever reports the distress experienced by her mother when she lost 30 years of summertime connections with her five step-siblings upon the death of her by-then widowed stepmother, at which point ownership of Treetops went directly to those in the direct paternal line. Both direct heirs and their now-excluded step-kin felt somehow "disinherited," including Susan herself, by the inevitable distancing of the step-aunts and uncles with whom she had shared her own childhood and adolescence. Cut off from a major piece of their own history, the step-relatives understandably severed nearly all contact with Cheever. There are obvious alternatives to this outcome, as we have seen above in a case where specific and congenial step-kin were granted lifetime use but not heirship, but that may be easier to structure in a fairly small extended family than in such a large one as Cheever's. Then comes the issue of retirement. Those who are sole owners, sharing neither title nor authority with any siblings or cousins, may sell their primary dwelling, spend the entire summer at the vacation house and otherwise lease a condo in Florida for the colder months. This in turn precludes any independent use of the place by their adult children, with resulting tensions that we have acknowledged above. At the same time, the second generation may be emotionally caught between the needs of their own children and the demands of their aging parents (even as we have seen above that the elders cater to their needs more than the reverse). Thus they may be increasingly questioning "the contract across generations" whereby their ability to enjoy the summer house may be sacrificed to the well-being of increasingly long-lived elders. We have seen that they are crucial to the success of relationships between their own parents and their children and grandchildren (Bengston and Harootyan 1994; Hill 1970), so any departure from this role has serious implications.

> We are somewhat reluctant to turn over complete control of the cottage to our kids just yet. In retirement, we think our time has finally come to spend much time there each summer, and to be in effect the primary occupants for a number of years. Having never had use of it alone until my parents died, much as we love our four kids and grandchildren, we want an empty nest much of the time we're there. Still, we do plan to share the cottage with our kids more than my parents shared it with us. (Second generation on Cape Cod)

One obvious solution would be to build another house for the children on the same property, if it can accommodate it, or to buy adjoining or nearly adjoining lots. If either is possible financially, many families do just that.

> My brother has the original house, and we bought the house next door. Then we acquired still another house, which we rent or let our adult children use. Two of the cousins have married into other island cottage-owning families, so they have other places to stay when we're full. (Third generation at Mackinac Island)

If the place becomes winterized and the aging founders decide to live in it full-time, what had been the family vacation house becomes their primary residence, what they think of as *home*. If so, it takes on a slightly different connotation for their children and grandchildren: if their parents live at the formerly "summer" house all the time, it upsets whatever sense of equality the children may have established among themselves through sharing its use or taking autonomous turns. What had been a house which belonged to everyone, in equal sociability, comes to be filled with the furniture and the role structure with which the now adult children had grown up. In turn, long-buried sibling rivalries may resurface, which will make it more difficult for the founders to reach agreement with their children about how they are going to pass it on. Such difficulties can also occur when permanent residence by an heir displaces the founder instead:

> One of my daughters was disinterested and the other and her husband got full-time jobs in the area, and asked if they could live in the big house full-time. That was fine with me, as I had always preferred the coziness of the little house which I have continued to use during the summers. They had the big house winterized, and my son-in-law gets along much better with the "natives" than I do, which in turn has made life easier for me when I am there. But while I am in the process of passing on full legal title to them (I don't want to give it all up until I die), they have started a lot of probably illegal construction of out-buildings for which I am probably liable. Yet given all their contributions, what can I say? (Founder in the Berkshires)

One uncle found work in the area and asked to be allowed to winterize the place at his own expense and live in it full-time. Grandmother approved, but she left it to my mother as well as to him in her will. As it is now "home" to him and his family, even though he moves out during our annual stay to a smaller cottage he has built down the road, he acts very proprietary. Mom says it's as if we can stay there only "on suffrance" and she resents it. At the same time, all of us first cousins get along just fine, so perhaps it will work itself out when it all comes down to my generation. (Third generation in Vermont)

If one such summer house can be winterized for permanent use, so too are neighboring houses likely to be. What had been a summer colony of escape from the serious routines of everyday life then becomes just another suburb. Summer residents can come to be seen—and see themselves—as transient interlopers ignorant of the real concerns of the year-round community. Under these circumstances, the heirs may be perfectly happy to sell the place to the highest bidder and lose their own history in the process. It is no accident that so many of my published sources devoted explicitly to summer houses are elegiac: their authors have already lost the summer house or expect to lose it. Such accounts reek with nostalgia for the innocence of perpetual childhood which the summer house provided even for the adults, unmitigated by any sense of the complexities and responsibilities of co-ownership to which my respondents attest. Still, as these latter also report, whether or not the ashes of the founders have been scattered on the beach or buried in the shadow of a favorite resting place, the place becomes sacred in a way no primary dwelling can be.

This is true not just for members of the extended family, but also for long-time friends who have become "like family" over the years, who have visited the summer house every summer (with or without their own children along) and who have witnessed and partici-pated in all of the family changes over time. Often a couple the founders embraced when both were starting their married lives, they become quasi-aunts and uncles and their chil-dren quasi-cousins to the growing summer-house owning family.

In the course of time, even as their own circumstances change, such family friends retain an aura of unchanging stability in the eyes of the family members who see them only once a summer for a few days, or only every other year, and *always* at the summer house, not elsewhere. If the summer house itself has permanence in family memories, so too do these genial family friends, who serve over the years as alternative role-models, sometimes even alternative "parents" to the children and grandchildren with whom they have shared only brief summer days.

> Martin and Sally used to come every Fourth of July weekend, and I grew up feeling secure that they and their kids (older than I was, so not really close) would always be there. Then for several years it seemed as if there was a lot of tension, even though they and my folks tried to hide it during their annual visit, when they came without their kids. They still took me out sailing and doing risky adventuring than my parents didn't want to do (and maybe didn't even know about). Then Martin came by himself for a couple of years and I gathered that he and Sally had divorced. Then he came with Pete, who fitted in just like the "uncle" Martin was—actually, better than Sally had been an "aunt"— and the two have come every year since. Well, of course now I'm old enough to understand the situation, and as I kind of grew up with it, seeing how close Martin and Pete are together and how much I enjoy them both, I've realized that what matters in relationships is that you truly be yourself, including whatever sexuality you were born with. And then you can be comfortable, and so can everyone else. If Martin and

Pete hadn't been part of my summers from adolescence on, I don't know when I would have realized that. (Second generation on Cape Cod)

Such yearly-visiting family friends may have a particularly strong impact on the children of the founders. Their parents' friends may well have been present more consistently over the years than their "overlapping" aunts and uncles. Such friends may become more intimate than their own kindred, as they are always met in a setting of leisure built upon the ideals of sociability, as extended family members are usually not so restricted in mutual get-togethers.

In his novel Crossing to Safety (1987), Wallace Stegner captures the critical role such a couple play in the lives of their friends' children, whose mother has called for a reunion at the summer house where she is dying of cancer. After dinner, they talk together on the porch of the "Big House (which) overlooks a lot of family history." The family friend tells the story:

It is less a conversation than a series of recollections, reminders, and questions. We are affectionately scolded.

— Doesn't your conscience bother you? All the time 1 was growing up, (we) Morgans and (you) Langs were part of the same family, back and forth ...and up here every summer. Then you go and move... and quit coming...

— You know, you really do belong here! You and Mom and Dad were always so in tune. I remember you going off to those Sunday evening concerts that Mom started .... They used to play phonograph records through a loudspeaker from the town dock and everybody'd gather in canoes and rowboats... We'd watch the four of you row away and as soon as you were around the point we'd tear the place apart.

(Your mother) knew that. She thought it was good for you, once a week...

— You were so much a part of us, like aunt and uncle. Meals and swims and hikes and picnics and expeditions... (Mom) never found anybody else it's so much fun to do things with...You made this a happy place for all (of us).

What are you saying? You made it happy for us. We were privileged visitors. (Stegner 1987, 235-8)

In Stegner's novel, the visiting "aunt and uncle" help the adult children deal with their mother's dying, just as coming back to the summer house helps them work through many unresolved issues of their own married lives and friendship with this family.

Like Susan Cheever's memoir, Stegner's novel pays homage to the love enhanced by the collective "selves" engendered in mutually tempered and fond relationships expressed through sharing a summer house. Lucky folks indeed, to have it and know it. As recipients of family generosity, such friends contribute to its transmission to the next generation:

> My mother's college roommate Betsy, a never-married business-woman, used to come with her close friend Cora and Cora's Aunt Pearl for the last two weeks of the season, and they would close the place up. Well, one year my husband and I endowed the place with a waterbed, which we set up on the deck so that the water was heated by the sun. Dad was horrified: he thought it would invite scandalous behavior in public, or something. But then Betsy and particularly Aunt Pearl thought it was marvelous, and as Dad had great respect for Betsy, that made our the water bed okay, and we set it up for years.

> They came every September, even when Betsy and Cora were in their 70s and Aunt Pearl was in her 90s! But then Aunt Pearl and Cora died, and so did my father. And when Betsy was dying of cancer, she asked Mother if she could come back and sit on the deck and watch the sunsets. She flew in for a week, and Mother took care of her—I think she was scarcely able to eat at that point—and they sat together as Betsy had wished. Betsy flew home in a hospital plane and died ten days later.

> I learned something about giving from the heart, watching her and Mother together that I will never forget. (Second generation on Cape Cod)

Such a collective sense of identity and ownership, experienced over many years of shared summer activities with both extended family members and friends, shows itself even in trivial "life-course" issues caused by the inevitably growing vegetation surrounding the house. Friends are usually part of the "work crew" involved in major projects such as pruning and witness t he quarrels between those who insist that "nothing be changed" I rom summer to summer and those who insist that the view changes if one doesn't cut the greenery way back.

> If we're to see the water at all, we have to prune the trees and mow the meadow. Well, someone always insists that nothing be done, and then of course when we do it, they say they thought of the idea. But meantime it's unpleasant, and the friends who helped with the pruning are roped in as witnesses to one side or the other, but then we all end up with gloriously hilarious memories of the fighting and the work and the fun involved. (Fourth generation in Maine)

> We have to keep cutting back the scrub oak and other bushes in front of the deck if we are to see the harbor from the living room. I did this year in and year out, and

finally complained to my sister. She got her son-in-law to do a major job of grinding up the bush and extending the perimeter of cleared land. I thought it would add maybe another five feet, but when we got there for our turn at the place, we found that he had pushed the "lawn" out at least 30 feet, all of which will have to be watered and mowed. I hit the roof? But by the next year, when we were there, the larger space seemed appropriate, and as we had a new dog, for once there was room for him to run without a threat of ticks. Don't know that I've ever apologized to my nephew-in-law for screaming at him, though! (Second generation on Martha's Vineyard)

Rather than simply prune the excess, some use the inevitable growth of vegetation as a means of reinforcing collective ties to the summer house:

> Whenever we cut back the bushes or thin out the garden, we take cuttings and get them started (we have mason jars of cuttings all over the place) and then give them to anyone who uses it, family or friends. Once we are back home, it keeps our sense of connection as we tend our home gardens "in absentia" from the summer garden. (Second generation in New Hampshire)

When such summer house activities are added to the routines of everyday life at home, or when stories, pictures and memorabilia are shared at holiday gatherings of family members, the summer house plays a major role in their sense of identity and continuity. In fact or in memory, it is the site for rituals celebrating the ever-changing yet eternal life course events they experience. But while such developments are inevitable with the passage of time, the structures that perpetuate their celebration at the summer house require deliberate planning. How families organize such structures is the subject of the next chapters.

PART FOUR

FAMILY ROLES AND ORGANIZING STRUCTURES

CHAPTER 12

"MATRIARCHAL" PRINCIPLES: WORKING AND SCHEDULING

How do families as individual and diverse as are my respondents show any common patterns in the ways they organize their use and support of a summer house? Surely each family is unique! So they are in many ways, but as I interviewed one respondent after another, I kept finding the same basic principles at work, even as each family apparently thought they were unique in any particular practice. Here we consider those practices, in this chapter focusing on the informal and "personalized" structures of authority over the summer house typically instituted by women. In the next chapter I review the various formal, "impersonal" legal structures of authority more typically instituted by men.

Whatever the particular form of its exercise, authority over the summer house by the founders may be taken for granted as an aspect of their parental roles, both by themselves and by their children. As these roles have usually differed, in most cases with women being the "kin-keepers" and men handling management of household property, so too have the forms in which that authority is typically expressed, with whatever happens at the summer house determined in large measure by the forms it takes "at home" on a routine basis. The forms of expression of that authority have different ramifications for the success with which its heirs share it and pass it on, in turn.

> Authority is a matter of legitimacy. As a right, it exists not in the one who exercises it, but in those who accept it... At the very least, authority must be maintained through ritual...

> The types of power and influence usually attributed to women tend to be impermanent and cannot [readily] be transferred to others. Men tend to become experts

in authority through their experience in authority systems of larger scale outside the family.

> The inequity between the sexes is usually not based on the fact that women lack rights, but on the fact that their rights are apt to define women's sphere in a way that leaves men with more general access to power. (Curtis 1986, 172-3)

To be sure, such traditional separation of spheres of influence is changing, but the younger generations (among whom women are as active in "authority systems of larger scale outside the family" as are their brothers or husbands) have typically not yet inherited the summer house. Whatever their sense of autonomous authority in their everyday and professional lives, and regardless of their own achieved mobility in social class or feminist terms, such women inherit a situation in which their mothers and aunts were more likely to have exercised authority in the summer house through the kinds of *informal* practices which we will examine here, while their fathers and uncles more frequently worked through more elaborate and *formalized* sets of rules, although among the inheriting generation women are as engaged as are their male relatives in setting up new formal structures and in the revision of old ones. Nonetheless, these are described in the next chapter in terms of the patriarch who typically has initiated them rather than in terms of those who may presently execute or revise them.

In any event, whether the family traditions be informal or legally institutionalized, there are only a limited number of forms and norms of behavior attendant to keeping a summer house in a single family over several generations. Legal forms are understood to be limited in type, if not in detail, but much the same is true of the informal ones. In interviews with my respondents, I kept hearing about the same ways of keeping extended family members both engaged and amicable in the more than life-long project of supporting a summer house, yet each family seemed to think it had invented those particular techniques. If what needs to be invented is a wheel, it is not surprising that all such efforts appear to be very wheel-like. And many of these techniques, maintained as part of the family tradition, carry more "formal" weight than do the legal structures that may also have been put in place and which may be attended to on a pro forma basis only. So important are these practices that it is unlikely that the children will manage to keep the place collectively after she is gone if some such traditions have not been established, based as they are on the motivation of reciprocity as discussed above, regardless of the legal structuring.

In Chapter 13 we will examine the formal legal structures set into place primarily by the patriarch, if only as part of sound estate planning. If some legal structure for the sharing of the summer house among the heirs has not been set into place when he dies, or if he was so totally motivated by efficiency that the heirs were not consulted, the children have a harder time deciding on the optimal structure—or living with that which was decreed. Moreover, if such a structure has not been established by the time of the third generation, as we have seen above it may be very difficult for the cousins to agree. Both reciprocal and efficient motivations and the resultant practices appear to be necessary and symbiotic, appearing in Remi Clignet's motive for structuring an inheritance that typically combines them both: ascriptive equality (discussed in Chapter 3).

We've seen in Chapter 5 the amount of work most families take on in maintaining the material property of the summer house themselves rather than hiring expensive and hard-to-find local tradesmen. To make sure this work is done willingly and with a minimum of complaint, typically the founding matriarch establishes its practice through her own summer house routines which she teaches to her children and grandchildren. These often become so ritualistic that the latter may find difficult (though not impossible) to change them after she dies.

Such "matriarchal" activities are not usually limited to "kin-keeping" or "inside" work such as cooking and laundry. For example, if the matriarch oversees decorative plantings around the house, selecting flowers appropriate to the locale and fertilizing, watering and weeding them herself, she is also likely to oversee even the outside work related to the house and grounds which is often relegated to the menfolk, such as painting and mowing. She is also likely to be the one who establishes the timing of certain annual maintenance tasks, such as collective work staining the decks every July 30th when family members may be overlapping in their use of the place. Whether she is directly in charge of the outside work or not, it is likely to be her standards of style and neatness that establish the measures that at least some of her children and children-in-law will expect each other to live up to when they are in charge.

Such ritual activities of work and play start upon arrival and run until all have departed from the summer house and it is closed for the winter. Many families have specific phrases of greeting and farewell. Others practice particular behaviors such as running to greet the water, ringing the porch bell or raising the flag even before unpacking the car upon arrival, and comparably bidding farewell just before leaving. Each respondent with such rituals has started the story in the same way: "This is what we always do when we get there, and when we leave." There are other family traditions, some newly invented as occasion requires:

> We decided to name the rhododendrons on either side of the porch steps after my parents, who had planted them. Now we introduce our guests to "Mother" and "Father,"

we offer them a libation when we are having drinks out there, and we all feel that they are still with us. (Second generation in Michigan)

That's the only place I cook swordfish and bluefish over the grill. It's the only place where I trust them to be freshly caught, especially as we have often caught the blues ourselves. Of course, it's also the only place where I cook at all, whether it's fish or steak! So we have particular summer meals there that are special, partly because I cook instead of my wife, but also because of the family involvement, shucking corn and all, and the special menus. We have enough time to savor both the process and the food! (Second generation in Nantucket)

Every five years, we have a birthday party for the house. Everyone tries to get there: last time over 60 people showed up! (Second generation in Wisconsin)

For the 100th anniversary of the house, my cousin organized a big reunion—87 people came, so obviously they couldn't all stay there. But instead of priority on residence at the summer house being by generation, as it has always been, it was given to those who had come the greatest distance and least frequently. We thought this was the best way their loyalty to the family would likely be maintained. The rest of us found rooms in town. It was terrific! But whether we'll continue with this new pattern, I'm not sure—and now that I'm one of the elders, finally first in line for "reservations," I'm really not sure I want to! (Third generation in Maine)

Many take back home with them a specific summer house practice to help the youngest generation retain their attachment to it over the long months (or even years) between visits:

We always set out seed to attract the goldfinches that suddenly appear almost as soon as we have filled the bird-feeder when we arrive, just as my parents did. Any kids in the household are given the task of refilling it, sometimes more than once a day. One year when we overlapped with my brother's and sister's families, on a rainy day someone had the bright idea that each of the young cousins build a birdhouse or bird-feeder from the scrap lumber in the garage.

The birdhouses all stayed there, to be set out and sometimes even filled by nesting pairs of various kinds of birds in succeeding summers, but the feeders all came home to be filled to attract local birds. For all of the kids, this has kept alive an interest in the natural world and a sense of the inter-connections between the home and the summer environments. (Second generation in Martha's Vineyard)

Many record such family traditions in a house memoir. What starts out in many families as a summer house guest book becomes more elaborated in others. Not only guests but also family members contribute to what is soon understood by all as a house "log," in which all record whatever happened on "their watch." In time, those who grew up at the summer house can review—and show their own children—their childhood experiences; extended family members who do not visit at the same time can learn of their siblings' or cousins' hard work and devotion to the place.

We always used to start whatever we wrote with "Dear Grandma." Now that she's gone, I'm not quite sure who it is I'm writing to—but I still write it up, just the same. (Third generation in Nantucket)

If the matriarch has not started such a house log, it appears to be such a good idea that those in the second or even third generation have sometimes managed to establish the practice. The summer house becomes the ideal repository for family photograph albums, as well: rather than have the full family history diluted by dispersing such photos among heirs, according to line, it becomes enhanced by their being made available to all who return. (We have seen above an instance where family reunion pictures were made into calendars sent to all members, to remind them at home of their connection through the summer house.) And today, with so many families videotaping their activities, the house log can take new forms.

We decided that we needed to record the history of the house before everyone forgot its early days. So my sister and I wrote to our parents, aunts and uncles, as well as our cousins—there were 18 families altogether— asking for stories and pictures, and memoirs from old family friends who had visited as well. Then we put it all together, with separate sections for each family which they could "subscribe to" individually or get a partial set—maybe just of their own direct line—or the whole thing if they wanted. It's several hundred pages long and still being added to. One full copy stays at the house, of course. It's terrific for a rainy day! (Third generation in New Hampshire)

We had all our old family movies put on videotape to watch at home after the projector died. Then when my niece and nephew endowed the summer house with a VCR (even though my younger brother puts it in the closet when he's there so that no one in his family is tempted to watch it), we brought our family videos up there. We've since added more recent videotaped material, much of it taken right there, so that others can see what was going on when they weren't around. (Second generation on Cape Cod)

In houses at which family members take turns, a check-off list of what to do before leaving becomes mandatory and sometimes even becomes a formal contract. It helps if this has been put into place by the founding matriarch, but it is so necessary that later generations have no problem instituting the practice even if they haggle over what must be included.

We use bottled water for drinking, and the one thing you do not do is leave without restocking it. We've had no trouble agreeing to most things, but how to handle family pets is a present bone of contention. Some say "don't bring them at all" and others say "just add to the exit list that if you've brought a pet, you must leave a flea bomb for the next folks." But of course, the only people who complain about a pet that has been there before their time slot are those who have to deal with the fleas and the shed hair (or the allergies to them) and these may have been left not by the preceding family but the one before that. And then they say that of course their dog couldn't possibly be responsible! (Third generation in Vermont)

Whether we are there just for a weekend or for a couple of weeks, following my late mother's insistence we are expected to defrost the freezer and clean out the refrigerator of everything except basic provisions like milk, juice or bread. We've found that if a casserole is thoughtfully left in the freezer for the next folks, it is likely to be ignored: while we grew up eating the same food, we don't seem to like the same food any more. We are also expected to clean the oven. That way whoever comes last and closes up doesn't have to deal with a full summer's worth of partially-used jars of food or built-up spills and scorches. (Second generation on Cape Cod)

What starts as an exit list at turnover time can become more elaborate, especially when certain tasks recur at distinct times during the summer months and are not shared by all. Both routine and non-routine jobs are listed, whose completion by those who came before or after might be unnoticed by others if not recorded.

We call it the Boast Book. It started this way: there is so much work to be done to keep this place intact that there had to be a listing of whatever people discovered that needed to be done that they couldn't do themselves, either for lack of a particular skill or because it happened just before they left. So they would record the new tasks —fix the torn screen door, for example—and then whoever did the work would write in that it had been done. Now cousins who seldom see each other compete through the Boast Book for family approval based on whoever accomplishes the most. Suggestions are left as well, such as that every summer we paint one side of the house. That way a single family can do the job that year, and in four years it is all done and we start all over. We've adopted that one as it made so much sense. (Third generation on Martha's Vineyard)

We list the sweat equity jobs as well as the work that people have hired out and paid for. We seem to maintain a fair balance between the former (usually done by the younger generation) and the latter (usually by the somewhat more affluent and less energetic elders). At least everyone can see who volunteered to do or pay for what. (Second generation in Nantucket)

I decided to list all the jobs that needed to be done and how many hours each would usually take, so that we could calculate how many hours of sweat equity were needed a year and divide them equally. Since we grade the private road ourselves and plow it in the winter when we come up for cross-country skiing, along with dealing with all the boats, you can imagine how long this list is. But my kids and my brother's kids told me that they would pitch in whenever we called, and that they didn't like all this calculation as it seemed to interfere with their sense of giving back. And I must say enough hands always arrive for a work weekend to complete the required tasks. (Second generation in the Adirondacks)

Even the young kids take on one of the listed projects. One of my daughters decided that her job this year would be to clean out the bathroom closet, which obviously hadn't been done for years, even though it's always on the list. She found a shopping bag full of toilet paper, with a sales slip dating from 1955! (Third generation in Pennsylvania)

While these examples all come from the Northeast, where the Protestant work ethic is most prevalent as we have seen in Chapter 5, the practice of such a job list is followed everywhere. Other techniques accomplish the same end, regardless of region of the country.

We're usually there with at least one other family, so many people of at least two generations are usually involved in dividing the work along with the fun. We have "meister hats," painters' hats each labeled with whatever that task is. Everyone gets one, so everyone knows who is to do what, according to age and ability. If a fireplace needs replenishing, we call for the "wood-meister." If it's sweeping out the kitchen and living room, we call for the "floor-meister." And so on. It makes something of a game with people of all generations wearing the hats while "on duty," and we all enjoy playing it while the necessary jobs get done. (Fourth generation in Virginia) Opening and closing are always both work weekends and family reunions. We set up tents to accommodate the overflow, and everyone brings food and drink. Older cousins watch out for younger ones, and everyone learns how to do something, everyone pitches in, and somehow we manage to set it up or leave it as it should be. (Third generation in Wisconsin)

To involve all the in-laws (even though they don't have voting rights), let alone the later generations in the direct line (who do), we have various committees who report at our annual meeting, usually held at the start of closing up. The Boats Committee, the Buildings and Grounds Committee, the Housekeeping Committee, whatever —someone reports and we then decide together what changes to make or financial charges to assess. As the "treasurer," I come in with the annual accounting, and then the "secretary" sends a newsletter of the final accounting to everyone. We try to make it playful, with lots of joking and pompous and official-sounding statements, so it almost sounds as if we we're a big corporation. Now that I think about it, we run the summer house as if we were. (Third generation in New Hampshire)

So much for getting the work done fairly after the founders have died, when no single authority is there to determine the distribution of necessary chores. What about the delicate task of scheduling—of assigning who gets use of the summer house, and when? This job is overwhelmingly in the charge of women, starting with the founding matriarch who then typically passes on that role to one of her daughters or a daughter-in-law. Alternately, there are informal negotiations among the female members of the next generation on the assumption that they are in charge of their respective family members' summer schedules.

So far, with only three families to be considered, we've just negotiated who will take which weeks at Christmas when we all get together or at least talk on the phone. It's complicated enough, what with one brother teaching summer school and another having kids in camp, but it will start to get even more complicated as our children grow up and marry and may want to use the place on their own, and we don't have any formal mechanism to allow for that. We'll have to come to that pretty soon. (Second generation in the Berkshires)

After my mother died and we were on our own, my sisters and I tried to continue the informal ways she used when she would invite us to stay, asking for our preferences and trying to honor them. We soon realized we would have to get more structured, as none of us have enough authority over the others to say, as she might have done, "You'll just have to wait your turn for early August." Even rotation of choice isn't a perfect solution, as we're all aware that both of my sisters' families can readily come only in August, so if I choose to take some of that time, one of them is unlikely to come at all. Yet my husband is increasingly resentful of the fact that we always end up there in late June and early July before the water is comfortable enough to swim in. We're working on it. (Second generation on Martha's Vineyard)

While all four of my children will inherit the house equally, its management goes to my youngest daughter. She's a landscape architect and lives closest, so she is trusted by the others in this regard, and she does the scheduling too. We don't have any formal rules, but my daughters and sons all know what to do, and so do most of my children-in-law, so it will work out. So far, they've often overlapped but they don't all want to be there at the same time. So far, so lucky! (Second generation on Puget Sound)

I'm the third out of four siblings, and as the only one not a lawyer and also as the only female, I don't attempt to act as my mother did. Pulling off a matriarchal number would not be possible. But as I provide much of the sweat equity as well as scheduling when the others come in (and they all want to come in at the same time), I've decided that my role is that of "camp director." There are only so many beds in "camp" at any one time, and whoever "enrolls" first gets them. (Second generation in Michigan)

Many women choose to take on this role; for others, it is simply expected of them, because they are assumed—even by their brothers or even brothers-in-law who may have been the ones who actually inherited the summer house—to be more sensitive to potentially different views of fairness that may be held by different family members and to deal with them appropriately. In Chapter 3, we discussed this propensity in terms of the motives which underline the making of wills, in that women are seen to be more willing to sacrifice efficiency for the sake of the contingencies determining perceptions of fairness among various family members. This becomes particularly important when there is no formal agreement settling the issue of how both the second *and* the third generation are to be treated equally in their scheduled use of the summer house, following the conflicting norms of inheritance.

Should its use be divided by second generation lines only or should members of the third generation have a right to independent negotiation with the scheduler regardless of their parental line? Should ownership shares determine time-shares, or should they be disconnected? Some of my respondents match them to the day, others ignore the form by basing scheduling decisions on other criteria altogether. Obviously, the number of heirs, their respective ownership shares and other interest in the property, as well as its legal structure will contribute to the answers. Given the variables to be juggled to arrive at optimum fairness for all concerned, women are overwhelmingly given the task of this calculus.

If second generation heirs are sons only, a formal structure of timesharing and/or rotation of choice is almost inevitably instituted as part of the by-laws of whatever legal agreement they reach for shared ownership of the summer house, rather than the scheduling being delegated to a sister-in-law. This may be due to the fact that none of their respective wives may have enough standing among them to act with independent authority in the role of scheduler: without such authority, a sister-in-law would presumably exacerbate any fraternal rivalry.

One man showed me the precisely detailed records he had kept of his summer house partnership with his brothers, based upon elaborate rules for rotation of scheduling and the sharing of expenses. When I asked him if this formal process was effective because the partners were all men, he said: "That has nothing to do with it." His wife interjected: "That has *everything* to do with it!" Such rules can become very explicit:

> "Check-out time" is noon on Saturday and "check-in time" is 5:00 p.m. There is a long list of tasks to be performed, with a check-off sheet to show that they have been done. If the departing family has hired someone to clean the place rather than do it themselves, the five hours between scheduled slots allows for this to be done. Of course, if the families in successive time slots want to overlap a bit, that is up to them, but keeping it structured this way saves a lot of hassles and hurt feelings if requests for a variance aren't accepted by others. (Third generation in Massachusetts)

Thus the construction of the family—the respective numbers of brothers or sisters inheriting, to say nothing of which generation is in charge—largely determines the practice of informal negotiation or structured rotation of days and weeks of use. Once a legal structure to support the summer house is agreed to (see below), rules of scheduling, including priorities and sequence, are often written into the bylaws regardless whether the person in charge of scheduling is male or female:

> July 4th weekend is always a particularly choice time to be there, as the entire lake community gets involved and there are fireworks, and all that. Because my brothers and I wanted our kids to all get to know each other—they'll be carrying it on after we're gone, after all—we have taken ourselves out of rotation for that week and set it aside for our kids. So July 4th Week is Cousins' Week. They come in with none of their parents around, and figure out how to deal with the necessary work and enjoy the place together. A few are now married and their spouses come along, and we stay out of it all. (Second generation in New Hampshire)

> Serving a term as the trustee in charge of scheduling and also serving as secretary to the trust, every January I send out to all the heirs the minutes of our last annual

meeting along with an accounting of our operating costs and any income from daily use fees. At the same time, I send the summer calendar of the last two years noting who has come during which weeks. This reminds everyone of the inevitable inequalities of use-time between those who have come each summer and those who haven't, so that when I then receive the "requests for reservations" for the coming summer, everyone knows who will be given priority based on infrequent use and who will come at the end of the line, priorities written into the trust by my great-grandmother, who set it up. (Fourth generation in Maine)

With two lines in the family, we divide the season in mid-summer, on August 1. The family with August closes up, usually at Labor Day, but then they get the first half of the summer the next year, which means that they are the ones to open up in late June, as well. Thus they have to deal with whatever they have left undone or poorly done at close up, by themselves, and there is less likelihood of resentment by the other line.. (Fourth generation in the Adirondacks)

While I have here followed the typical patterning of roles with women dealing more directly as "kin-keepers" while men deal more directly with legal structures and formal management, there is often a considerable mixing of styles and of roles according to who is available to take on the responsibilities. Especially in the "play-form of association" analyzed by Georg Simmel (discussed in the *Introduction*) that is typically built into the leisure activities of a summer house, family members feel more free to act as the spirit moves them even in the "Protestant-ethic" territory of New England:

My mother died when I was young, and Pop always had to take on a sort of double role when it wasn't typical for men to nurture four young kinds. Well, he figured out how to do it, and the summer house was a large part of it. He cooked, he fished, he accepted things being messy. His friends were artists from the "colony" nearby and they all mixed up what were the fairly restricted gender roles of that period. My brothers and I, as well as my cousins (because my mother's family all came too), all grew up there with a freedom we didn't have anywhere else. I have grandchildren of my own now, and Pop's Place still has a magic of being totally safe yet allowing freedom to take whatever risks you want. (Second generation in Maine)

Because such play and free sociability are the major function of summer houses, they serve as "sacred hearth" not so much because the patriarchal "Lares and Penates" are there, as a respondent noted earlier, but because they are grounded in traditionally informal and "feminine" practices distinct from the "masculine" rationality inherent in the law courts and the market place. That men need such playful locations and, indeed, invent and oversee them without the engagement of women, is obvious in the analyses of Huizinga and Simmel, who posit no specific gender distinction to these characteristics found in an experience such as successfully owning and passing on a summer house. Ofcourse patriarchs and their sons and grandsons support and perpetuate the playful aspects of such summer leisure, along with any necessary work. However, if that play is to reaffirm the innocence and exuberance of childhood, protecting individual idiosyncracies even as it provides the security of loving rituals and special rules (as Cheever and others have analyzed it above), practices which embody a "matriarchal" sense of authority would seem to be crucial to its success.

The "patriarchal" structures to be discussed in the next chapter—perhaps "paternal" would be a better term in this connotation —should then be understood as the means to the end of keeping safe the "maternal" hearth rather than as ends in themselves. At the same time, that hearth cannot be sustained for long without such protective institutions, as we have seen evidence above in cases when establishing formal and legal structures for the inheritance and use of summer houses have been ignored.

CHAPTER 13

"PATRIARCHAL" PRINCIPLES:
LEGAL FORMS AND LEGAL COUNSEL

Professional advice as to how to find, buy, build and legally structure the ownership of a summer house is readily available, starting with "How To" guides found in many public libraries and via the Internet (Diesenhouse 1997; GeRue 1996; Scher & Scher 1992; Small 1997). However, most such sources say nothing about the factors of family structure or sub-cultural values which provide the context in which one or another of the alternative legal options is preferable. While the preceding chapters have described and analyzed those contextual variables in detail, this review of the standard legal forms for shared ownership of property such as a vacation house is still couched in highly generalized terms so that the best "fit" with the specifics of any single case can be more readily determined. The following discussion is based on information provided by attorneys Harrison Gardner, of Madison NJ, and Thomas Loikith, of Fairfield NJ. It is not to be construed in any way as legal counsel, let alone as advice regarding which option to select in any specific instance. However, if there is any lesson from this discussion, it is that any legal structure for shared ownership and responsibility of a summer house or any other vacation property is better than none. The unintended consequences of inadequate provision lor the future on the part of the founders, "letting them work it out after I'm gone," have been all too obvious in the preceding examples, and are almost entirely negative for the success of the enterprise of "passing it on."

Regardless of the legal structure decided upon, the same issues must be resolved so as to be reasonably equitable and efficient. Thus there must be some formal provision to ensure that no one needs to work too hard at the management of the property so that all family members can then get on with the primary purpose of enjoying mutual sociability and play.

The agreement must facilitate:

1. Ease of implementation of the legal structure.

2. Perpetuation of equitable funding and use.

3. Ease of administration, considering:

   a. Who does it, out of how many participants?

   b. Provision for turn-over of administrators

   based on terms or age or competence.

4. Relation of these issues to access and use.

5. Anticipation of and provision for contingency and change.

For example, here are both positive and negative cases which illustrate the third and fifth issues just noted, respectively showing the kinds of issues that must be anticipated in settling on an adequate legal structure. In these specific cases, the decisions are being made by members of the second and third generation, recognizing the structure and the needs of a variety of later generation cousins:

As one of my brother's children is mentally incompetent, we had to structure the trust to deal explicitly with the matter of competence among the full voting members, including in this regard the continued competence of my brother and me as we age. We will need to be replaced at some point! (Second generation in Connecticut)

We set the "retirement" age for trustees at 65, which is probably before my sisters and I will think we should relinquish authority over the place to our children and maybe before they will be willing to take it on, but a least it will force the resolution of who takes more or less responsibility while we are all still mentally and physically capable of doing so. We seniors will still be there in advisory capacity, after all—if the juniors turn out to be interested in our advice. (Second generation in New Hampshire)

My grandmother appointed two of my cousins, brothers who had been in business together, to be the official managers of the trust she had set up to sustain the property. They had a falling out over their business which then spread into the trust management, and it is now really chaotic. As a family we are so divided with different people siding with one or the other brother that even though we have reached nominal agreement about term limits and thus replacing them with other cousins, no one has been willing to force the issue: pride and vengeance just keep getting in the way. The last time we tried to discuss it in person, fourteen cousins showed up, several of them bringing along their own lawyers! (Third generation in Delaware)

To be sure, lack of resolution up to the third generation is not inevitably harmful: we've seen above cases whcre first and even second cousins have managed to reach agreement on both the legal structure and its implementation. It helps to know that informal as well as formal provisions for resolving ownership and use issues can be reflected in every alternative legal structure, which appear to work best when the following rules of thumb apply:

1. If the legal structure is too detailed, requiring micro-managing by professionals, it will be the source of conflict between those with and those without such professional knowledge, and preclude the very kind of amateur and egalitarian involvement that the summer house is supposed to provide for.

2. On the contrary, if the legal structure is too loose, there will be insufficient guidelines upon which all can agree when any informal patterns need to be changed as circumstances change, and rights ofuse and obligations of support will inevitably become unequally distributed.

If only as a part of sound estate planning, as we have seen, most founders begin the legal restructuring of their property whereby their heirs will share ownership of the summer house, Gifting fractional shares to their heirs while they are still alive may remove it from their estates altogether, as well as bringing the heirs into more responsible roles in its management.

However difficult it may be for founders to relinquish authority over the summer house, more and more of them have taken advantage of the 1987 changes in estate tax law which increased the gill exemption, thereby allowing them to transfer ownership to their heirs incrementally, within a comparatively few years. The act also raised the floor for probate to estates of more than $600,000 (it is to rise to $1,000,000 by 2006). Accordingly, since 1987 only 32,000 or so estates have been probated annually, less than a quarter of the annual total in the decade prior to that date (Johnson & Eller, 1998: 85).

However, such *inter vivos* transfers of ownership do not necessarily mean that the *motives* of the founders (or their heirs who may need to do their own estate planning) are different from those characterized by Remi Clignet as efficiency and reciprocity (discussed in Chapter 3). And legal counsel and resultant action do not necessarily result in peaceful agreement among the heirs who are affected.

With such generalities in the background, consider in turn a variety of legal structures, each with specific implications regarding the degree to which all family members are likely to participate, as well as implications for income and estate taxes. (Attorney Stephen J. Small [1997] provides a very usable summary of the estate tax consequences of the respective legal alternatives.) Aside from individual outright ownership, such as founders start with, forms of joint ownership are here listed in order of escalating formality and complexity, requiring increasing amounts of professional help to establish and administer, hence increasing fees paid to lawyers and other fiduciary agents.

Joint Tenancy

Joint tenants own equal shares of the property as a whole, with the provision that upon the death of one, the surviving joint tenants inherit those shares, i.e. they are not distributed to the decedent's other heirs by will or intestacy, nor is the property itself subdivisible by shares. Of the few of my respondents who have this legal structure, most are second generation siblings who have inherited it with the property and keep it only for the sake of convenience while they work to reach agreement on another structure with provision of inheritance down the lines.

Like the next two forms of tenancy, its major advantage is the comparative ease by which a new tenant's name can be added to the list of owners by having it put on the deed on file, without having to redraw any formal agreement that details its management and use. However, one does not want to change the deed this very often, and, more important, even then the procedure does not subdivide the property into shares.

In any case, such an ownership structure still needs to be supplemented by a separate agreement to spell out the legal responsibilities among the joint owners. Ignoring this aspect of joint tenancy, a few founding widows among my respondents have simply added their children's names to the deed, thereby avoiding legal fees as well as any discussion with their children, the fellow joint tenants, about more detailed administration. There are, of course, ramifications in terms of estate planning and any misunderstanding that may occur due to the absence of legal counsel. Here is a widow who is mistaken in thinking that joint tenancy with her children reduces the value of her share and increases theirs as nominal joint tenants of the property:

> As each of the children has come of age, I've just gone to the courthouse and added their names to the deed. They'll get my share when I die in equal measure, but as my equity in the place is reduced, it won't be such a big part of my estate. (First generation in New Hampshire)

In fact, as this widow has provided the entire funding for this summer house ever since she and her late husband built it as well as the fact that in joint tenancy, the property is indivisible, her equity is assumed by law at 100%. The surviving joint tenants will discover that the entire property is part of her potentially taxable estate.

A particular form of joint tenancy, *tenancy by the entireties*, involves only husband and wife, each with sole right of survivorship. Should they divorce, if they retain joint ownership of the house they become *tenants in common*.

Tenancy in Common

Here, as above, tenants own undivided shares in the whole property, as when children are left equal shares of ownership in a summer house upon the death of their parents. These shares become part of their own estates when they die and are taxed accordingly. Thus they are subject to probate and estate taxes on only that portion of the assessed property but not on the whole, as in the case in joint tenancy. In time, however, this subdivision among tenants in common can still become an administrative nightmare:

> There are seven deed-holders in the third and fourth generation, with differing shares in the property (from one sixth to one ninth, according to how the shares were divided in the second generation) with 25 families among those seven lines. We are agreed that there will be no further division, so these shares will come down intact in each of the seven lines. We allocate use and responsibility according to the proportionate share although everyone in the direct line gets an equal vote. So far, the deed has been left to whichever heir(s) could most afford to contribute to the upkeep. It gets pretty complicated, but so far it's working out, maybe because the cottage has been in the family for nearly a century and this is how we have traditionally done it. It's probably about time we get more formal about the administration, as those in the next generation are unlikely to be as obsessive about running it as I have been. (Third generation in Vermont)

The major problem with all forms of single ownership and tenancy in common is the difficulty of dividing the property into fractionalized shares for transmission to multiple heirs in the future, however easier such forms may appear to be in terms of adding on additional tenants in the present.

Further, any decisions about the use or disposition the property require agreement among all the tenants in comma If one wants to put on a conservation easement and another does not, or if one wants to sell and the other three do not but can't afford to buy him out, nothing happens—unless the one takes the other three to court to force the desired action. In effect, veto power is accorded to each tenant in common, regardless of how many there are. In such fashion are family feuds created that last into the next generation.

Associations and General Partnerships

These are unincorporated organizations which opera based upon a partnership or association agreement coveril membership, the sharing of income, expenses and patterns use, and the transmission of any member's shares to fellow association members, partners or other heirs. In terms of their operation, there is no difference between an association and general partnership. The association or partnership is the legal owner of the property and shares are distributed according to the agreement. This can be a fairly complex document, specifying rights of inheritance and membership as well as attendant obligations, and like the legal forms to be discussed below, can include "rights of first refusal" regarding buy-outs and other restrictions on the transfer of ownership. Annual meetings and accounting for tax purposes are not mandatory but are strongly recommended, and should be part of the agreement. However, some find the "flavor" of an association to be more informal and egalitarian than that of a general partnership or trust:

> My father set up a trust for the support and maintenance of the multi-dwelling property my siblings and I have inherited. We're from very traditional and conservative stock, so naturally there is one rebel, one of my brothers who never got over the Sixties and who remains an ardent left-winger. He keeps pressuring us to become an association because it sounds more egalitarian and it is against his political principles to be a "trustee" of anything! (Second generation in Vermont)

If there is any difference between associations and partnerships, it is that the latter are typically organizations of two or more people intending to be co-owners of a business for profit, although they can be used to structure the ownership of property which is not intended to be a profit-making entity, like most summer houses and other vacation homes in winter resorts. Accordingly, they are regulated by the Uniform Partnership Act which has been adopted in most United States jurisdictions.

Most people are familiar with such partnerships as law firms or medical practices (although these are increasingly being placed by professional corporations). As co-owners, partners old an interest in the property itself, in the partnership itself, and in the management of both. Should there be a profit (i.e. if the house is rented and income exceeds carrying costs), the partners share the profits and individually pay taxes on them. If there is a loss, they all share in the loss. On the death of a partner, his or her interests are vested in the surviving partners unless the partnership agreement provides for its inheritance by other heirs. In either case, partnership interest (like associate interest) is probate property, i.e. it is included in the estate upon which heirs or remaining partners may need to pay inheritance taxes.

Of particular importance is the fact that partners have *unlimited* liability for another partner's wrongful acts and for *all* other debts or obligations of the partnership. A corollary assumption is that partners are equal in their obligations to the partnership. Summer house heirs, unlike law partners, are likely to be geographically scattered and may find it difficult to get together to consider every aspect of management of the property. Thus one attorney recommends that the partnership agreement establish a "managing partner," and further provide that the responsibility and the burden could be changed from time to time.

Limited Partnerships

A subset of partnerships are those which designate two, categories of partners: general partners who carry personal responsibility for management of the property and also liability for any partnership debt etc., and limited partners who hold no such rights or liabilities unless they are actively involved in management of the partnership. As with general partnerships their structure is governed by the partnership agreement an state law; indeed, they are chartered just as corporations are. Limited partnership interests, like general partnership interests, are personal property that can pass to heirs through will or intestacy.

Most of my respondents who have decided to include the next generation in their partnership have followed this form, with provision for transition to the rank of general partner typically (but not always) by only one member of the general partner's line at a time. That person is designated either by primogeniture with her line, by election by siblings and cousins, or by volunteers with rotating terms. Thus the total number of general partners remains fairly small, typically "by line" even as the number of limited partners may be increased.

> My sister and brother and I were in our late 50's and mid-60's when my mother died, leaving the place to us equally. Our total of eleven children ranged in age from 20 to 30. We wanted to include them in some formal fashion as the best means of cementing their loyalty to the property, and a limited partnership seemed the best way to do it. We have a provision in the agreement that when each general partner turns 70, one of his or her line will be elected by the others in that line for a three-year term. The retired general partner then fills the role of "elder statesman." None of us has yet reached that

age so I can't report on how that will work, but so far the cousins are increasingly involved in the operation of the place yet don't have any liability for it. (Second generation on Martha's Vineyard)

Corporations

As with associations and partnerships, title to real property can be held by corporations. In most states, laws pertaining to setting up a corporation as well as those determining tax reporting are "extensive, somewhat convoluted and at times burdensome," in the words of one attorney, and hence more costly to establish than partnerships. However, as with partnerships, ownership of shares is considered intangible personal property rather than real property or tangible personal property, and in many states is thus exempt from inheritance taxes. In other states this is not the case, so it is important to determine the rule in the state where the property is located: it may be the determining factor as to what legal form is set up, and where.

Further, from the perspective of the owners of summer houses or other vacation homes, one of the most important advantages is that unlike a partnership, a corporation limits the liability of the shareholders. If a guest falls off the deck, breaks his neck and sues for damages, all he can take is the assets of the corporation (presumably the summer house itself), not those of the individual shareholders as would be the case for general partners or members of an association.

As is also the case for partnerships, ease of succession is enhanced as ownership interest can be readily fractionalized and distributed among multiple heirs. Transfer of ownership fractions can then take place through annual exclusion gifts (presently up to $10,000 for one donor, up to $20,000 for a married couple) to each member of the next generation(s). If such gifting is started early enough, the entire property can be transferred out of the estate in this fashion. (We've seen such an example described in Chapter 3.)

Whether or not the summer house is to be rented will surely contribute to a family's decision to opt for an association, partnership or a corporation, and if the latter, which kind. If the house is to be rented to non-family members, protection from personal liability through corporate ownership may be the determining factor, as tenants are assumed to be more willing to sue for injury than are kinfolk. Choice of type of corporation may be determined by the alternative tax implications. As with partnerships, in one form of corporation (an "S" corporation), any profits or losses flow directly through to the shareholders and may thereby affect their income taxes. In the alternative form (a "C" corporation) the corporation itself pays taxes before any remaining profits may be reinvested or distributed to the shareholders, who then add them, in now reduced amount, to their individually taxable income.

This "double tax" is why some attorneys (for example, Stephen J. Small [1997]) strongly advise against the use of a corporation for the joint ownership of land. Clearly, the degree of profit or loss that may be expected from any rental of the summer house— let alone the possibility that it be sold, inevitably affecting the income taxes to be paid by the corporation itself as well as the individual shareholders—will contribute to their decision about which form of corporation to use, if any.

> Accepting the advice of our lawyer father, my siblings and I decided to go for an "C" corp. After mother died, he had gifted all of the ownership shares to us even though he has continued to run the place as he sees fit without consultation with any of his children. However, he also had the good sense (and has the money) to decide to rent it from the corporation at seasonal rates. After paying the carrying costs, including the corporate taxes and any we may owe on what nominally comes down to us, we put the profits into CD's to serve as an "endowment" to keep it going after he dies. In this way he has engaged us in the financial management of the place without really giving up any of his authority. As long as he is physically capable of handling it (and as he is there all summer to manage it while we just take turns coming to visit), we all benefit. (Second generation in the Adirondacks)

Limited Liability Companies

Limited liability companies have only recently been instituted as a hybrid form combining features of both partnerships and corporations. (Indeed, they are so new that many states do not permit them and in those that do, case law is very undeveloped.) In practice, LCCs operate much like limited partnerships and "S" corporations, with obligations spelled out in an operating agreement but with somewhat greater flexibility.

Trusts, Nominee Trusts and Qualified Personal Residence' Trusts (QPRTs)

As sub-categories of Trusts, let us take the two latter first. *Nominee Trusts*, rather than having a sizeable financial base typical of trusts in general, simply reduce the complexity of real estate transaction records in that no new trust document, certificate of incorporation or partnership agreement needs to be recorded with each transaction. Thus transfers of shares among the heirs are greatly facilitated.

Legal title is vested in a nominee trust of which one of my sisters and I are trustees, and a partnership among all of the siblings is the beneficiary of the trust. The reason is to simplify transfers of interest among the partners: if the partnership were the direct owner, the partnership agreement would be a public document and every change would have to be filed. We act as a partnership but legally we're a trust. (Second generation in New Jersey)

Qualified Personal Residence Trusts provide for a reduction in estate taxes at the time when heirs will inherit full ownership of the summer house, without the owner relinquishing lull ownership in the meantime as is the case with incorporation.

With a QPRT, the owner may transfer [the] residence into [a] trust for a set period of time, during which the owner may enjoy use of the house. The value of the property—which is a gift for tax purposes—is discounted to take into consideration the owner's use of the property for the term of the trust. If the owner of the property dies before the term of the trust ends, the property passes to heirs... and is subject to estate taxes as if the trust never existed, ...at its market value at the time of death. If, however, the owner is still alive when the term of the trust expires, title to the property automatically passes from the trust to the beneficiaries [and] the value of this "gift" for gift-tax purposes is the discounted value established when the trust was created. (Diesenhouse 1997, 8)

The length of the term of the trust can be set at will to accommodate the anticipated remaining lifetime of the donor and/or to spread out the gifting of portions of its ownership to fit the annual gift provision of $10,000 to each of the intended beneficiaries. Further, such changes in proportionate ownership need not be recorded every year, as they are all under the umbrella of the QPRT. Under incorporation, as noted above, ownership of corporate shares equivalent in value to the annual $10,000 gift provision can be readily transferred and removed from the estate according to the federal and individual state inheritance tax laws, so a QPRT merely to facilitate this transfer is unnecessary.

As for *Trusts* in general terms, many founders provide that the remainder of their estates be placed in a will or testamentary trust to cover the operating costs of the summer house after they die, if their assets are large enough to permit it. Thereby their children and grandchildren will not need to cover all of the costs themselves, and also they are able to make use of very considerable estate tax benefits associated with this legal structure. (Such trusts can be set up to begin during the founders' lifetimes as well.) As with all trusts, the further advantage is that those who establish them can specify exactly how they are to be administered, by whom, and with what degree of term limits. The intentions of the founders can thus be ensured through future generations. (I am here ignoring the option of a revocable trust, whose terms can be changed by the donor at any time, and consider only irrevocable trusts generally implemented after the death of the founder.)

However, there is sometimes insufficient flexibility provided for the trustees when changed circumstances demand action in violation of the trust agreement. For example, if a will trust has a clause precluding sub-division or sell-off of any portion of the property, the beneficiaries would be unable to do so even if this would be the best way of raising funds to supplement the trust income, which during inflationary periods is unlikely to generate enough interest to cover all operating costs. One can go to court to change the trust but that is expensive and time-consuming.

On the other hand, sometimes the flexibility offered to the trustees is too great. Here is a case where the founding widow established a trust, the trustees being her four children, of whom only one is still alive. Evidently operating on the principles of "let them work it out after I am gone," the founding widow (and her lawyer, presumably on her instructions) did not specify how trustees were to be replaced or how their shares were to be inherited.

> There are now 28 families with rights to use the place, represented by 6 trustees, two per line, with one of the four lines being represented by a lawyer as the heirs there are legally incompetent. No one knows what will happen to their shares when they die.

> We're pretty flexible—in-laws have even succeeded to trusteeship when the blood-relative incumbent trustee died—but we have no terms of office and no way of prioritizing decisions or authority. Our family is truly Scottish in that *nothing* is ever said until after the fact, so it makes it very hard to plan ahead . As I'm not a trustee, I was willing to become the manager, which I find is a totally thankless, time consuming, hard job which often earns me the anger of other family members, especially as the trustees really don't do any advanced planning to provide guidelines for managerial decisions. (Third generation on Lake Ontario)

Another problem may arise when there is a limited number of trustees and no personal ownership of shares, in that a sense of participatory ownership on the part of all the beneficiaries may be inhibited. Finally, all trusts ultimately come to an end, leaving to the heirs the problem of restructuring their legal agreement and the continued financing of the property.

> The trust set up by my grandmother is to run out upon the death of the last of her heirs who was born before she died in 1947, so it will run well into the twenty-first

century. It was pretty flexible in its provisions, as well as sensible (the two managing trustees are to come from different generations, and serve for terms of three years with a maximum of three terms), but even now it doesn't begin to cover the costs. With over 100 heirs, no one gets a chance to use the place every summer, so their loyalty gets weakened along with their willingness to support it. We charge daily users' fees, which helps, but when something big comes up, like replacing the deck, it's very difficult to reach agreement on how to finance it. (Third generation in Maine)

As we have seen, given their financial advantages trusts are often combined with one or another form of collective responsibility, such as an association or partnership, for the ongoing flexible management of the property. By themselves, they do not necessarily provide even a guidance structure for the heirs to help them deal with new problems that inevitably develop, other than by establishing a sound financial base for their resolution.

As tax implications for each of these alternative legal forms vary from state to state, involving those of both the state in which the summer house is located and those in which the heirs reside, experienced estate lawyers should be consulted as to the optimum form for the particular circumstances. An attorney practicing in the vicinity of the summer house is most likely to know what kinds of legal structures are advisable for such property according to the regulations of that state, and has the further advantage of being accessible to all heirs who return to the place, rather than being perceived as the personal lawyer of only one of them. On the other hand, in summer colonies with a particularly active real estate market, the few full-time operating attorneys may not be so accessible after all:

After my parents had died and I was trying to make sense of the very complicated trust-cum-partnership they had worked out with their attorney on the Vineyard, I found that I had great difficulty getting through to him. In a way I can understand it, as since they died there has been a great deal of new construction and sales on the Vineyard so there is more work to be done by the few local real estate lawyers than they seem to be able to handle. The situation is compounded by the fact that my brothers and I haven't yet decided how we want to change the partnership agreement. I'm now talking with my own attorney but he doesn't have the same authority with my brothers that the local old guy would have had, who after all dealt with my father. (Second generation on Martha's Vineyard)

To be sure, one's own lawyer is more likely to be conversant with one's own tax situation as determined by the regulations of the state of primary residence, so in this case, each of the brothers might be advised to bring his own lawyer into the picture unless the siblings can work out an agreement among themselves prior to consultation about its legal implementation.

This latter course is certainly preferable. We have seen above instances where several family members (siblings or cousins) were attorneys, yet their warm family relationships were sufficient to override any basic litigiousness inherent in their profession as they determined the optimum agreement and form for their collective ownership and operation of the summer house. In other families, even without legal training various members can be argumentative for the sake of argument. if they are not to waste their inheritance in legal fees, family solidarity (if not necessarily warmth) must prevail. The next chapters provide models for those who may want some guidelines by which to organize the discussion about setting up a formal agreement. Consensus about the ground rules then becomes the starting point for agreement about the resulting document.

PART FIVE

REACHING AGREEMENT

CHAPTER 14

ECONOMIC PRINCIPLES OF FAIR DIVISION

In Part IV, we considered first the informal structures of authority over the summer house, typically instituted by women, followed by a discussion of the formal, legal structures of authority more typically instituted by men. While the two types of structures are often instituted simultaneously by the founders and have identical ultimate purposes, the evidence shows that the formal structures accomplish their ends only if the informal ones have been successful in instilling in the heirs a deeply-felt loyalty to their shared inheritance. The legal structures can thus be seen as resulting from the operation of the informal practices, as well as from the motives of the founders as analyzed by Remi Clignet. The form and effectiveness of any resultant legal structure are also affected by the form and effectiveness of the *process* by which agreement on it is reached, which is the subject of this and the next chapter.

What are the ways in which agreement might best be reached among heirs as to how to manage and use the summer house? Here we consider first the abstract principles which govern collective decisions about sharing or dividing scarce goods, according to several economists. Not surprisingly, economists have devoted much attention to formulas for dividing goods equally so that the division is "envy-free." I present their work here in order of increasing elaboration, as the first explanation which is offered becomes more detailed and more subtle in the later examples.

In his book on exchanges within families and groups, Oded Stark (1995) includes a brief discussion of sharing the inheritance of summer houses. However, after running through various mathematical formulas and distinctions made in "prisoner dilemma" games between "cooperators" and "defectors," (in the case of summer house heirs, the latter being those who may insist on being bought out or who want use of the place but are unwilling to take any responsibility for it), he concludes that matters of genetic and/or cultural inheritance are most important in determining the outcome:

> Those who inherit a genetic tendency to cooperate are more likely than others to enjoy the benefits of cooperative siblings. Similarly with cultural inheritance; altruism can prevail when individuals are likely to interact with others who share the same role model. (Stark 1995, 132)

In sum, the abstract economic principles of rational-choice theory demonstrate that happy families (cooperators) are all alike; unhappy families (defectors) are unhappy in their own separate ways! The respondents to this study provide examples of both. However, that Stark resorts to this level of explanation suggests that at least some economists can't explain how such transfers and exchanges work on principles that are not obviously rationally self-interested. (He does not refer to work by the authors cited below.)

H. Peyton Young (1994) advances us further by pointing out that even among those intending to cooperate rather than defect, the first step in reaching decisions about equity in the sharing of goods is to determine priority.

> The evidence suggests that indivisible allocations are often handled by confronting the indivisibility directly instead of trying to circumvent it. He who has the greatest claim gets the good; the others do not.... [But] most often priority is based on a mixture of criteria. (Young 1994, 14)

According to Young, the three basic methods of equably dividing indivisible goods are: randomization (throw of dice or lottery such as the "duking it out" we saw in Chapter 3 as the method preferred by the elderly Boston lawyer to determine sole heirship among his four children); rotation (taking turns); and conversion (i.e. sell-off). Application of each method should be based on principles of impartiality and consistency. Assuming that taking turns rather than a lottery or sell-off is the method of choice for most who intend to pass on their summer house to succeeding generations, subsequent and sequential questions show what decisions are needed in the construction of an equitable method for allocating turns (1994, 164-166):

> 1. What form should the allocation take (e.g. how many days or weeks at the summer house for each "member")?
>
> 2. What are the eligibility criteria (e.g. anyone in the direct line or by generation with seniors first)?
>
> 3. What counts in the distribution of the allocation (e.g. need, ability to pay, other contribution)?
>
> 4. What are the relevant principles underlying the allocation (e.g. length of time wait-

ing or other deserved-ness)?

5. What are the relevant precedents within the family's history?

6. How should competing principles be reconciled?

7. What incentives to continue does a rule create?

Young sees these questions as steps to follow in any discussion about how to equably structure the inheritance and use of a summer house:

> This list of seven steps provides a framework for analyzing equity in concrete situations. It contains both normative and procedural elements... The reason equity is important... is that it *coordinates* and *legitimates* distributive choices. Equity principles are the language in which we discuss and justify such choices. (Young 1994, 166-7 [his italics])

Jon Elster presents a more elaborate listing of principles for prioritizing such allocations in his study of how institutions allocate both scarce goods and necessary burdens (1992, 70-112). His breakdown of underlying principles is particularly useful in teasing apart the various motives that family members may differently bring to the discussion. Seeing them listed is helpful in deciding which are legitimate in any particular family's situation and which are not. As listed here, those marked with an asterisk (*) have been used by at least one of my respondents.

1. *Egalitarian*:
   *absolute equality
   *lottery
   *rotation

2. *Time-related principles*:
   *queuing (first come, first served)
   *waiting lists
   *seniority

3. *Status-related principles*:
   *age
   gender
   ethnicity/race
   *other physical features/disabilities
   freedom (vs slavery)

nobility, caste, civil status
*family status
*residence
*occupation, education
religion

4. *Other properties*:
   *individual level of welfare
   *efficiency
   *contribution, deservedness
   *character

5. *Mechanisms based on power*:
   wealth
   *influence (including negative: nuisance)

6. *Mixed systems*:
   *linear point systems (different weighted criteria)
   *intuitive trade-offs
   *post-allocation trading

As to which allocation principles would be followed by whom, Elster notes (apparently without awareness of Remi Clignet's 1995 work, discussed in previous chapters, but fully congruent with it) that there are typically different "types of motives based on the desire to promote self-interest, equity and efficiency" (180-182). Actors at "first, second and third orders of decision making" differ. Accordingly, from our prior discussion, one might here consider them as members of different generations trying to reach agreement together while the founders are still alive. If the grandchildren are included in the discussion of the optimum formal structure, what motives are likely to be present?

First order actors—founders—are likely to speak for *efficiency* on global principles (e.g. each child should inherit equally), at least as they open the discussion. Second order actors—adult children of the founders—are likely to favor *equity* at least as much as efficiency as both should be locally understood (our circumstances differ including the number of children we have). Third order actors first cousins—are likely to be more motivated by *self-interest* (how often can we ever get there; how can the management be set up so that no one need take on the whole load?).

Clignet would reconfigure these motives according to a different assignment of "levels" but in essential agreement. Presumably first order actors would be founding patriarchs, with motives of *efficiency*; second order actors would be widowed matriarchs with motives of equity based on *reciprocity*; third order actors would be the heirs operating from motives of *ascriptive equality* based on revered precedent. Analysis of these two similar orderings together raises the question of how third-order actors might be operating from both motives of *self-interest* (Elster) and motives of *ascriptive equality* (Clignet). From the evidence presented by my respondents, both are likely to be operative at the same time, even if not openly acknowledged at outset: heirs may disguise issues of self-interest through the rhetoric of appeals to precedent. It would help all to recognize that likelihood.

In any event, regardless of level of actor, for Elster violation of different principles has different results: "Inequity has a higher scandal-arousing potential than inefficiency" (182). Seen in terms of generation rather than in Elster's more abstract terms of "orders," his conclusion is not surprising. From the point of view of the heirs, fairness as contingently determined (thus potentially including precedent or need) is far more important than efficiency, as they can work out rules to expedite the latter by themselves more easily than they can determine principles of equity.

Moreover, Elster goes on to provide basic rules of thumb for determining the priorities upon which to base implementation. if the basic purpose is to enhance the well-being of all judged eligible to share in the summer house through their use of it, then the following rules should be followed:

The commonsense conception of welfare may be stated in four propositions, each of which modifies its predecessor:

1. Maximize total welfare.

2. Deviate from that goal if necessary to ensure that all achieve a minimal level of welfare.

3. Deviate from [that requirement] in the case of persons who fall below it because of their own choices (e.g. one family member earns less than the others because of career choices; another needs rental income having more children to support).

4. Deviate from [that principle] if their [choice]... is due to severe poverty and deprivation. (Elster 1992, 240).

The last proposition would hardly apply to people with summer houses, but some of my respondents do have family members who, through their own choices (typically involving drugs) are impoverished. Given the Protestant Ethic or simply the expectation of a shared family culture (note Stark above on the sources of altruism), this last principle receives no support in such families, however useful the other principles may be. If followed, it would lead to the selling of the summer house to alleviate the poverty—and they are unwilling to do that. Instead, they punish the deviant family member by ostracism. In such largely informal mechanisms (although sometimes formalized in "no buy-out" provisions in family partnerships or corporations), they follow the patterns of how neighbors settle boundary disputes and co-ownership of property analyzed by Robert Ellickson (1991).

Based on a case study of boundary disputes among neighboring ranchers, Ellickson calls them "co-owners" in that they share a specific ecosystem whose over-all health affects each rancher, even as mutual boundaries such as fences need to be mutually maintained. Under the circumstances, disputes about boundaries are inevitable. Ellickson discusses the informal sanctions used to punish defectors (who don't cooperate in resolving boundary disputes) rather than rewards being given for cooperators. Regarding those who share ownership of property:

> The theory of norms developed in this work predicts that these co-owners will rarely consult law. Because co-owners tend to be intimate, they can usually be expected to rely on informal rules and self-help sanctions to keep each other in line... Anticipating future difficulties over sharing, co-owners may prepare a contract governing their relationship... [but a] strict accounting of past inputs and outputs would be transactionally costly and signal a lack of trust. (Ellickson 1991, 274-5).

As we have seen in previous chapters, informal sanctions often build upon and indeed, strengthen the application of the formal sanctions built into whatever legal structure is agreed to. But what happens if the informal sanctions and processes fail, when the second or third generation can't agree—perhaps never having been consulted, or having changed their minds as they matured into new responsibilities? Ellickson is talking about "intimate" neighbors, not kinfolk whose level of intimacy may either enhance or preclude the power of public shaming over a lack of mutual trust. It is one thing to have none of the neighbors speak to you again; it may be easier to risk such ostracism within a family where forgiveness and reconciliation are more likely, among some family members at least, if only because the costs of private defection are so much greater to those abandoned.

Accepting different and irreconcilable values among participants which make informal sanctions and even public ostracism ineffective, economists Steven J. Brams and Alan D. Taylor (1996) provide a readily-understandable procedure to follow, called "Adjusted Winner." In a circumstance where a cake or other object can't be divided ("you cut, I choose"), how are goods divided among several actors with different value principles?

Regarding summer houses, one heir may put greatest value on maximizing income, another on coming in August, yet another on being there alone with no other family, another still on doing as little work as possible in upkeep. All such principles or characteristics are to be listed for all to consider and among which to determine their own priorities. (See the discussion of Matlack's procedures in the next chapter.) Then all participants get 100 points to distribute among the lot, based on their own value preferences. Almost inevitably, each person gets whatever he or she placed most points on. Thus if being at the summer house in August is more important to me than having solo use, I may have to share residence with my kin; if solo use is more important, I may have to settle for a stay in June before the water warms up. And if maximizing income or minimizing work is most important, I may have to rent out my own allocated time or hire someone from outside the family to do my share of the work. After first choices are allocated, a formula provides the means whereby the rest is split so that each participant ends with approximately the same number of total points.

We have seen this procedure approximated in Chapter 8, in a case in which one founder distributed $250,000 in Monopoly dollars to each child and child-in-law, and another $10,000 to each grandchild, to indicate preferences as to various items in his estate. If a single family had gotten together and bid for the summer house, they would have owned it outright. In fact, that did not happen: my respondent felt that no single family wanted to cause envy among the several lines, in addition to which they particularly enjoyed being there with each other, so that single family ownership did not appeal.

Brams and Taylor have applied this procedure to widely varying cases, finding that often people gave up tangible rewards in order to avoid appearing greedy or selfish. Obviously, rational choice may include far more components than financial self-interest.

By allowing players to set their own value preferences and win at least that which they want most highly, Brams says his system is "envy free." To be sure, in nasty divorces and child custody suits (and sometimes even in the inheritance of summer houses), preventing others from having what they want may be what you most want yourself, but Brams' structure provides a procedure by which some of the above more abstract principles determining equity and fairness can be applied in real-life situations.

CHAPTER 15

PROCEDURAL PRINCIPLES BASED ON MEDIATION

With the contributions of the various economists on the table, let us consider the advice of Louis R. Matlack, former business executive, professional mediator, and second generation heir to a summer house held by a family trust with the ten members of the third generation as beneficiaries with undivided interests. We will hear from various respondents in this section as to what has worked for them as well as what hasn't, illustrating the economists' and Matlack's principles of mediation in general and here applied to reaching agreement on both the informal and formal structuring of sharing an inherited summer houso and illustrated by my respondents. While traditional negotiation was based on an industrial model in which management argued from a basis of greater *power* and labor argued from a basis of greater rights, the present views on negotiation start from the point of identifying the various interests of the several parties. Part of the process of determining what the various interests are, and how they might be met collectively, can easily lead to developing a general mission of "family interests."

Most adults under 60 have had some experience with the organizational mandate to agree upon a mission statement, so starting with an effort to agree on a "family mission" regarding the vacation house should be possible as well as beneficial. The mission is to express an ideal concept of maximum family benefit from shared use of the place, in terms of the collective interests without regard to the sense of comparative power or rights that the respective individuals may have.

To start the discussion going, useful open ended questions include: "What does this summer place mean to you?"; "What is really important about it to you and your immediate family, and why?" Answers will usually include explicit values as well as family relationships and income-production, which may involve implicit value factors as well. (Matlack 1998)

He goes on to specify a key step: encouragement of clear expression of the values to be enhanced through collective ownership of the summer house, as well as each listener's understanding of these values. If the authoritative founders have not initiated this process, for the second generation it may be to circulate written "visions" among themselves. Sharing these descriptive visions with the next generation is one way to invite their participation by an expression of their own visions. Hear from one respondent whose family decided to follow Matlack's advice:

Once we got specific about what we actually meant by "family solidarity," which we had generally agreed was an important part of our collective vision for the summer house, it turned out that our definitions weren't altogether the same. What was interesting was that the major difference was by generation. The cousins were much more relaxed about how it had to be expressed than my siblings and I were: the kids saw no particular need for all of us getting together annually or even making sure that everyone had time at the cottage every year, maybe because they took more for granted that we would share the place equitably and that the "solidarity" already existed. Of course, they may also just have assumed that my brother and sister and I would work it out, as senior members of the family, and they would deal with the fall-out of our decisions when it came. (Second generation in Rhode Island)

Obviously, the goal of the discussions resulting from such an exchange of visions is to develop a practical agreement about how to manage the family's vacation place. As various family members contribute their views and concerns, commenting "round-robin" in a face-to-face discussion or through a circulation of drafts, a working text evolves. Professional advice on ownership forms, inheritance and property taxes, major maintenance costs and the like are to be shared among family members to elicit further questions, interpretations and alternative suggestions.

While some second generation heirs may want to settle things among themselves before bringing their children into the discussion (whether or not the latter are all of sufficient maturity to take any responsibility for the place), many have opened the discussion to the third generation from the beginning, with considerable success. The cousins frequently contribute to greater agreement among their respective parents through their mediation of any latent sibling rivalries. Their collective presence, along with that of their "silent-partner" parents who have married into the family, help to keep the entire discussion on a collegial and adult level.

Brams' and Taylor's procedure may be useful here in helping all participants acknowledge that they may legitimately hold different values and motives, all of which should be understood as contributions to the collective mission. For example, especially if the third generation members have been born in unequal numbers to the second generation, almost inevitably a conflict will emerge between those subscribing to the norm of inheritance which holds that all second generation members should inherit equally (presumably the siblings with fewer children) and those who follow the norm that third generation members should also do so (presumably the siblings with more children). In such cases, the inclusion of cousins in the discussion I om the outset may be crucial in developing a stable, workable agreement about how to equably manage the vacation house, as they will speak from their own self-interest which may include more equity among them than some of their parents might anticipate.

According to Matlack, at various times in the process of developing a workable agreement all of the family members should meet face to face to talk out their concerns. This is most valuable for the initial sessions. Typically many families show an avoidance of candor and forthrightness among certain family members, and more openness among others.

Certain areas of primary but often unacknowledged conflict are likely to surface, given enough reassurance in the process that they will be taken seriously and the one who voices them not blamed outright. These concern the differences in income that are likely to be found among extended family members by the third generation, if not by the second, and the imputation of differences in personal merit and its related social status. We considered such issues in the early chapters of the book, and it is important to be reminded of them here. Individual family members are likely to judge each other according to whatever level of achievement they have attained, according to their own values, and to denigrate those of others and thus the presumed worth of their contribution to the discussion. If all can acknowledge at outset that each has a legitimate "class interest" in the proceedings and the outcome, each may participate more freely.

At least acknowledging that such "old" patterns may be troublesome in the "new" summer house management scheme can suggest pitfalls to be addressed... very tenderly. Creative solutions to these pitfalls developed carefully over a limited time will strengthen the ultimate agreement.

Developing a workable family vacation home management agreement is not family therapy, but the process can improve how a family functions. (Matlack 1998 [his italics]).

Today there are many media for easy communication among family members and there respective professional advisors as they work through this process: email, overnight delivery, conference calls. If family meetings cannot be held at the summer house itself, holding them at neutral sites such as an airport motel equidistant from all participants can contribute to the atmosphere of equality upon all participants and thereby enhance the discussion. Whether the conference is called by the founders or members of the second or later generations, in-laws are to be included in the discussion even if they have no rights of inheritance, and ideally also all legally competent adult descendants. In sum, everyone who is a potential independent user of the vacation property should be included.

After careful preparation with advance reading materials, he initial family conference starts with all participants speaking about where they presently are in their thinking about future enjoyment and use of the summer house, without comment from others. Even if some participants are reticent at first, it is essential t hat all speak and contribute to the composite image delineated by these comments. Permitting agnostic non-participation can have consequences as much as does determined involvement, especially if the non-participant is a "silent partner" in-law.

Early in the process, family members must become very clear about their decision-making rules, whether they be based upon voting, consensus, founder decision, or some other method. (The economists cited above agree on this point.) Matlack's experience suggests that simple majority voting among the comparatively small numbers making up most families can be destructive. Even super-majority voting, with a decision requiring a majority of two-thirds or three-quarters, can be non-productive. The preferred alternative is clearly consensus decision making, as practiced by Quakers and others for centuries.

One simple decision making rule could be that every participant must either accept the final draft agreement as workable, even if it contains terms seen as undesirable, or not stand in the way of its acceptance by the group. However, if any participant continues to object while making a clear statement of what needs to be fixed for the agreement to be acceptable to him, the draft agreement is not accepted until that issue is resolved and consensus reached. A mild dissenter may choose to stand aside while still agreeing to abide by the rules being established, and let the group go forward with consensus but not unanimity. Deciding "how to decide" at the beginning of the process prevents serious roadblocks later. (Matlack 1998 [his italics])

After establishing a written rule for future group decisions, the participants begin to create a working agreement by building on the common themes of their visions. At an absolute minimum, whether or not the provisions are expected to be written into the formal legal structure, a practical agreement must address three fundamental issues: time sharing, work and cost sharing, and future governance mechanisms. The basics of these should become part of the legal agreement even if the specific details should be included only in the supplemental written agreement.

Additional issues can include more specific ground rules for normal use involving water and fire safety standards, ecology protection standards (e.g. limiting the number of overnight users to the maximum acceptable to septic systems loads), as well as guidelines involving plants and animals, both those seen as "members of the family" whose health is to be optimized as well as those seen as weeds or vermin to be destroyed or evicted.

These are as important as the formal governance issues that are likely to be written into any final legal document, such as those involving possible buy-outs, rotation and replacement of the management committee, and any limitations on decisions to change basic furniture, color schemes or "atmosphere" features. if non-family renters are to be permitted, a whole panoply of additional issues arises. (Matlack 1998)

In Chapter 13, we considered a variety of legal structures, each of which could accommodate such a working agreement. The focus here is on how family members can most readily agree un the principles to be set forth in any such legal structure. Given such prior consensus, when they hire a lawyer to finalize their decisions in whatever legal form best meets their needs (including its tax implications) the process will run smoothly and efficiently. It is crucial to reach agreement on how they can most readily implement the legal structure over time, with provisions made for altering it should changed circumstances make it unworkable.

Moreover, given the expense of legal counsel as well as the adversarial positions such consultation may bring out among family members, it would make sense that only the basic principles of the agreement be "enshrined" in the legal documents, so that the legal structure need not be changed even when details of the implementation agreement may need to be. Thus prior to consulting a lawyer to draft the formal legal structure (be it an association, partnership, corporation or trust), family members should reach closure on an objective accounting of where they stand, including remaining uncertainties and disagreements:

1. What is agreed to? What are the priorities? What can or should be deferred until later (e.g. when next generation members are mature enough to participate)?

2. What are each participant's suggestions for dividing up the issues and the work to resolve them?

3. Including areas of disagreement, what are the obstacles to be overcome?

4. How might they be dealt with?

For example, regarding time sharing among families of unequal sizes, can the season be divided one year by the number of siblings and the next by the number of cousins? Can there be an allocation of so many weeks of "prime" season and so many of "off" season? Regarding tasks of maintenance, must all participate directly ("sweat equity") or may some pay for such work to be done by professionals or other family members?

Matlack further suggests that the person who organizes the process leading to an actual face-to-face meeting of the family members should probably not be the person who presides over it. The organizer must be in the direct "bloodline" to have sufficient authority to bring the process to that stage, but the presider of the meeting should be the one among the entire adult kindred, regardless of generation and including in-laws, who can maintain the greatest neutrality. Others family members can be asked to take such roles as drafting pre-meeting "white papers", taking visible notes of the discussion on a large flip-pad for all to see, or taking and later circulating the minutes.

Care should be taken that some individuals do not over-compromise or avoid taking a stand on particular issues, as these will remain festering otherwise, especially if they concern the interests of in-laws. Such issues may include the fact that some may not want the situation organized at all. Why? Comparably, there may be issues that some people want to avoid discussing which others insist upon bringing to the table, issues that from either perspective may be seen to be personally "non-negotiable." However, all such personal topics are relevant and important to the collective understanding that is to emerge, if only to discover what obstacles must be removed if agreement is to be reached. Throughout the discussion, any individual's motives must be accepted openly, as otherwise they may be impugned. This is facilitated by use of non-personal language: the focus is to be kept on interests and ideas, not on personalities.

These are Matlack's rules of procedure, based on a Quaker heritage; it still took him, his two brothers and their ten adult children two years to reach closure on their trust-cum-partnership agreement as amended drafts were circulated. As we have seen above in the discussion of motives and the likely implementations of structures, a process such as

Matlack suggests itself becomes part of the resolution. Hear from those who have tried to follow such a process intuitively, without knowledge of his principles of mediation:

We decided to make the place a rallying point for the West Virginia branch of the family to celebrate their roots, by giving them first choice in next year's schedule. We asked if there were any other family members they might like to overlap with. We thought it was important that they felt fully included if they were to be willing to be responsible as future owners, and so far that is working out. (Third generation in Maine)

When my father was diagnosed with Parkinson's, he got me and my four brothers together to arrange for our taking over the ownership and maintenance of our summer house. With his advice we set up a limited partnership. After he died, we worked together to develop fairly detailed rules for scheduling, financing and so on, and with provision for the eventual retirement of each general partner and his replacement by one of his own children, so that the lines stay intact. Each of us has by now gifted our shares to our children, so the 18 of them own it outright. We have our differences, of course, but we stay out of each other's way when we need to, and it has worked very well. There will be 67 coming for a family reunion this summer! (Second generation on Cape Cod)

There are several lawyers among the cousins and we finally decided to incorporate, or we would never manage to hold to the informal arrangements my mother and her brothers have for taking turns on the cottage. The cousin who drew up the agreement practices law in Texas so that's where our Maine cottage is incorporated. And even though all of my uncles are also lawyers, my mother has been the "matriarch-in-charge" and she has made it work. But it needed to be formalized for the rest of us, and she helped us all the way. Email sure made it easier for us to reach agreement among all four branches of the family. (Third generation in Maine)

We knew we would have do structure something to supplement the trust my grandmother had set up, as it no longer covered expenses. Also, as the family had grown, we had no provision for deciding how to schedule who could use it when: just dividing the summer into thirds, as we had always done, no longer worked. So the trustees arranged and billed the trust for a very long conference call, with family members patched in from Arizona, California, Missouri and Scotland to "attend" the meeting at the summer house where those who could get there were assembled.

While the trust allowed the trustees to do whatever they thought best for the property, so they could have set up a supplemental legal structure on their own, they felt it was important that such major decisions be made collectively. We had sent copies of alternative possibilities around in advance, with some specific questions to think about. Of course various family members had been in touch with each other about the questions, as well, so the conference call—lengthy as it was—was sufficient that we all agreed to the final partnership form. (Third generation in Wisconsin)

Considering Ellickson's and Clignet's respective analyses of motives, discussed above, it is certain that participants in any discussion about use of a summer house will not only have different ones but as Matlack notes, motives will be impugned to others that they may or may not have (or be conscious of). Open discussion, without accusation, may reveal any hidden motives even to those carrying them, and at least they can then be considered and evaluated. If some motives remain masked because they seem shameful, it can lead to later difficulties:

I always thought that my sister was my parents' favorite, and then when her second child turned out to have severe developmental disabilities, my widowed mother bent over backwards to give her family priority in the schedule for use of the summer house, and fewer responsibilities. Now that mother is gone, the pattern has been set and it is impossible for my brother and me, and our wives, to ever speak openly about what we felt was unfair about use of the place, even as certainly "life has been unfair" to my sister and brother-in-law in terms of what they have to do in caring for my disabled nephew. There is still a latent resentment that is very difficult to overcome in any dealing we have with our sister, and the respective cousins perpetuate this resentment. (Second generation in the Adirondacks)

While we have met and talked and talked, we are as far from reaching agreement as we were at outset, and it goes way beyond the realities of the shared property. For some family members it is concerned with pride and vengeance. The majority of the family doesn't want the discussion to sink to this level, but because the decision-making authority in the family was invested in the minority who, in turn, are invested in fighting over this, we all get dragged along. These discussions have tapped into family rifts that had lain beneath the surface for years, decades even. I suppose it's better that at least we are talking about what we never dared to talk about before: if we keep on talking, I have to believe we'll reach a comfortable closure on both how we handle the summer house and maybe everything else about our shared estate that has been bothering my cousins. (Third generation in Connecticut)

The difficulties in reaching agreement and staying there, over time, are obvious. In the absence of strong and generally accepted norms of inheritance as well as those which might determine status within the family by age or gender, let alone by achievement or occupation as discussed in Chapter 2 and alluded to above, the views of siblings and cousins are likely to diverge. All the more important, then, is the process through which agreement is reached, and further, that there be provisions on the process through which changes to the original agreement may be considered. If mutual trust is enhanced by the process itself, family members will be more willing to discuss any problems that emerge about its implementation in confidence that a resolution can readily be found.

In sum, "fair play" in establishing basic ground rules contributes to subsequent fair play by those who follow them. If the basic principles are understood (as with baseball, players have different but equal roles, individual members of teams take turns at bat), new situations can be accommodated without having to check the document of agreement each time, even as it is there to resolve any disputes. All equipment that is at risk of damage even with normal use, such as boats, is the cause of frequent need to revise the operating agreement:

> As part of the formal agreement we reached last year, we included a provision that boats were privately owned and not to be shared with other extended family members when they were visiting without express permission. Well, my sister and I own the canoe in common, and operating autonomously as she had before, she let our cousin, who was having his turn in the other house, keep it in the water and use it after my sister went home. You can imagine what happened: he took it out in weather that was too rough for it and he ran it hard on a rock and damaged the hull. He paid for the repairs, but it was unpleasant for awhile, as I thought my sister should have checked with me before she let him use it after her departure. If she had been there, she would have known it was unsafe to take it out, and she wouldn't have let him do so. But because we trust each other's good will, we've marked this down to lack of forethought on the part of both of us rather than lack of judgement on her part. We should have been clear with each other from the beginning that common ownership meant common decision-making. So we're now more aware that we need to pay scrupulous attention to the terms of the formal agreement before we make any decisions that might affect someone else. (Second generation on Lake Champlain)

> We had so many problems over assigning blame or responsibility for damages done to the boats—routine wear and tear, really—that we finally made a provision in our operating agreement that every family makes a boat-use deposit of $150 when they

come to the house. Each incoming family is responsible for checking the boats when they arrive, even if they won't be using the boats: if any damage is found, the previous family is billed from their deposit. The deposits are returned at the end of the summer if no damage has been incurred, but people can opt to leave the money in the boat fund, which goes for a new boat every ten years or so. This procedure has taken any fear of blame out of use of the boats. Now we feel we can play and have responsible fun without worrying about liability all the time. (Third generation in Maine)

Given trust and commitment to the principles underlying whatever formal agreement is in place governing collective use of a summer house, the sense of playfulness that Huizinga analyzed as crucial to the survival of civilization is enhanced. As quoted at greater length in the *Introduction* and particularly relevant to the mission a summer house is to fulfill, he noted:

> Play is not "ordinary" or "real" life. It is rather a stepping out of "real" life into a temporary sphere of activity with a disposition all its own... It endures as ...a treasure to be retained by the memory. It is transmitted, it becomes tradition... It creates order, it *is* order. Into an imperfect world and into the confusion of life it brings a temporary, limited perfection. (Huizinga 1955, 8-10 [his italics])

During the few days or weeks any family members may spend at the shared summer house, away from the routines and stresses of their everyday lives, instead following the ritual practices established by the founders as well as those accruing with time and experience, they are likely to feel a sense of sociability that is rare in other contexts. As Simmel understood it, sociability is based upon an assumption of equality among those who participate in this "play form of association" which has no ulterior end in itself but instead is "oriented completely about personalities" (1971 [1910], 132). With this taken for granted as the primary mission of the summer house but with recognition that its shared ownership requires them to go "beyond personalities," family members may avoid getting so caught up in the calculation necessary to support it that they lose sight of why they are doing it at all, on the one hand, or on the other become so lost in trying to accommodate their individual tastes and values that they lose sight of how their mutual interests might be met.

CONCLUSION

We can now pull together these multiple lines of evidence and argument. Of the many factors that contribute to any single family's experience in the inheritance and use of a summer house, some operate at the societal and cultural level, making it more difficult to perceive them, let alone to understand how they affect me and thee in our ownership of our private property. These macro-level factors include the social history of the inheritance of land and the inevitable role of stewardship that goes with it, as distinguished from the inheritance of more liquid and readily divisible forms of wealth. One result of this history is that when land or real property is to be equally divided among heirs of the same generation, conflicts are almost inevitable. Such equal division carries expectations of comparable personal use benefit as well as shared financial responsibility, but there are no norms which govern such sharing.

The situation is compounded further by the norm that heirs of the same generation should inherit equally, even though members of the third generation (cousins) are unlikely to be born in equal numbers to members of the second (siblings) so that any legacy from grandparents may or may not reach them in what they consider "fair" proportions. An additional complication is the norm that family members should never discuss money with each other, lest it interfere with their sense of mutual equality. Accordingly, because these discrepant norms are differently written into estate law and expressed in the general value system, their inconsistencies are largely unrecognized, let alone raised for re-evaluation. In turn, provision for the passing on of a summer house to multiple heirs is unlikely to deal adequately with the inevitable conflicts built into the explicit and tacit rules governing such inheritance.

Mitigating these conflicts and providing considerable social "glue" are the over-arching cultural values that have been literally built into the design of a summer house. These are often deliberately cultivated by its founders in their own practices among like-minded members of the surrounding summer colony. Similarly important are their specific serious-yet-playful family rituals associated with the summer house, distinct from those practiced by family members in their everyday lives. Under contemporary conditions, when women have ceased to monopolize domesticity just as men no longer monopolize the world of work outside the family, such rituals embodied in the shared material property of a summer house have become all the more important in its continued joint ownership.

> These new family rituals [have] acquired tremendous emotional appeal because they [assert] a symbolic unity of family activities and schedules that [has] ceased to prevail in [everyday] reality. For this reason, they remain powerful symbols of a stable family life for most of us today... [However,] the people who seem most satisfied with their family relationships often mention the ways they have reworked older rituals and values. (Coontz 1997, 119)

Such reworking may well happen incrementally and without deliberation, as family members, including increasingly "extended" kin and in-laws, negotiate their inter-relationships so as to achieve greater harmony in their shared use of a property all hold dear, yet which none are likely to be able to afford to maintain alone. As we have seen, such relationships show many basic patterns leading to more—or less—successful outcomes. These patterns include the motivations with which summer house "founders" plan the disposition of their estates as well as the legal forms they settle upon, after more, or less, consultation with their intended heirs.

The patterns also include the informal rituals, found to be so important by my respondents that consciously revising them may be difficult. Their importance to the stability of family life is recognized as well as by Stephanie Coontz, the foremost contemporary historian of the American family, quoted above. Yet as she notes, satisfaction is also found in "reworking" them, as members of younger generations inevitably do when their circumstances change—especially as no one is able or willing to assume the patriarchal and matriarchal roles of the founders and insist that nothing change despite a collective sense that *something* must. Indeed, in many cases the creativity that contributes to the satisfactory revision of some now-traditional practices is taken to be part of the family's inheritance from the founders. As stated by the heir who recounted her grandfather's playful auction of the various items of his estate, using Monopoly money (as noted in Chapter 8):

> Grandpa's view was that you can only keep this going with creativity, not with law, and that legacy is going to help us settle the issues now that the younger generations are in charge. (Third generation in Missouri)

Thus any "ideal" set of family rituals and traditional practices, combined with the "perfect" choice of a legal instrument to structure the equitable and agreeable inheritance of a summer house by successive heirs, may still be insufficient to pass it on: in addition luck, creativity and the motivation to use them may be necessary as well. Those of my respondents whose families include fifth and even sixth generation heirs, all having some share in the use of the collectively-owned summer house, show that it is possible—and they serve as inspiration to those of us at earlier stages in the process that it can indeed be done.

However, in our focus on the family dynamics of sharing a summer house, as influenced by the wider social and cultural norms and practices, we have not yet discussed why anyone else should care about how successful they are in passing on such legacies. In a much-fragmented and multi-cultural society, filled with conflicts based on social class, race, ethnicity, age, religion and other cultural and political value systems, what difference does the successful sharing of a summer house make to the common good, other than as the grounds for mutual envy by the vast majority who do not own one?

Noted sociologist Peter L. Berger, who developed the concept of the "social construction of reality," provides another useful concept in his discussion (with Richard Neuhaus, 1977) of what he calls "mediating structures." These "stand between" individuals and micro-order institutions such as their families, and the macro-order institutions of civil society such as political or corporate entities of enormous scale. Why are such mediating structures so crucial? The level of individual and the nuclear family is so particular that it is difficult to generalize from its experience to some greater understanding of and personal relation to the over-arching social, political and economic institutions of a globalized and bureaucratized society . (How can someone who shops mainly in the local deli or boutique understand the motor vehicle agency, let alone know how to complete her income taxes, or have an idea on what our trade policies should be?). Berger's analysis shows that the "mega-structures" of contemporary global society are experienced by most as so "abstract", so "unreal" despite their enormous power, that they cannot *generate* the stable values that people need to live by—whether they then work to sustain those mega-structures or work to oppose their effects. Without stable values, people can scarcely trust and build upon their own experience, having enough consistent faith in the future that they believe in the efficacy of their own actions in ensuring it "for themselves and their posterity."

Fortunately, in between the micro and macro levels just denoted are a host of potential "mediating structures" that embrace and support individuals, providing experiences of personal and collective meaning. Such structures thereby generate and sustain the values and the systems of interpretation that their subscribers need, in order to operate in the utterly impersonal "value-free" world of post-industrial, global society. Among these structures are neighborhood groups, institutions of religion, education, social welfare, and a panoply of voluntary associations.

Obviously, many "mediating structures," such as neo-Nazi or other organized hate groups as well as those of fundamentalist ethos, promote and sustain values and systems of interpretation which are utterly alien and even destructive to a civil, multi-cultural and multi-racial society. Certainly some mediating structures turn their members away from the values which permit—let alone foster—the practice of "live-and-let-live" that is necessary in at least some public realms if all are not to be in total conflict against all others. To the degree that summer colonies reinforce class distinction or racial or ethnic exclusion, as surely many do, it could be argued that they should count on the negative side of the ledger: they may contribute to the sense of social identity of those who own property within them, but in such a way that the effects on the wider society are inimical to the general welfare. I would argue, however, that summer houses have the potential to serve as benign mediating structures in ways their owners may not be conscious of, particularly after they are successfully passed on by the founders and collectively maintained by later generations. In a society as age-stratified as ours, gated communities with residency restrictions based on eligibility for the AARP (if not on race, religion or income) are symptomatic. So too are political conflicts over the collection and distribution of tax monies for seniors through Social Security and Medicare on the one hand, and for children and juniors through public schools and Medicaid, on the other—decreasing poverty rates among the former while those among the latter increase. In such a society, any institution which fosters multi-generational connection and caring is beneficial.

It is not simply that activities at a summer house are almost inherently trans-generational in their fostering of family solidarity. Perhaps more important is the egalitarian sociability that is one of the chief qualities of successful summer house sharing. In a playful, leisure setting affirming the quality and value of social experience rather than its quantity or price (following the analyses of Georg Simmel and Johan Huizinga discussed in the Introduction), any assertive or distinctive characteristics of its separate owners and their guests are subsumed by and into the collective solidarity. Only after it has been internalized into the social identity of those who participate in it can that sense of egalitarian sociability be extended to outsiders.

This is not just a case of learning "good manners" and habits of pitching in to help when needed. Any sub-cultural group teaches the same to its members, according to its values. Rather, it is the teaching of "fair play" in the sharing of a summer house that is most important here. As we have seen, this sense of fairness is learned—sometimes with difficulty—through the process of reaching collective agreement about how the summer house is to be maintained if members of an extended family are to continue to enjoy its use. The process determines—indeed, *becomes*—the end product, just as Huizinga has shown us that *play for its own sake is necessary for civilization*.

If this line of argument is unconvincing to those who continue to regard play and leisure as unrelated to the serious and often tragic circumstances in which we find ourselves, consider the parallels between the values taught through the shared ownership and use of a summer house with those found crucial to effective social programs designed to restore health to America's troubled cities.

According to Lisbeth B. Schorr, whose analysis of such successful programs, *Common Propose: Strengthening Families and Neighborhoods to Rebuild America* (1997) has received encomiums from pundits and politicians from right to left of the spectrum, seven key attributes are critical. Successful programs:

1. Are comprehensive, flexible, responsive and perservering.

2. See children in the context of their families.

3. Deal with families as parts of neighborhoods and communities.

4. Have a long-term... orientation, a clear mission and continue to evolve over time... [in this regard] like the successful corporations described in Peters and Waterman's *In Search of Excellence*, they are "tight" about their mission and simultaneously "loose" about how the mission is carried out.

5. Are well managed by competent and committed individuals...

6. [Who are] supported to provide high-quality, responsive services.

7. Operate in setting that encourage practitioners to build strong relationships based on mutual trust and respect. It is the quality of these relationships that most profoundly differentiates effective from ineffective programs and institutions. (Schorr 1997, 5-10).

She goes on to note the importance of "smallness of scale" and "a warm, welcoming climate that conveys a sense of safety and security" (12).

Without question, all of the above characteristics are found in extended families who manage to pass on a summer house from generation to generation. While Schorr's social programs typically deal with impoverished clients whose motivations are determined, in part, by the fact that they have no alternatives—that they are desperate for *any* secure support structure—owners of summer houses typically have many alternative ways of spending their leisure time and money. Their on-going *voluntary* participation in the collective ownership and use of a summer house is the result of the values that it has instilled in them, that they pass on to their children in turn. There they learn to participate fully and freely in the on-going activities and institutions of the wider civil society, in the extended kindred of "the family of man." Summer house owners have the opportunity— and in the eyes of most, the obligation—to capitalize on their legacy for the public good, practicing and extending its lessons of conservation and civilized rules of play to their other social relations as they go about their everyday lives. Having learned self-discipline, restraint and concern for others during their leisure time at the summer house, they are more likely to demonstrate those qualities when they leave it for their work in the market place of the global economy.

Is the societal effect of this "character-building" likely to be trivial? I can think of no way of measuring it accurately, but as there are six million "second homes" in the United States with a collective user/owner total perhaps six to ten times that, surely there is a large and highly positive social impact of these privately-owned and individually-determined family vacation properties. What many summer house owners regard as their "havens" of escape from the complex struggles inherent in the "outside" world become, in fact, their means of cultivating the qualities necessary to sustain and even improve it.

For those of us fortunate enough to be included in this category, the message is clear: Keep the faith—and pass it on.

THE WORKBOOK

HOW TO PASS IT ON

[Note: Avoiding sexism in pronoun use is difficult. I have opted for alternating genders rather than continually using the awkward "he/she", "him/her" .]

INTRODUCTION

This workbook was originally written to accompany my sister Judy's book, *Passing It On*. Judy realized that her book, which she had initially intended for the academic sociological community, was long on theory, without a lot of suggestions. Since I had been consulting with her on the book, and she knew I could write in a more colloquial style, she asked me to do a workbook with some practical ideas.

I will be referring to her book, but also to a book written after she was gone, *Saving the Family Cottage, by* the late Stuart Hollander. Both of these books are designed to help families maintain and use to best advantage what Judy called "summer houses" and what Stuart called "family cottages". Millions of families have one of these; in fact, one out of every twenty dwellings in the United States is a second home. These homes are of immense value to the families, both emotionally and financially, but not a lot has been written to help families use and pass them on in peace and to best advantage of all members.

There has been a fair amount published about dealing with these homes as financial assets, most of this aimed at an affluent audience, despite the fact that many families owning such property are of modest means. Judy's book was the first to look at family dynamics, how families operated in order to use their summer houses to best advantage of all members, and to prepare for orderly passing on of the property to younger generations.

Stuart acknowledged his debt to Judy, and growing out of his experience as an attorney in a vacation area of Michigan, explained how and why the development of a Limited Liability Corporation (LLC) is the best legal route for a family to take in preserving and bequeathing a family cottage.

I will be explicit about this now; our original legal advice was very poor and I recommend that you ignore it. Judy and I were educators, not lawyers, and we were speaking out of our experience with our family home. Stuart Hollander was an estate lawyer and worked with many families who owned second homes. I strongly encourage you to purchase Saving the Family Cottage and follow his legal advice.

Where I feel that Stuart's book fell short was on the family dynamics involved at arriving at an agreement for a Formal Operating Agreement. That is the focus of Judy's book and my workbook, so I see the books as perfect complements to each other. Working with all three will give you the best advice at home to preserve your family cottage.

Judy's book grew out of our family's experience in owning summer houses on Nantucket Island. Yes, THE Nantucket Island of immense wealth and cachet. All I can say is, "it weren't that way when I was a young'un," and I deplore what has happened to it.

From 1949 until 2003, we vacationed on Nantucket. For the first ten years, we used the cottage of family friends. Then in 1959, my father bought ten acres of beautiful waterfront land in an area called Pocomo, and built a three bedroom summer cottage. The land cost a thousand dollars an acre.

Recently, I learned of the purchase of a four bedroom cottage on three-plus acres of land in Pocomo, three acres being the zoning minimum, for more than five million dollars. The buyer then tore down, or as they so sweetly say, "scraped" the existing dwelling, and will spend millions more building his McMansion. So, five million for three acres. That works out to $1.67 million per acre. You can figure out the percentage increase.

This suggests why we no longer own our family cottages.

In 1969, my parents built a second cottage on this property. The idea was that they would use it, while my sisters, brother and I would divide up the time to use the first cottage. This sounded like a fine idea but using the first cottage was not a smooth process. Judy and my late brother Bob, second and first born respectively, were both strong-willed individuals with some not-so-latent sibling rivalry.

Judy and I would often discuss the problems we were experiencing. Judy was a sociologist and at one point she wondered what the sociological literature said about families sharing a summer house. To our surprise, no one had ever studied and written about this very common phenomenon.

Judy was a dynamic person so she thought that she would be an ideal scholar to do such a study, and she was right. We discussed the design of the study and she started recruiting families to participate. Through word of mouth and newspaper ads, she started to get families in the New England area. Gradually she expanded geographically to the mid-Atlantic states, the Midwest, and even Far West. Ultimately, she studied seventy families, trying to focus on what made it possible for them to maintain and pass on a summer house, in some cases, to the fifth and sixth generation.

Her intention all along was to write a scholarly text for an academic audience, and she hoped to find a university press who would be willing to publish it. To the great good fortune of hundreds of families, she was unable to interest a university press.

Judy was a true force of nature and ideas were always percolating in her super-sharp mind and one of the best ones she ever came up with was the decision to aim the book toward a wider audience, publish it ourselves, and use the internet to market it. I would write the workbook and she also asked me to help edit her manuscript to make it more accessible, "dumb it down", to a general audience. I made a number of suggestions, a few of which she adopted. Idea people like Judy are usually not very good about taking suggestions, but I did get her to eliminate some of her parenthetical statements. Quotes from theorists were another matter. I miss arguing with her.

So I wrote the workbook, which was fun, found a student who proved very adept at developing a website, Judy found a place to print the books, and a distributor, and we were off and running. Through word of mouth, different journalists learned of her study and the books, and she was interviewed for The Boston Globe, The New York Times, Forbes Magazine, some regional New England newspapers, and she appeared on local New York television. Sales of the books started slowly but grew to a gratifying level where we had order a second printing.

Through all this period, she was battling breast cancer. She was diagnosed with a virulent form of the disease in 1993, had a mastectomy and very aggressive chemotherapy and hormonal treatments, which kept the cancer at bay, and never denied what was happening to her. Everyone who fights cancer is courageous in my book, but her drive to forge on was monumental.

She had had metastases for awhile but in late 2001, the disease spread to her liver and she lost the battle in March of 2002. She was 64. Perhaps it's a good thing that we no longer have the Nantucket cottages because it would be there that I would miss her, and my parents and brother, more acutely.

I am glad that she didn't live to see the eventual sale of the cottages. After my mother died, and through a needlessly complicated process, my brother Bob and my nieces inherited one of them, and my sisters and I had inherited the other. Owning and maintaining them was becoming increasingly expensive; in the last year we had our cottage, taxes were $17K. For a non-winterized, plain and simple summer cottage! I won't tell you about our electric bill.

First Bob and his daughters, and then Judy, our sister Janet and I reluctantly decided that we could no longer maintain the properties and we had to sell. Judy knew that we had no other choice but she hated the decision. She let me handle everything about it, both because she didn't want to deal with it, but also because she was getting sicker.

The long, complicated and painful process of selling our place outlasted her. It wasn't sold until the Fall of 2003.

Meanwhile the books kept selling and I was happy to keep that going. Of course I wish she had lived much longer, but especially because a few months after she died, I was interviewed by a writer for The Wall Street Journal, and the subsequent article produced a boom in sales such as we had never imagined. She would have loved to see that.

Though we made some money from the books, she was far happier knowing that she was helping people who were struggling to peacefully use and maintain their summer houses. My parents had raised us with a strong ethic of doing for others, and though her life was cut short, writing and publishing the books gave her more satisfaction and happiness than anything else she did in her career. She was a wonderful teacher but the consulting she did with those who contacted her was as gratifying as working with her students.

In the spring of 2007, I was contacted by Stuart Hollander, an attorney in Traverse City, Michigan. He explained that he was very familiar with Judy's work and had written and published a book called Saving the Family Cottage.

When I read it, I saw that it was just a natural fit to the work Judy had done and the books we had written. We knew that the area where we were weakest was on legal ownership of the summer house, and some of the advice we gave was not very good.

Stuart's argument that a Limited Liability Corporation, an LLC, was the best form of ownership made perfect sense.

On the other hand, what I thought his book needed was more discussion of how an extended family can work together to come up with the formal by-laws for the LLC. Stuart had worked with a number of families in developing LLC's, a lot of them first generation, what Judy called the "Founders". Not to put the work down, but it's not hard to come up with an agreement with Founders.

Judy had studied families in their third and fourth generation, even one with a fifth, with cousins and second cousins trying to come together to create a formal operating agreement that would work for as many as fifteen or twenty households. Following her death, I had talked with many of these people and knew that they needed a lot of help in the preliminary stages of talking and working out an agreement, long before they would ready to draft an LLC.

Stuart and I talked about all of the issues that families faced and how we might work together to integrate his work with Judy's. In July of 2007, while my wife and I were visiting her family in Michigan, Stuart and I met in St. Ignace, on the Mackinac Straits.

We discussed how I might modify my workbook so that it would dovetail with his book. In that way, we would have a three book sequence, a "trilogy", as we literary types like to call it, that he could publish.

This was not to be. Stuart died suddenly in August at the age of 54, leaving his wife and a college-aged son and daughter.

So that is what has led to what you are about to read. I think you understand the purpose of this workbook, but being a teacher, I can't leave well enough alone, so I will sum it up.

This workbook is designed to help families, whether first generation or fourth, come together to produce what I am calling a Formal Operating Agreement (FOA). This will serve as the by-laws of an LLC, if that is the route you choose to go, governing the ownership, maintenance and inheritance of their summer house or family cottage. Even if you choose not to form an LLC, a Formal Operating Agreement will be very beneficial, despite the hard work it will take.

This process can, and often is, lengthy and involved and usually takes a lot of time and energy. Two or three people, whether Founders or second and third generation members, will have to drive it.

These "Drivers" may have to bring together a number of differing and often conflicting ideas about what the family should do with their special place. It can be a maddening process but it is well worth it.

If you, dear reader, are to be one of these Drivers, you may already realize that to succeed, you need to be a Paragon of Unconditional Positive Regard for every family member, and a Mortal Manifestation of Divine Patience. You will be able to do this, because of your innate goodness but more importantly, because it is so important.

The FOA and subsequent LLC that your family may develop will enable your family to happily enjoy their special place for many years and through succeeding generations.

Hopefully they will have the sensitivity to put a small plaque somewhere in your family cottage honoring you and the other Drivers.

Even if they don't, you will be able to say to yourself, "I dun good". Congratulations!

CHAPTER ONE

THE PLAN OF THIS WORKBOOK

As a teacher, I have been trained to identify to my students the goals of a course, and then the specific objectives of a particular class. Then I identify what we are going to do to achieve those objectives. I don't want to make this too pedagogical and make you squirm in your chair, as you did in seventh grade math, but it does seem to be a good approach to take with this book.

After all, it is a "workbook" and you know what that means. Yes, you're going to have to do some work, not just read. I'll get to your homework later, but don't worry; there won't be any quizzes or a final exam.

In the Introduction, I described our overall goal, developing a Formal Operating Agreement (FOA) that could serve as the by-laws for a family Limited Liability Corporation (LLC).

I will describe the plan for the rest of the book, but first a word about the problem of terminology. Judy called the dwellings under discussion "summer houses". When I asked her why we couldn't call them "summer homes", she said that there was an important sociological reason for this, and after all, her book was originally intended for scholars. So the term to be used was "summer house". I never understood why.

When Stuart Hollander sent me his book, I saw that he used the term "family cottage" to describe the same dwellings. Sibling loyalty aside, I immediately saw that this was a better term. After all, the second homes for many families may be fall hunting cabins or winter snow lodges, and they are often occupied in the spring. "Family cottage" also had a warmer feel to it than "summer house".

So from this point on, with an apology to Judy, I will discuss "family cottages".

In Chapter 2, we will look at the Importance of Family Cottages. You are probably very aware of it but it is important to consider the factors that make them so important.

Some of your siblings, cousins, and descendants may not have thought about all that makes a family cottage so special, and even the more abstract ideas are good things to have in mind as you work toward an FOA.

In Chapter 3, the discussion will be about the Difficulties of Owning a Family Cottage. Again, you may know many of these, but if you are a Founder or a member of the second generation, you might not have considered some of the difficulties that are more likely to emerge with the third or fourth generation.

Chapter 4 will present two fictitious families, the Madisons and the Murphys and the issues and difficulties they face with their family cottages. These families are similar to those of many of you reading this book, and you will undoubtedly recognize many of their issues as ones you're also dealing with.

In Chapter 5, I will discuss patterns of Informal Operating Agreements (IOA). Whether they realize it or not, all families have these and they encompass significant matters such as who is going to get to use the cottage and when, and how expenses are handled. The IOA also deals with questions like what food should be left in the refrigerator for the next occupant and who does the weeding in the flower plot.

It is very important that families identify what their IOA is. Members may disagree with certain ideas and argue that, no, we don't have to leave eggs for the next occupant.

Knowing what the IOA actually is is an important requirement in determining what the FOA should be. So the first step in the process toward an LCC, or any formalized document, will be to write explicitly and to everyone's agreement what the terms of the IOA are.

Once the IOA has been described, we can move on to Chapter 6 and the first steps toward the FOA. At this point, we move from the past and present to the future, from "what we've been doing" to "what we will do". There are two things to be done at this point. One is to interview attorneys to discuss what you and your family are doing and just what you will need legal help with.

The second is to write a Family Mission Statement, almost like a Preamble to the Family Constitution that is represented by the FOA and LLC, and this will be covered in Chapter 7.

At this point, I will indicate that I will continue to talk about developing an LLC, even though your family may choose to go another route in terms of coming up with a legal document governing use of your family cottage.

In Chapter 8, we will discuss the issues that need to be discussed in order to develop Policies and Practices to be outlined in the LCC. Your family will be able to identify many of these but one thing families have difficulty doing is planning for the future, looking at the issues that will emerge as people get older, new generations come along, and the family cottage itself ages. So we'll look at how your family can develop their Policies and Practices for the FOA and how your attorney can use these in writing your LLC.

This chapter will also discuss how to develop these Policies and Practices. You can probably anticipate that this will be a lengthy part of the process. Some of you are third or fourth generations and you're thinking about all those cousins, siblings, all those aunts and uncles, grandparents, sons and daughters, grandchildren, step-parents and step-siblings and step-children, dogs and cats, birds, pet tadpoles... "AAARRGGGHHH!!" you say. "I'd rather try to get the Republicans and Democrats in Congress to agree!"

Okay, it isn't always an easy process and it may take a long time. But we have already identified you, a Driver of the process, as a person of unconditional positive regard for others and of infinite patience. In the end, your virtues, and those of your fellow Drivers, will carry the day and the Policies and Practices will be decided, with all of the "i's" dotted, and all of the "t's" crossed.

At this point, all that remains is to put this bright and shining FOA into legal terms in the family LLC or other legal form.

Chapter 9 is a happy send off to you and your family and I will happily "pass it on" to you.

A WORD ABOUT THE WRITING TASKS

Now, let's get to the matter of the "work" in this workbook. Before you begin reading any further, I want you to get a good, substantial notebook. At certain points, I'm going to give you writing tasks, (but ones that you do not have to turn in to me for treatment with my red pen). Some room has been provided below each question to jot your first thoughts but I believe that a companion notebook is much needed to accommodate your fullest answers. For some you may also come to find this notebook becomes a cherished deposit for wonderful memories that apart from this structured means of committing them to paper might be otherwise forgotten in time.

While there will no doubt be some of you that may not at first appreciate the need for the writing tasks, or are not generally fond of writing, I urge you nonetheless to come back to them and complete them diligently. Certain things we discuss are going to stimulate a lot of thoughts and feelings on your part, and all of these should be recorded. The opportunity these exercises offer in getting out and putting down your thoughts on paper is essential. These are your thoughts and your notes—nobody else need see them but you'll need them to work from. The FOA and LLC will be written documents as well so you may as well start the writing process as you read.

I also strongly urge you to obtain additional copies of this book to give to the rest of your family members. While this can appear self-serving, I believe you will agree that the scope of information presented here should be in the hands of each family member with whom these issues are to be worked out. Your family's collective notes will be of great value in this process.

CHAPTER TWO

WHY FAMILY COTTAGES ARE SO IMPORTANT

I realize that to some degree I am preaching to the choir but I do want to discuss why family cottages are so important. One of Judy's respondents summed it up succinctly, "*It's where we do family!*"

It's at the family cottage where we often see extended families, Grandpa, Aunt Trudy, and Cousin Ralph, in a more relaxed and fun way than during Thanksgiving or Christmas dinner. By definition, we're on vacation or holiday, with the stresses of work, of school, of the usual family issues, at least temporarily forgotten. There are fun things to do, swimming, boating, hiking, cookouts, or just relaxed, guilt-free reading. Even if the available activities are minimal, it's still a joy.

Passing It On goes into much more detail on this issue, including both theorists and quotes from the subjects of Judy's study. This is just a reminder.

As my kids were growing up and we went to Nantucket every year, I was aware that they had a lot more activities to choose from than my siblings and I did when we borrowed the cottage of family friends. We had nothing more than a rowboat, no outboard or sailboat, and the island had far fewer fun things to offer. I can't remember much of what we did on a daily basis, besides playing on the beach, but I do remember the cottage and how much we loved being there.

In my childhood and that of my kids, we did not have television available, and I think our evening activities in particular were more varied and involving than flopping in front of the evil electronic eye.

I recall one summer after I had become a father, and when we arrived, my kids immediately raced around the cottage, just as my sister Janet and I used to do. Then I heard them say in indignant tone, "What is this doing here? " I went to see what they were talking about and it was a new television. My brother's wife was completely disabled and one year, my nieces had gotten her a television and VCR. That is what my kids were offended by. They seemed to understand that a television would actually detract from the ways we enjoyed the cottage. I was very pleased at their indignation.

A week or so later, I recall looking around our large living/dining room. Some of our friends were there with their kids and over here, two people were working on a jigsaw puzzle, my friend Elliott and my son Jeff were making a model boat. Meanwhile, my wife was reading, my daughter Donna and her friend Jessie were watching hermit crabs in our saltwater aquarium, and out the picture windows, I was aware that a spectacular sunset was starting to develop. This scene could have never happened at home.

Family cottages are important not just for the fun times and the chance to see extended family, but they are also a means for families to pass on important values. As Judy put it, "The summer house is the family's emotional "sea anchor", steadying the direction of related individuals by linking them with their shared past and pointing them toward the future with a kind of collective identity."

Through the summer houses, we pass on values that are cultural and may include important ethnic and racial traditions. In many areas, there are colonies of families of a particular ethnic or racial ancestry. Judy studied African-American colonies on Martha's Vineyard and the eastern shore of Maryland, and also found a colony of Finnish ancestry on the Upper Peninsula of Michigan.

Particularly in New England, the "Protestant Ethic", as defined by German philosopher Max Weber, is alive and well. This is the idea that work must come before play, that hard work is important, not just for what it accomplishes but for the cultural values we learn from it.

While the Protestant Ethic may not be as conscious a cultural value in other parts of the country as it is in New England, I think the idea of work "along with" play, if not "before", is important for reasons other than those illustrated above.

As you well know, but your children may not, family cottages require a lot of work, from daily chores, to physical maintenance of the building itself, to dealing with legal and financial matters during the off season. It is important that children learn this as they grow up by pruning shrubs, helping to paint the barn, or just taking out the trash.

If anything, it is more important that they do this at the family cottage than their year-round home. They will eventually be managing this place and they are never too young to learn that in no way are the family cottage and vacation time there "free". They can be given little tasks when they are four or five.

Fond and doting parents understandably want their children to enjoy carefree vacations, but "carefree" doesn't have to mean "work-free". If they don't grow up understanding through their contributions just what is involved in owning their family cottage, learning this when they take over the property may come as a shock.

It certainly was for me. I was the third born, and second son, and my father discussed property matters with my brother Bob, not Judy or me or my sister Janet. When Judy, Janet and I inherited our cottage, Judy was chafing at the bit to take charge of everything and I let her. Then as she was dying, she literally dumped folders in my lap and said, "Here, it's all yours." She never even gave me the password to the Quicken spreadsheet.

It was a painful learning process for me, in a number of ways.

So the concept of "sweat equity" is a good one to instill in all family members, and the learning should begin early. If your progeny are to become owners of the property, they need to learn to produce a little sweat to earn their share.

Judy found that one characteristic of all families who where equitably maintaining their family cottage is that they kept some sort of log, each family recording their stay, who joined them, memorable things they did, etc. Often they record what they did to maintain the property. This can be mundane, e. g. "We cleaned the oven," or major. e. g. "We've-shingled the shed roof." They can also note potential trouble spots, e. g. "In our last week, hot water was rather iffy."

It is important that the tasks undertaken be recorded, both to make sure that they are done and to avoid duplication of effort. Whoever exercises oversight of the entire property can see that necessary maintenance jobs need to be undertaken, e. g. "I think we need to call the plumber about that hot water heater. It's at least twenty years old."

Another benefit from a work log, as opposed to a play log, is that it can help promote healthy competition among branches of the family. If I see that my cousin did a major job of cutting back brush, I'm going to look for something that can match or top that.

Whether a family log is kept or not, I think it's a good idea to keep your own personal log. Family cottages and our stays at them serve as markers for changes in our lives. Summers blur and you may not recall whether a particular event happened five years ago or fifteen.

We are likely to remember our first years there when we were kids. Then as we hit adolescence, we moved away from our families and toward our peers, and perhaps our first employment was a summer job nearby. We bring our fiancés and fiancées to meet family there and perhaps take our honeymoon on the premises. We bring our babies there and see the first year that toddlers can appreciate that this is a special place. We are likely to try to offer our kids some of the same pleasures we enjoyed in our youth and thereby establish family traditions that we treasure.

As the older generations age, they slow down but enjoy seeing their children, grandchildren, and great-grandchildren. As they approach the end, final summers may be especially treasured.

I'll never forget the summer of 1985, my father's last year. My folks were in their cottage and my siblings and I rotated through ours. Though he was visibly deteriorating, it was still nicer to see Dad there than it would have been visiting their home in New Jersey, and I know that he enjoyed it more. I stayed on longer than my wife and kids and spent more time giving care to Dad and Mom It was a precious opportunity to give back to them some of the love they had given us.

It was not long after that that I started keeping my own log, and though we no longer have the Nantucket property, I will always value the log. Initially, I just recorded the dates we were there, which family members we overlapped with, and what the weather was like. I also recorded when my siblings used the place.

There was a practical purpose behind doing this. We were having more difficulty dividing the summer slots among ourselves and I wanted to keep a record or who had used it when. I wanted to know whether Judy was correct when she complained that Bob always got warmer August when she had to use cooler July.

Each year the entry became longer, including our guests, how many bluefish we caught, what my kids did, the sunsets, and even memorable meals. If I had thought of starting it earlier, I would have had my kids make an entry each year.

WRITING TASKS
—You can come back to this later but don't put it off too long.—

1. As quickly as you can, in whatever sort of shorthand you want to use, write down some of your fondest memories of your family cottage.

Big or small, major or minor, write down everything that comes to mind. You may have a lot of years to cover and if it'll help, you can go chronologically or just put your mind on "Scan" or "Shuffle" and let it meander where it will. When you've recorded a bunch, put the notebook aside, but make a point of coming back to it later. Even if your conscious mind continues to read, your unconscious mind will be on "Search" and other memories will pop up in an hour, as you go to bed tonight, or tomorrow as you head to work.

2. Even if it's February, write a log of last summer's stay at your family cottage.

Revisit this as memories will surface while you prepare dinner or watch television.

continue on the back...

CHAPTER THREE

WHY OWNING A FAMILY COTTAGE CAN BE A PROBLEM

When people first get a family cottage, whether they buy or build it, they rarely see it as anything other than a joy. These folks, usually a couple whom Judy called "Founders", are delighted that they have the discretionary income to afford such a place, even if it is a spartan two bedroom house with few amenities. Their kids are equally delighted and for many years, things go swimmingly, often in more ways than one.

Founders often do not anticipate the problems that their children, grandchildren, and great-grandchildren may run into. Some farsighted individuals who have sufficient money may establish a trust for future generations to financially maintain the house, but often this is the extent of planning for the future.

Some founders do anticipate future ownership problems and set up an LLC. If you are one such Founder, I honor you. However in Judy's experience and mine, subsequent to her death, most families have not had such wise Founders. Typically, they may set up a trust fund which their descendants find is inadequate as land values and taxes increase, sometime outlandishly so.

Even if an LLC has been set up, the terms may deal more with legal and financial matters than family dynamics, such as who gets to use the cottage on the Fourth of July weekend, or what determines that an individual is now deserving of his or her own slot, rather than sharing time with parents.

Of course it is hard to plan for what grandchildren will need when you don't know how many there will be, and the ones you now enjoy can still sit on your lap. Yet when they, and their cousins, get older, they are going to have their own ideas on how to best utilize their family treasure, and these may be different than those of the Founders.

With grandchildren, there are now three generations and simply dividing up the precious prime-time summer weeks is becoming more difficult.

Consider typical Founders, whom I'll call Fred and Marge. They have three children, Leah, Carol, and Nat. All of them marry and have two kids themselves. As the cousins reach maturity, they want to have a summer slot for themselves, not use the cottage with their parents.

Fred and Marge are still alive and kicking, and while generous with the cottage, they now find that there are eleven family households, including themselves, who want some time during those prime weeks of July and August. That's about nine weeks and eleven doesn't divide into nine very easily. Even if you add the end of June and beginning of September, if Labor Day is late, giving each household a convenient week can be a big challenge.

Traditionally, the male Founder has handled the financial and legal aspects of ownership, while the female Founder sees to matters of usage. So it is usually the woman who does scheduling. While in our culture there is a heartening relaxation and reexamination of traditional gender roles, Judy found that they seem to be more operative when it comes to the family cottage.

Naturally, the Founders take care of things and as they do, they establish both implicit and explicit rules for their families and these apply to the family cottage. In addition, families often establish traditions with the cottage and they may be very attached to these. The rules and traditions may be more rigorously maintained with the summer house than they are at home. Because of the effort and sacrifice necessary to establish the family cottage, Founders may be more insistent on the rules for the cottage than with an everevolving family life at home.

Such "top-down" decision-making can lead to problems. As Judy put it, "Top-down decisions by founder patriarchs are usually based on the motive of efficiency. . . However, such self-determined arrangements. . . may also contribute to more conflict than to less as the once beloved patriarch comes to be seen, by his heirs, to be dictating from the grave.

"Of course no one intends to cause problems for his or her children; rather, founders see themselves as merely exercising power on behalf of their children, not in their own self-interest."

Usage of the summer house usually goes smoothly for a number of years. Even as the Founders' children establish families of their own, three generations often use the treasured cottage without serious problems, that is, while the grandchildren are young.

Yet, as we have seen with Fred and Marge, as the cousins grow up and become heads of families themselves, problems start to grow, and not just in connection with the allocation of summer slots. The cottage is starting to age and is requiring more expensive repairs and maintenance. In many areas, like Nantucket, property values have zoomed to cosmic levels and the trust the founders established may no longer be sufficient to cover taxes, much less the other myriad costs of maintaining the place.

How is this cost going to be supported, and by whom?

While brothers and sisters are usually able to get along as they are growing up, once they establish their own families and want things for their own kids, latent sibling rivalries may surface, especially over the family cottage. It was learning about a family she knew where siblings became so combative that the family was torn apart, and the family cottage lost, that helped spark Judy's interest in doing her study. As she did her research, she found that this case was unfortunately not that rare.

If siblings are fighting among themselves, this influences their children, the cousins. Even if there is no unusual conflict, the cousins may not know each other very well. The bonds among them may exist more in theory than in practice. They live in different parts of the country and follow more diverse lifestyles. They may come to question some of the patterns that their grandparents have established for the family cottage, e. g. "I know you all got up at eight to raise the flag with Grampy, but I don't see why I should have to drag myself out so early when I have to work till eleven. Besides, no one but us can see the flag."

When I was fifteen and my parents built the first Nantucket cottage, we established a pattern of putting on a record called "*The Beloved Choruses*", by the Mormon Tabernacle Choir and Philadelphia Symphony. A favorite cut was Haydn's glorious anthem, "*The Heavens are Telling*". It just seemed to suit our joy at being so fortunate to be in such a heavenly place.

When I tried playing it when my kids were young, I got the plaintive, "Daaaad, why do you have to play that stuff? "

The patterns that Founders begin are usually informal, even when they become well-established. It hasn't been necessary to write anything down. Good heavens, families don't need constitutions, do they? This is the attitude that Founders, and usually their children typically have. They all feel that, "We can work it out among ourselves."

This belief may be held more strongly by the women in the family, and they are the ones most responsible for maintaining the implicit usage patterns. They may be more resistant to the idea of formal agreement, even as they age and consider what their family will do when they are gone.

Judy says, "The notion of 'letting them work it out after I'm gone' is typically held by women (a few male respondents voiced it as well), often those who had not been engaged professionally as had their husbands, and who are less comfortable with the idea of relying on legal structures to resolve internal family matters." (132)

In the next chapters we will look at some of the issues that develop as families expand and extend. What I find interesting is that it is often the third generation, the cousins, who realize that existing policies and practices are inadequate, and not just because they want a summer slot to themselves. Many of the people who contacted Judy and have contacted me since her passing, expressing a need for help, have been from the third or fourth generation of a family.

In some case, aging members of the second generation realize that something needs to happen in order to preserve the family cottage. In such cases, I encourage the individuals contacting me to enlist the active participation of their children and nieces and nephews. If you are a Founder, I would encourage you to involve your children immediately, and even grandchildren if they are even near adolescence. As I will discuss later, as a family develops an FOA, it is best if the "Drivers" of the process represent more than one generation.

If you have been experiencing some or many of the problems I will discuss, you know that they are not going to simply disappear. Rather, they will increase in number and amplitude as more generations come along.

WRITING TASKS

1. Identify some problems you see existing now in your family's usage of their cottage.

Try to identify these without reference to family members, i. e. "Standards of cleaning the cottage for the next family members are not consistently followed," rather than "Those good-for-nothing kids of ours and their cousins always leave the place an unholy mess."

2. Describe problems in communication and understanding among family members that may underlie these problems. Again, try not to make these personal.

You could refer to the problems that happened two years ago with scheduling, and how miscommunication led to misunderstanding which led to frustration and anger. Again, be sure to not even imply that one or more family members was at the root of the problem.

continue on the back...

CHAPTER FOUR

TWO FAMILY SCENARIOS

Judy was sometimes asked what a "typical" family situation was and this is a question for which there is no answer. Families and their cottages vary too much for there to be any "typical" situation.

What follows are two hypothetical families derived from details of the many families that Judy studied. As you'll read, certain details are likely to resonate with you, producing an "Ah ha!" recognition reflex, i. e. "Yes, that's exactly what's going on with us."

In your reaction, pay attention to your feelings, not just your cognitive recognition of similarities. As I will emphasize, your feelings, and those of everyone in your family, need to be identified in developing a Formal Operating Agreement. Yes, these feelings may be negative and discussing them can be messy. That's the way it is with emotions.

Yet all emotions, including negative ones, need to be recognized and, here's the tough part, validated, or they may sink either the development of the FOA or its implementation. No one is ever "wrong" to feel as they do. You may think that someone is ridiculously touchy or grossly unfair to feel as they do. You may yearn to say, "Get over it!", but the feelings must be accepted as real and not dismissed. This is one of the hardest aspects of this whole job and I cannot emphasize it enough.

You will also have to help your family members that even "unfair", "ridiculous", "absurd" emotions must be understood as valid, meaning they are real, and they cannot be dismissed.

ABOUT THE WRITING TASKS IN THIS CHAPTER

After I describe the first family, the Madisons, I'm going to ask questions about what you think they should do about some of their issues. After each question, I will leave some room for you to jot down your immediate response. If you are going to share this copy of the workbook with a family member or friend, you can write your response in your notebook. Of course, I strongly recommend that everyone has his/her own copy. At the end of this chapter you will find a family tree diagram to help you visualize and keep straight the Madison family. Likewise, you'll find the Murphy family tree that we'll also be considering.

THE MADISONS

The Madison family owns a three-bedroom cottage on two acres of waterfront property on Cape Cod, Massachusetts. Carlton Madison, the Founder, bought the land and built the cottage in the early 1960's, and named it "Whispering Grasses". He has been dead for eight years. His widow, Ginger, is now 84 and lives in the Albany, NY area. She is still physically and mentally energetic and likes to spend four for five weeks each summer at Whispering Grasses while some of her children are in residence there with their families. She is proud to be the matriarch of the family and loves to talk about her four children, their spouses, and her seven grandchildren. She would be delighted to show you the snapshots she carries with her everywhere.

As issues have developed and some conflicts surfaced, she has encouraged her children to, "Talk it out; just truly listen to each other with love in your hearts." She dismissed a recent suggestion that it might be a good idea to develop a Formal Operating Agreement. The idea of any structured legal agreement, and an association or corporation, is anathema to her, as it would seem to violate the principle of shared love among all family members, to which she has devoted her life.

Ginger has been able to maintain this view in part because Carlton established a trust fund to cover taxes and maintenance. However, land values on the Cape have been booming and there is an ever-increasing shortfall of $10-15K which the family must make up. She has had difficulty in understanding the urgency to do something formally about this.

In addition, as is often the case, the trust says nothing about how the cottage is to be used, who gets which weeks, how repairs are handled, etc. What is clear and fully understood is that when Ginger dies, her four children will inherit Whispering Grasses in equal measures, according to the 600 year old English tradition of "Tenancy in Common"

Chapter 5 of Stuart Hollander's *Saving the Family Cottage* has an excellent discussion of the problems associated with this legal principle.

The four Madison children and their spouses are as follows, in order of birth.

Thomas, a successful attorney, is married to Stacy, an interior decorator. They have four children and live in the Boston Area.

Doug, the second born, is married to Gwen, and they are both social workers. They have two children and live in New Jersey.

Silvia, the only daughter, and her husband Rob are both professional craft-makers and live in Mystic, Connecticut.

Fred, the youngest, lives in the Chicago area with his wife Karen. He has a small advertising agency and she is a buyer for a department store. They have no children.

The four Madison offspring divide up the nine prime summer weeks of July and August into specific two week slots. They schedule these with Ginger, rotating first, second, third choice on a yearly basis so that she can visit with two, and hopefully three of them during her own mid-summer stay. They sometimes negotiate swaps of slots based on children's summer schedules and individual preferences. These negotiations are not easy and there has been some tension round them, especially as they still go through Ginger. And occasionally, she has forgotten to write down someone's request.

Because of their distance from Cape Cod and because they also enjoy Lake Michigan, Fred and Karen come east just once every three years. When they do, they get first choice, though the other siblings only get first choice every fourth year. When they don't come east, the other sibling families can have three weeks.

However, Doug and Gwen, and sometimes Silvia and Rob can't take more than two weeks, so there have occasionally been days or even a week when the place is not in use. This has been a course of some frustration but the two couples are reluctant to give Thomas their extra days without some form of compensation.

The siblings could certainly do the negotiation of summer slots among themselves, but Ginger likes to have her say in it, especially since she uses the place during some of the time. Her name is on the deed to Whispering Grasses but more important is the implicit authority as Founder which she has always enjoyed.

The increasing shortfall from the trust fund is now being made up equally by the four siblings, as was stipulated in Carlton's will. The outlay has been no problem for Thomas, but it is something of a difficulty for Doug and a real problem for Silvia. Because he uses the place just once every three years, Fred questions why he should have to pay 25%. Thomas has said that he is willing to pay all of the shortfall but in return for that, he wants three full weeks and first choice of slots each summer. So far the others have not agreed to this.

Other issues have surfaced and are causing increasing tension and conflict. None have been resolved and they are threatening the peace and solidarity of the Madison family. These issues include the following:

Thomas wants to add another bedroom and bath to the cottage since it's very crowded for his family of six, especially when Ginger is with them. He would like to take on a home equity loan, with all sharing the payments, but as with his suggestion on the tax shortfall, he has gotten no agreement. He could afford to build the addition himself, but is reluctant to do so and let the others benefit from his generosity. He points out that he has replaced appliances without asking for compensation.

Thomas is the only one of the four with the time and resources to come down to the Cape for a few days in June or September. Doug and Silvia feel that because he can do this, he should not get a crack at first choice in the prime months.

Further, Thomas' firstborn child, Carlton II, was married two years ago and his first grandchild, Ginger's first great-grandchild, is expected in a few months. Carl has mentioned that he would like a summer slot of his one, which has taken Thomas' three siblings by surprise.

Of Ginger's four children, Doug is the closest to her emotionally. Ginger is also fond of his wife Gwen, who has similar tastes to her own, as her daughter Silvia does not. So Ginger prefers to come to the Cape for all of Doug's slot, spending a week or so with whoever precedes and follows him. Doug is willing to allow this, but he is beginning to resent the fact that he and Gwen never have the place to themselves. They have never been able to invite another family to share their slot, as his siblings have done.

Silvia and Rob enjoy using their skills to work on the cottage and land and are acknowledged to have put far more "sweat equity" into Whispering Grasses than anyone else. They have made a number of repairs which have saved a good deal of money, give the cost of hiring local service people. The two are sailors and recently purchased a sixteen foot sailboat. Given the relative fragility of the boat and the trickiness of local winds, they have asked that no one else use it, though it remains on the property when they are not there. This is the first instance of a piece of property being owned by only one branch of the family.

Thomas is resentful of this since he has guests who come every year, staying in a nearby motel, who are experienced sailors and he would like for them to be able to use the boat. Fred and Karen have done some sailing on Lake Michigan and would like to try saltwater sailing as well, and they are also miffed that Silvia and Rob are adamant that no one else use their boat.

Silvia is frustrated with her mother's conservative tastes and would like to spruce up the cottage. On her own, she threw out the musty old drapes for the living room picture window and made new ones of much brighter colors. No one else likes the new drapes and angry words have been exchanged over the imperious way in which she made the change.

Since she is the only daughter, she feels that it is her right to eventually assume her mother's role as arbiter of decisions about furnishings and décor, just as Thomas has handled legal and financial arrangements. However, Ginger usually talks first with her daughters-in-law, Stacy and Gwen, and is influenced more by them, especially since Thomas has paid for most of the changed in furniture and furnishings. This adds to Silvia's resentment.

Spending just one out of every three summers at Whispering Grasses, Fred and Karen find themselves drawing away emotionally from the place. With no children to join them in summers there, Fred lacks a link his siblings all have. In addition, Fred is five years younger than Silvia, his closest sibling, and he has never felt equal to his older siblings. He is tired of the increasing bickering and conflict over some of the issues concerning the cottage. He and Karen have thought about reserving their slot each year and then renting it for the two years they don't come. Knowing how ticklish this might be, he hasn't raised the question with his siblings, but he would like to.

Indeed, he has mentioned a couple of times to Thomas that after Ginger dies, he might like to be bought out of his share of the property. Thomas has not mentioned this to the others. He knows that Doug and Silvia would be unable to contribute to a buyout. He might be able to handle this himself, but he also knows that if he owned half the property, with Doug and Silvia each owning just a quarter, there would be even more problems.

As an attorney, Thomas is also aware that the Commonwealth of Massachusetts will hit them very hard on the inheritance of a second house, especially since it is still entirely in Ginger's name. He has talked with her about considering ways to give the property to the siblings before she dies, but she seems incapable or unwilling to understand the importance of this.

Finally, the winds and salt air are tough on Cape Cod houses. Whispering Grasses desperately needs a new roof and coat of paint on the extensive trim that sets off the pine shingles. Moreover, many of the shingles are cracked and rotting and they need replacement. Local estimates for this work have been in the range of $15-18K.

Silvia and Rob are willing to do the work if others pay for materials and they get extra time and first choice of slots for three years. Though they are very skilled in a variety of crafts, neither has done any roofing or shingling. The matter is under discussion.

WRITING TASK (THE MADISONS)

Listed below are the questions the Madison family is trying to resolve. In the space provided or in your notebook, give your immediate response to each question. If you rethink a question later and want to change your mind, that's a good thing.

1. Should Ginger remain in charge of scheduling? If not, who should handle it?

2. Should Fred and Karen get first choice every third year if the others get it less often?

3. Who could or should use the cottage if there are periods when it's idle?

4. If Thomas assumes a greater burden of the expenses, which he is better able to do, should he be compensated with extra time or more frequent choice of slots?

5. Considering the growing age of the grandchildren, should Whispering Grasses be expanded? If so, how should this be financed?

6. If Thomas can come down in June or September, should he still be eligible for the same July or August slot?

7. *Should Thomas' son Carl be allowed a slot of his own, or should he negotiate with his father for part of his time? As Carl's siblings and cousins get older, when should they get their own slot? Age/? Marriage? Children? This is one of the thorniest questions and there are no easy answers.*

8. *Should Ginger rotate whom she stays with? If she continues to spend more time with Doug, should he receive some compensation?*

9. *What is Silvia and Rob's "sweat equity" worth? What about the sweat equity of the others? Can a sweat equity-to-use equation be developed?*

10. *Since Thomas has assumed financial management, should Silvia assume her mother's role vis-à-vis décor and furnishings? If Thomas assumed more of the cost of the cottage, should the role then devolve to Stacy? Come to think of it, should this be an exclusively female role?*

11. *Should Fred and Karen be allowed to rent their slot? If so, to whom? Who should get the rental fee?*

12. *What about the general idea of rental to defray their expenses? How should this be handled?*

13. What should they do now to avoid ruinous inheritance taxes when Ginger passes on?

14. Who should paint, roof, and reshingle the house, and how should this be financed?

15. What plans should be made to revisit these question and others on a regular basis?

16. Can you think of any other questions the Madisons need to deal with if they are to develop an FOA?

ADDITIONAL WRITING TASKS

1. List any of these questions, or ones like them, that your family is currently dealing with.

2. List any questions that your family is now currently dealing with that you should be discussing. Then give your answers to the questions you have identified.

THE MURPHYS

The now-deceased Founders, George and Frieda Murphy, built a three bedroom log house, "Pine Haven", on five acres of land in the Allegheny Mountains of Pennsylvania in the late 1940's. The wooded land is beautiful and there is a lovely trout stream meandering through their property. The cabin has a large living room with dining area, and huge working fireplace; their eat-in kitchen completes the downstairs. Upstairs are the three bedrooms and full bath. There is a large roofed deck around three sides of the house.

As their children, George Jr. , Philip, and Rose, started families, the Murphys attached a large shed-roofed addition to the back of the cabin. Up to six children can sleep there, dormitory fashion, and they love it. There is a half bath in one corner of the addition.

Over the years, as all families do, the Murphy clan developed what I have called an "Informal Operating Agreement" for Pine Haven. There is a semiformal structure for finances and use, but what really determines how things are done is tradition. All the children and most of the grandchildren remember how George Sr. and Frieda did things and they try to carry on in that tradition.

George Jr. has inherited from his father oversight of details regarding the cabin. He handles all paperwork and has arranged the summer schedule with his late brother, Philip, and Rose. Philip and Rose were happy to let him do this, and there were few problems among the three until Rose divorced Stan Porter when her son Will was small. She then married Jim Pearson, a divorced father with a daughter named Lisa. Rose and Jim have since had two children together.

(See family tree at the end of the chapter.)

George Jr. usually hosts a large family gathering right after Christmas at his home near Pittsburgh. It has always been expected that all the Murphy family would attend, no matter how far away they live. At this gathering, issues concerning Pine Haven have been discussed and assessment of expenses has been made.

However, as the clan has grown, some members of the third generation have started to resent the necessity of coming to George Jr. 's home. Some have to travel quite a distance during the holiday season and then stay in motels, as his house has just two extra bedrooms. The "Cousins", as they are known, also feel that since they have had little say in decisions, their presence should not be required.

George Sr. and Frieda died within a short time of each other, leaving Pine Haven equally to their three children, and there was little inheritance tax. As they were all in comparatively comfortable financial circumstances, George Jr. , Philip, and Rose faced few of the difficulties we have just seen with the Madisons. The siblings and their families happily divided July and August into three week slots, usually taking the same ones.

After Philip's untimely death to cancer, his widow Corinne was granted what are essentially "partner's" rights. George Jr., Philip, and Rose always divided expenses equally, and since Corinne has partner's rights, she is expected to pay for her third. However, as Philip's investments have not fully compensated for his income while alive, this has been difficult for her to manage. Her children, Jason and Carol, have helped her out, to the extent that they now pay two thirds of her share, about 22% of the overall expenses.

The Murphy sons' families and their children have always been closer to each other than to their Porter/Pearson cousins. It is complicated enough with Will Porter, their same-age first cousin, with whom they have less in common than among each other. Relations with all of Rose's children, Porter and Pearsons alike, are compounded by the fact their Pearson step-cousin, Lisa, has come to Pine Haven with her father and step-mother Rose, and loves it. She would like to be considered on the same plane with the other cousins, but they do not consider her as an equal.

You're already getting a sense of the increased complexity of the issues in the Murphy family as compared with the Madisons. Second spouses, half- and step-siblings, and cousins create all sorts of questions, but that has been increasingly the norm for families over the last fifty years. People have fewer kids, but divorce, remarriage and blended families more than compensate for the reduced birthrate in adding to the complexity of ownership.

Let's look at more of the Murphy family circumstances.

Under the lead of the Murphy cousins, the eight consanguinary cousins (excluding Lisa) have discussed the current arrangements. They don't like the fact that they must negotiate with their parents for time at Pine Haven. This is especially irksome to Jason Murphy and Carol Cable, since they pay so much of the expenses, as well as George Murphy III, the oldest of them all.

Three years ago, the eight met and drafted a proposal to their parents. Their suggestion was that the eight cousins and their three sets of parents be considered on equal terms, making eleven family "units" eligible for summer slots. They further proposed that the summer be considered as including the last week in June and first week in September, so that there would be eleven weeks of summer. Each unit would initially draw straws for a selection process, after which, choice would be rotated, first choice going to eleventh and the others moving up. Swapping or even sale of slots within the family would be permitted, but not position of choice.

One unit could also agree to share with another unit, so that it would be possible that individuals could spend two, or even three weeks at Pine Haven. In addition, expenses would be divided by eleven and that figure would be a weekly user fee.

George Jr., Philip's widow Corinne, and Rose listened to the idea, discussed it and have rejected it. They see nothing wrong with the current system. Naturally this has caused some anger in the third generation toward their parents. George III, a successful accountant, is particularly angry with his father, who, he feels, has never given him credit for being an intelligent and competent adult. His cousins Jason Murphy and Carol Cable are also very angry since they are already paying expenses yet have little say in management of the property. Finally, Will Porter, Dan Pearson and Amy Schmidt are very upset, but more with Jim Pearson. They feel that their mother Rose would be willing to make the change, but that Jim's influence caused her to vote against it.

Jim's ability to influence Rose may be partly due to the fact that she is showing early signs of Alzheimer's Disease. Though just 65, she is getting forgetful, confused about the family tree, and is subject to abrupt mood swings. Her mother Frieda died from Alzheimer's so there is a strong probability that these symptoms are those of this awful disease.

There is concern for this on many levels. One of the biggest concerns is that since Corinne inherited partner's rights upon Philip's death, there is precedent for Jim Pearson to claim partner's rights for himself if Rose becomes incapacitated. Jim is a strong, self-made man, a successful industrial contractor, and the Murphy cousins have never been comfortable with him. He dotes on Lisa and as we have seen, the cousins have largely excluded her. If he becomes a partner, it is likely that he will push for her inclusion in any formal agreement about ownership and use of Pine Haven.

Rose and Jim's son-in-law Gary is very successful in real estate and has proposed building a second cabin on the property to ease the pressure on use of the first cabin. He would finance it entirely by himself and asks only that he and Amy have first choice of two weeks at that place, with the rest of the use to be determined by the whole family. He is willing to consider their input in the design of the new cabin.

This proposal is very attractive but a bit unsettling to the others. It would be wonderful to have more room, but it seems that it would establish a precedent of one cousin having priority over the others. Would any children Gary and Amy might have inherit such precedence over the other second cousins? Naturally, expenses would increase as well. The fact that Gary is a cousin-in-law adds to the concern.

Most are willing to discuss the idea; however, George Jr.'s daughter Marlene Murphy is adamantly opposed to it. She is an environmental scientist already concerned about what is happening with increased development of their area of the Allegheny Mountains. The only logical site for a second cabin would be close to the trout stream. Though a septic tank would be pushed far away from it, and percolation tests done, she is concerned that it would leach into the stream, which has already had its pristine quality tainted by dwellings upstream.

The other cousins recognize her concern but there has been some personal resentment toward Marlene in the past. For one thing, her environmentalism is voiced in a particularly strident and critical manner. Worse still is the fact that a few years ago, without telling anyone, she installed a composting toilet to the shed-roofed "dorm" and encouraged everyone to use it. The kids don't mind but the cousins resent the fact that she did this without discussion.

She also took it upon herself to throw out some old, rotting porch furniture. It had definitely seen better days but had strong sentimental value. Sentiment and cooperative decision-making don't seem to be strong values of Marlene.

There is one other potential problem. For a number of years, cousins Steven and Jason Murphy have used Pine Haven for a week in November for deer hunting. The cabin is not winterized but they use the fireplace and bring along kerosene heaters and sleeping bags. Since they are usually accompanied by some friends and there is need for liberal use of eighty proof "antifreeze", there is some concern about the heaters. Marlene hates the idea that they are killing deer and some of the other family members who have been first to use the cabin in the spring have noted that clean-up and final closing of the property have not been immaculate.

Of greater concern is the fact that this week has never been taken into account as they negotiate summer use. This was discussed when the cousins put together their proposal to their parents, but since it immediately produced tension, it was set aside in the interest of achieving some consensus.

If you're a Founder, you may think that I have made this scenario unrealistically complex. If you're a member of the third or fourth generation, you probably know I haven't.

WRITING TASKS

1. Of the issues facing the Murphy family, which resonate most strongly with you?

2. Which represent questions your family is dealing with?

3. How successful is your family in dealing with questions it is facing?

4. Now take a crack at writing your family's history with your cottage, as I have done with the Madison and Murphy families.

Try to write it as objectively as possible, without criticism or praise of any individual's actions and behavior. You might ask a family member you feel comfortable with to do the same thing, then compare your scenarios. It is odd how often we can differ on what we consider to be the facts about our family's history, and it would be good to get someone else's take on it.

continue on the back...

The Madison Family

Carlton
deceased   **Ginger**

Thomas   **Stacy**   **Doug**   **Gwen**   **Silvia**   **Rob Simon**   **Fred**   **Karen**

Child   Child   Child   Child   Child   Child   Child

The Murphy Family

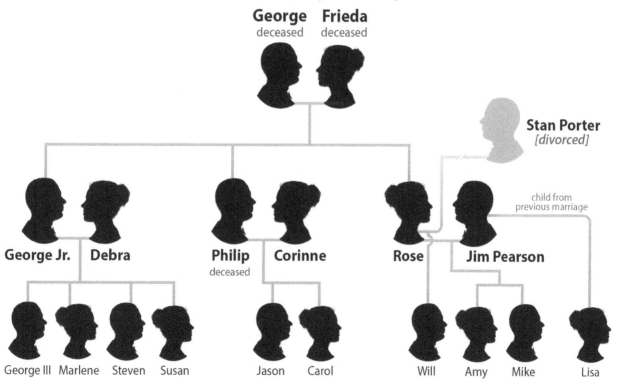

George
deceased   **Frieda**
deceased

Stan Porter
[divorced]

child from
previous marriage

George Jr.   **Debra**   **Philip**
deceased   **Corinne**   **Rose**   **Jim Pearson**

George III   Marlene   Steven   Susan   Jason   Carol   Will   Amy   Mike   Lisa

CHAPTER FIVE

TYPES AND PRINCIPLES OF INFORMAL OWNERSHIP AND OPERATION

In the original form of this workbook, I discussed types of "Informal Ownership". Of course, to be technical about it, all ownership is "Formal" in that it is a legal entity.

So it makes better sense to discuss "Informal Operation" since all families have what I am calling an "Informal Operating Agreement (IOA). This is developed from some explicitly stated, but probably not recorded, Policies and Practices, (P & P) as well as many implicitly evolved and evolving P & P's.

The first version of this IOA is what I will call Single or Joint. This is what we saw in the previous chapter with the Madisons. Founders build or purchase a family cottage and pass it on to their children. They make decisions and establish traditions for the P & P and expect their children to maintain them. The system is often patriarchal though the matriarch usually has a lot of authority when it comes to domestic matters.

As the third generation comes along and the extended family grows larger, families develop some form of Complex IOA, and this was exemplified by the Murphy family. Usually there are more established means for discussion of issues regarding the summer house, allocation of summer slots, and distribution of financial obligations. As with the Murphys, this may be done in an annual meeting. There is one family member, usually male, who handles legal and financial matters and presides over the meeting.

My focus in this chapter, and in the remainder of this workbook, will be more on families with a Complex IOA, because they are the ones Judy studied and with whom I have talked. If you are a Founder with a Single IOA, your task will be simpler but the principles I discuss will still be valid.

The hallmarks of the IOA are that it simply evolved over time and there is no document that articulates how the family cottage is to be used and maintained. As discussed, duties of operation often follow traditional gender roles.

When an IOA works well, it is usually due to certain key factors. Founders involve their children early in the work of owning the family cottage. Along with this, they encourage a more consensual mode of decision-making rather than exercising a top-down dictatorial pattern. Founders encourage their children to communicate and respect each other and they work to mitigate sibling rivalries that can flare up into conflagrations that can be very destructive.

When Founders fail to do this, we find the second generation may have difficulty managing themselves and the property. One of Judy's respondents said the following:

> My parents involved my brothers and me in their discussions of the best possible legal structure and process for transmitting ownership of the summer house to us. But we weren't really in charge until they had both died. Much as we get along well, we've learned how hard it is to go from their rather authoritarian regime to a participatory democracy. I now have more understanding of what the Russians have been going through in recent years!

Another respondent added:

> Whenever my brothers and sister and I had our "annual meeting" to discuss summer house issues, as our parents' health declined and we took over more and more of its operation, we found ourselves playing the old games of sibling rivalry based on traditional sex roles our parents had embodied. My brothers dealt with external maintenance and legal issues and my sister and I talked about things like replacing the washing machine or bedspreads.

What these comments illustrate is the importance of Founders planning in both explicit and implicit ways how their descendants can own and use their family cottage. The model of caring consideration which these Founders can offer is as important as setting up a monetary trust fund.

An interesting factor in the success of an IOA is the role of in-laws. They can have a very positive influence over the family or they can be very divisive. Families usually do not gives sons- or daughters-in-law the opportunity for direct input in decisions regarding the family cottage, but in-laws can have a great deal of what I will call "bedroom" influence.

One of Judy's more interesting findings is that daughters-in-law usually fit into a family better than sons-in-law. This is somewhat intuitive. As Judy put it:

> Given our society's patrimonial system of kinship in which the male line carries the name, and, usually, pride of place, women seem more willing to identify with their husband's family than the reverse, 'marrying in' to his family and thus to some degree 'marrying out' of their own family of origin. . . While some very secure sons-in-law readily fit in, generally it's easier to be a daughter-in-law to an entrepreneurial founder.

Joining a family, a woman may find it easier to assume a contributing role to the maintenance of the family cottage than a man would. I know I am treading on the mine field of Political Correctness here, but women tend to be more inclusive and willing to give the "new girl on the block" a substantive role to play than men, who tend to be more competitive and possessive of their traditional roles.

Obviously in-laws are very important to the success of informal ownership and a wise family will make a conscious effort to involve new in-laws in the life of their family cottage. In addition to the explicit things they do, Judy found that in-laws often have a positive implicit influence, what I called above "bedroom" influence.

She said:

> "One often overlooked strength that in-laws provide is the easing of any sense of structured inequality and rivalry among siblings based on birth order or gender; their presence strengthens the adult roles the siblings play, supporting their maturity in the tendency to become children again."

So just to make things pedantically clear, the following are, among others,—

Nine Characteristics of a Successful IOA

1. The implicit authority of the system is recognized and honored by all family members. Individuals don't make unilateral decisions, such as replacing an original and treasured couch, or booking guests for certain dates prior to allocation of summer slots.

2. Founders and other senior family members begin delegating responsibility to the next generation as they achieve maturity, not just when the seniors die or become incapable of handling it.

3. Founders practice the kind of democratic decision-making they hope their descendants will practice.

4. Children grow up contributing to the well-being of the cottage and develop the habit of working on or for it, not just enjoying it.

5. Some kind of log is kept of each member's contributions to maintenance and repair.

6. There is a check-off list to be done by a departing family so as to make the place ready for the next family. This can be anything from making sure that there are milk and eggs in the refrigerator or cleaning the oven, to putting away beach toys or flea bombing the house if there have been pets there.

7. There is also a seasonally-determined list of tasks for opening and closing the house and clearly understood mechanism for doing these, whether hired out or done by family members.

8. Family members communicate throughout the year, and not just about the family cottage. They have a sense of who each other are and what their lives are like. They care about each other.

9. Overlapping of slots among family members is common, assuming there is room in the cottage. While this is not necessary and sometimes not possible, there are many advantages to it. Members get to know aunts, uncles, nieces, nephews, and cousins in relaxing circumstances. They can learn different ways of enjoying the property. They can also discuss tasks that need to be done and work on them together.

Obviously, many of these characteristics will become formalized in the FOA to be developed.

IOA's break down when there is division among siblings, as with the Madison family, or the family becomes too large, as with the Murphy family and cousins have problems with each other. Members struggle to resolve problems but communication may be haphazard, and if the Founders are deceased or incapacitated, authority may be contested. Old wounds and resentments resurface and exacerbate the problems.

Conflict may be inter- or intra-generational. If Founders had operated in a top-down, authoritarian manner, the second generation, champing at the bit to be in charge, may operate in the same mode with the third generation, simply because they had to wait so long to be in charge. The third generation then becomes frustrated with their parents, aunts and uncles and may continue the dysfunctional pattern. This would be a sad legacy for Founders to leave and certainly not one they would wish for.

While it is important for Founders to model and promote a democratic mode of decision-making, Judy's research suggests that few Founders think beyond legal and financial concerns as they consider the inheritance of the family cottage.

Inter-generational tension and conflict is quite common, as we saw with the Murphys.

Parents often have difficulty letting go of their offspring and recognizing their maturity and competence. This difficulty is magnified when it is focused on one issue, like the family cottage, and one that inspires such strong attachments and emotions.

Intra-generational conflict may exist among siblings, as with the Madisons, or among cousins, as with the Murphys family Siblings customarily know each other better and may communicate more but they may also have more scars from the past that get opened in disagreements over the family cottage. Blending families and the rights and privileges of half- and step-children just add more complexity to the mix.

Even if the family lineage is pretty straightforward and vertical, cousins may lack the bonds that siblings have, may not know each other well, and may be even more widely dispersed around the country.

When my family decided we could no longer afford our Nantucket cottage, there were six cousins involved, along with me and my sister Janet. Judy was no longer with us when the sale was completed. Of the six cousins, one was in Florida, one in North Carolina, another in New Jersey, one in Massachusetts, and two in Washington. They get along cordially but see little of each other and don't communicate regularly.

If we had held on to the cottage and they eventually inherited it, an annual meeting among them would not have been feasible. Yet we made up a New Jersey "S" corporation and annual meetings are a requirement of such an entity. For many reasons, forming this kind of corporation is a bad idea, as I will soon describe and as discussed in Saving the Family Cottage.

In addition, my nephews Nat and Ian in Seattle have enjoyed the Puget Sound and San Juan Islands and did not often come to Nantucket. It is quite possible that eventually, they would have asked the other four cousins to buy out their shares in the corporation, which they would not have been able to do. The cottage would have had to been sold anyway, although with even greater likelihood of more painful emotions than we experienced when we did sell.

This situation and its complexities are not uncommon and they certainly speak to the need for a Formal Operating Agreement.

WRITING TASKS

1. Describe your family's current IOA, (you'll only need to describe it here—we'll draft it after the next chapter). List your "policies and practices" as they stand regarding all issues involving time-sharing, work and cost-sharing, and governance.

You can get a reminder of what these issues are from the descriptions of the Madison and Murphy families. You may also want to skip ahead to Chapter 8, on the formal issues to be addressed in an FOA. As you do this, try to leave out personalities and their interactions, both positive and negative. However, do include the things that frustrate you the most.

2. An alternative approach would be to write your family history as I have with the Madison and Murphy families. This will help you identify some of the issues around the P and P.

You may have done most of this for question #4 in the last chapter.

CHAPTER 6

DRAFTING THE FAMILY's INFORMAL OPERATING AGREEMENT

At this point in the original workbook, I discussed legal entities for ownership of the summer house or family cottage. This was based on consultation Judy had with an attorney and a professional mediator in New Jersey. We also knew something about it from what had happened with the Nantucket cottages, my brother and nieces forming an association, while my sister and I, plus our offspring, formed an "S" corporation, what we called Pocomo Corporation, after the Nantucket area where our cottage was.

The decision to form these legal entities was one my father made in consultation with my brother. Dad did not discuss it with me or my sisters, something that really upset Judy. Knowing nothing about business, I would probably have gone along with what Dad, a very successful corporate executive, recommended. Bob was very successful in the reinsurance business so he was also more knowledgeable about business and financial matters than the rest of us.

Nevertheless, Dad should have talked with all of us, and that is why I will continue to stress the importance of involving all family members, including children, in the decisions you will make in developing your FOA.

To come back to our original recommendations, I am, with humble heart and soul, and sackcloth and ashes, going to penitently recant the previous advice Judy and I made about legal entities of ownership. My recanting is based on discussion with Stuart Hollander and reading his book, which I have already mentioned a few times.

One of the biggest problems for us was that it was much more difficult to sell Pocomo Corporation than a standard property, and we got a lot less money for it. The money we did get was doubly taxed, first on the corporate level and then on us, the shareholders.

In *Saving the Family Cottage*, Stuart Hollander presents a strong argument for formation of a Limited Liability Corporation, and LLC, and offers many reasons why it works better than any other form of legal ownership.

Before I go further, I want to discuss the concept of the "Driver" as I have been discussing it. I don't think the term needs definition. Any process involving ten or more people is going to have two or three who push and steer it along, i. e. Drivers. While a Founder may also be a Driver, it is unlikely. Very few Founders are sufficiently far-sighted to plan for how the cottage will be used by their grandchildren and great-grandchildren. Indeed, they probably will not still be around when they come to full maturity.

Drivers are likely to come from the second and third generation, and they are likely to be self-appointed and/or recognized by consensus for their family leadership.

They don't have to have financial or legal expertise but if they to have it, it will be seen as a plus.

The duties of the Drivers will be to do whatever it takes to develop a Family Formal Operating Agreement, which can then be used as by-laws in the Family LLC that owns the cottage.

Following are some suggestions about Drivers and how they can best work: There should be a minimum of two, even if the family is small. Drivers need to bounce ideas off each other, which works because they are so rubbery and flexible to begin with. There can also be a lot of work and this needs to be shared.

If there are three mature generations in the family, it would be best to have one Driver from the Second and one from the Third. You don't want a team of Drivers who are just siblings, or first cousins, and who might be seen as primarily concerned only with the issues most important to their generations.

If one or two of you have decided that you can be Drivers, there is nothing wrong with recruiting one or two more family members to share the load. They might be from the next generation and will be flattered to be asked.

If you form a Committee of Drivers,, make sure that as much as possible, it has an equitable distribution of men and women. Maybe it should be called the Team of Drivers for it's almost a guarantee that at some point, you will want to become a Muleskinner with some members of the family.

When we were selling Pocomo Corporation, after Judy's passing, I tried to handle everything and I got in over my head. I didn't know how to delegate, though other family members offered to help, and I stressed myself out to the breaking point. Fortunately, my nephew Nat is a very bright attorney in Seattle and as he got into some of the legal and financial aspects of the sale, I let him take over a lot of it. He was very effective at this and his involvement curbed the growth of my incipient insanity.

Were we not selling but trying to develop an FOA, I would have enlisted Nat's help and possibly that of my son or daughter.

Following are some general tips regarding conducting the whole process.

It will probably take a lot longer than you hope for, especially if you have a large family. I can't give you a time estimate because it will vary with the size and makeup of the family. I would recommend that you not set a deadline, for example, of completing this before the next summer season. Actually, I would say that the longer and more methodical this process is, the more likely it will be that the FOA will work into the next generation and beyond.

Using email and other electronic media will greatly facilitate the process, but don't forget the effectiveness of the phone. Emails are just too easy to ignore, even reminders, but repeated calls cannot be ignored so easily. On the phone, when you get the "I've just been swamped, and the kids are just, yada yada, yada," excuse, you can still politely but firmly set a due date, e. g. "So shall we say by next Wednesday? "

Involve children and adolescents to the maximum extent that their maturity allows. This is probably going to be greater than you estimate, so don't dismiss that fifteen year old, long-haired, metal-blasting lout of a nephew of yours. He may surprise you with some of his insights.

Children and adolescents may not understand a lot of the legal and financial aspects of owning a summer cottage, but then again, neither do I, and I've lived through it. You know already that kids and teens will have opinions about how they like to use the cottage and why it's important to them. You may be surprised to hear their dreams about it in the future, and these are very important.

The biggest reason to involve them is that they are going to have to live with and continue implementing the family FOA. If they haven't been consulted, if their opinions don't count, it will be easier for them to dismiss the FOA as their parents' work, not something that they have to live with and live by.

It is not unlikely that you will encounter family members who think that this whole process is unnecessary and fruitless. They may be ones who are less attached to the cottage, or ones like Ginger Madison, who think that you can handle all problems if you just "listen with love in your hearts".

Don't dismiss or "dis" them. Without intelligent handling, they could later sabotage the process or implementation, claiming, "You all came up with this. I had no say in the matter. "That may have been their choice but telling them so at that point will not gain their cooperation.

Even if they don't want to contribute, keep them informed and circulate all drafts to them. It is likely that at some point, they will see something that engages their interest.

You might facilitate this by asking them about a specific issue that you know they care about, e. g. "I know you have strong feelings about building a permanent shed at the beach. We're talking about this now so I wanted to get your take on it."

Legal representation will be important at some point, but not in the initial stages. If you already have a family attorney, it is fine to let him/her know what your family is planning to do and how it will go about it, but you can say that his/her legal counsel is not necessary in the earlier stages. They will take many hours and you don't want them "billable".

Once you have hammered out the details of the by-laws of the FOA, then you can bring the lawyer in. You might want to present him/her with a gift of Saving the Family Cottage to read while you go about getting your family's cooperation. I think Stuart will be very persuasive that your family's decision to develop an LLC is a wise one.

Ideally, at this point in this Workbook, you have copious remarks in your notebook regarding the facts about your family and their cottage, and your feelings about them as well. If you skipped any of the Writing Tasks because you were so enraptured by my seductive writing, now would be a good time to go back to the ones you skipped.

The first task for your Team is to get family agreement on what your IOA actually is. You may be surprised that there is disagreement over matters you consider to be factual, but this is not unusual. You may find that some members say, "Of course we're supposed to leave eggs in the refrigerator for the next occupants," while others say, "No we don't. Eggs aren't good for you. We decided that we're supposed to leave Egg Beaters and whole-grained bread."

If there is disagreement, you can simply say that Practices differ over this issue and the Policy is unclear.

If you did the WRITING TASK at the end of Chapter 5, you already have a draft of your IOA to circulate. In addition to asking for your family's response to your version of the P and P, you can ask if there are major issues which you have overlooked.

It may take a few rewrites to get your IOA fully clear, but this is to be expected.

When you circulate your IOA draft, emphasize that you are trying to determine what your family P and P *actually are*, not what they should be. You'll get to that in due course.

The drafting of an IOA is extremely important because it will serve as the basis for a discussion of what your P and P should be. Saying, "Oh, everyone knows how we do this," is probably inaccurate and it will not be helpful as you address questions about the future of the family cottage.

So, no matter how many drafts it takes, get a written IOA that everyone agrees to, and then you can move on to the really fun parts of getting them to agree on the terms of the Formal Operating Agreement.

WRITING TASK

As explained in this chapter—Draft your family Informal Operating Agreement.

CHAPTER 7

THE FIRST STEP TOWARD
A FORMAL OPERATING AGREEMENT:
THE MISSION STATEMENT

Retired professional mediator Louis Matlack, with whom Judy consulted a great deal, often worked with families experiencing difficulties over their second home. Of the first steps he prescribed was to write a *Family Mission Statement*. Many corporations and institutions have Mission Statements describing how they see themselves and their purpose. While a large corporation may use its Mission Statement as part of a marketing strategy, a non-profit institution may truly describe its goals and those with whom it tries to work.

Since your family cottage is assuredly non-profit, even if it is incorporated, marketing is not a concern. However, a statement of how your family views your cottage, and what it most values about it, can help give direction to the development of your FOA.

While Mission Statements are by definition brief, usually fewer than two hundred words, and general, they are also positive and to some degree idealistic. An emphasis now on the positive values of your family's cottage will be a good place to start the more difficult parts of the process of developing your Formal Operating Agreement.

I think that the value of doing a Mission Statement at this point is that it looks toward the future, which needs to be both an implicit and explicit focus of your FOA. Hopefully, it also fosters the spirit of cooperation and goodwill that began with articulating your IOA. It should increase a sense of pride in who you are as a family and in the cottage you own, use and love.

These qualities are more important than the actual words of the Statement, something to remember as you go through the process of "wordsmithing". However, the finished Statement might be something that you would want rendered permanently in a form suitable for framing to hang in your cottage. It's an interesting document for visitors to read and a reminder to family members of what you treasure about your cottage.

As to the process of drafting the statement, many people, including me, see writing by committee to be about as much fun as doing your taxes or experiencing a bone marrow biopsy, so we want to make this as painless as possible. One way I would not recommend is to ask all family members to draft a statement and have the Drivers somehow boil them into a finished concoction.

If you as a Driver feel less than comfortable about doing the actual wordsmithing, your Drivers Team or Committee might ask two or three other family members, who perhaps work with words as teachers, writers, lawyers, etc. , to spearhead the process. This brings more family members directly into the overall process and lightens your load.

This is a place where I would strongly encourage you to involve a member of the youngest generation in your family. Children can certainly say what they love about their cottage, perhaps with greater passion than their parents and grandparents. And the future of the cottage is really their future and a good thing for them to think about. Even if the children are too young to actually lead the process, they should definitely be asked for their ideas as to what should go into the Mission Statement.

Whether the Drivers head this up or it's delegated to a Mission Statement Subcommittee, a good way to start is to ask every member of the family to identify three things they love about the cottage and two things they hope for in its future. These can be general, such as, "I love being with family" and "I hope to have my own kids come here someday". They can also be much more specific, like, "I love our pillow fights" and "I hope we can get a kayak".

This consideration of the present, which incorporates the past, and the future, suggests an approach to take for whoever is going to do a first draft. You might think in terms of three sections, one on the past, one on the present, and the final one on the future.

Whoever is in charge of the process should take the statements of the family members and put them into a draft for circulation and suggestions of amendments by everyone. Eventually a final draft can be circulated for approval.

This is not an easy stage of the process but it will go much more smoothly if you remember, and remind others of one important fact: Haggling over a word or short phrase is not important and can only lead to further bickering over more important matters. This is not a legal document with explicit implications for how your family enjoys the cottage. It is a statement of values and ideals that will hopefully guide everyone's enjoyment of your treasured cottage.

Below is what the fictitious Madison family, whom we met in Chapter 4, might have written about their cottage.

THE MADISON MISSION STATEMENT

The Madison family cottage, Whispering Grasses, stands as a tribute to its Founders and the patriarch and matriarch of this branch of the family, Carlton and Ginger. It was their hard work that built the cottage and they invested it with love. Their model of love and devotion can be felt by all as we enjoy summers of relaxation and bliss.

At Whispering Grasses, we relish in the time to forget the stresses of our regular lives and soak up recreation and relaxation. The sun, the water and the beach are focal points of our enjoyment. Working on the yard, in the garden or inside never feels like work; it is a celebration of our family's love. At the end of the day, sitting on the deck watching a gorgeous sunset while children play on the beach is an incomparable pleasure. Sleep comes easily in our snug beds.

We also love to reconnect with our family members, siblings, cousins, aunts and uncles, and learn more about their lives and their growth. We learn from each other new and exciting ways to enjoy the cottage.

We hope that Whispering Grasses will always be a place where the family can gather to celebrate the love of Carlton and Ginger. As the family expands and the cottage ages, we hope to come together in a spirit of cooperation to maintain and utilize this special gift. Each individual will find his/her own way of enjoying the cottage but will always recognize his/her own responsibility to maintaining it as the Madison summer home.

After reading the above Mission Statement, you may be wondering whether it is absolutely necessary—honestly and technically, it's not. Your family could develop a fine FOA without one but I think that it's a very good idea to develop one. And as I look at the clock and see we have five minutes before the end of this class period, I will sum up today's discussion and the reasons why a Mission Statement is a good idea.

1. It involves the whole family in a positive venture, emphasizing all of what is good about the cottage, and fosters a spirit of cooperation.

2. This involvement should include even young children, giving them an idea of what the whole family is doing and why it's important.

3. It can hang in a central focal point of your cottage, reminding all who occupy it why the family loves it so much.

4. It can also serve as a Preamble to your FOA, which in many ways, is a Family Constitution.

CHAPTER 8

LEGAL COUNSEL AND DRAFTING THE FORMAL OPERATING AGREEMENT

If you do not yet have a lawyer to draw up an LLC or other legal document, now would be a good time to find one. You may have a lawyer who handles your personal matters, or a lawyer for the whole family,—who perhaps executed the will of the Founders.

Despite your loyalty to this individual, if he* is not well versed in the issues surrounding ownership of a vacation home, what Stuart Hollander called "cottage law", I would recommend against retaining her.

Instead, I would look for an attorney in the area where your cottage is located. Such attorneys will be more likely to have experience with issues involved in ownership of a family cottage, as well as local matters such as zoning or environmental regulations.

If your vacation area is experiencing feverish growth, some of the local lawyers may be specializing in buying and selling of houses, not in their maintenance and orderly succession. Be sure to quiz a prospective attorney on her experience working with a family toward drafting an FOA or forming an LLC. (I hope the initials aren't confusing. I promise I will use just one other such grouping.)

Before you even begin interviewing attorneys, I think it is very important for you and the other Drivers to have read Hollander's book, *Saving the Family Cottage* (SFC). Even if you decide not to form an LLC, you should know the arguments for one. When you get your copies, available at nolo. com, purchase an extra for the attorney you retain.

This book is easy to read, even for those like me who are befuddled with legal issues and terminology. It is very persuasive that setting up a family Limited Liability Corporation (LLC) is the best way to ensure orderly passing on of your treasured second home.

The attorney you wish to retain may not have experience in setting up LLCs for ownership of family cottages but may have other good qualities. So ask him to read SFC so that then you can all discuss why you want an LLC and literally begin on the same page. Your attorney should research relevant corporate regulations in the state where your family cottage is located, and you might want to look into this as well.

Discussion of SFC will also define just what sort of legal counsel will be necessary and when, and then you can discuss legal fees. You won't need your attorney while you are hammering out a question such as how summer slots are to be allocated. You will need her when you get to such an issue as the right of a family member to demand a buyout of his/her share of the cottage.

I doubt that your attorney will volunteer to mediate the discussion of all the issues in the FOA, and you certainly don't want to be paying an hourly fee for this. However, if he is an experienced mediator and if there are issues where your family is at total loggerheads, then legal mediation may be a good idea.

Below are issues to be addressed in your FOA. I don't claim that this is exhaustive and there'll be issues I have overlooked, so if you think of any of these, be sure to add them.

I will leave space below each question for you to jot down your immediate response. You might also want to consider using the list of questions as a template to circulate among family members and get initial responses.

A number of these questions are addressed in detail in SFC, and Hollander discusses alternative answers that you and your family may not have thought about, so I am going refer to chapters from SFC for your consideration. In posing these questions to your family, you might want to suggest a variety of these answers.

One final piece of advice about your LLC comes from SFC, based on Stuart Hollander's extensive experience with clients who own family cottages:

I remind my clients that a cottage plan is fluid and flexible. This is critical to keep in mind. A plan can change. It doesn't have to be perfect. The important thing is to have a plan in place. You can tinker with it as time goes by. Do not let perfection be the enemy of the perfectly adequate. (p. 179)

If there are issues where the family simply will not agree, even with professional mediation, don't let this sabotage the whole process. It is possible to mention an issue on which there is now no agreement, but that this will be visited again in the future.

This brings me to one important clause in the FOA and LLC. One of the provisions in your LLC should concern its amending. You might want to put in a clause that calls for an informal revisiting in five years, with a formal re-appraisal every ten, as well as how this will occur.

There are three general areas to be addressed in the FOA: *Time-Sharing Issues, Cost-Sharing Issues, and Governance.*

TIME-SHARING ISSUES

1. What model of use will your family use, "Time-Sharing" (family units have season slots) or "Rooming House" (self-explanatory)? See Chapter 13 of SFC.

2. If you choose the Time-Sharing model, which is more common, how many "slots" per season will there be and how long is each slot? See Chapter 13.

3. How is the allocation of slots to be determined, and by whom?

4. If there are more "family units" than slots, how are slots to be assigned or rotated? (A family unit may be anything from a single person, to a single person and partner, traditional nuclear family, senior heir expected to share the cottage with children, etc.)

5. How is "family unit" to be defined and at what point does one have a right to a slot? Age, marriage, children, independent income? This is a very difficult question.

6. *Will certain slots, e. g. July 4th or Labor Day weekends, be more valuable than others? If you get one, do you have to give something up?*

7. *What about pre- and post-season slots? If your family unit can take one when the cottage would be otherwise empty, does this count against your right to a seasonal slot?*

8. *If you can't or choose not to take a slot when eligible, will you get first choice next year or lose your place in the rotation?*

WORK AND COST-SHARING

1. *Who opens and closes the cottage at the beginning and end of the season? If this is contracted out, how is it to be paid for? If family members perform this arduous task, how will they be compensated?*

2. *Will there be a "users' fee" to cover taxes and maintenance, and if not, how is each branch of the family assessed their share?*

3. Who will serve as Financial Manager? Should this position be rotated by fixed terms of office?

4. If a Founder has always managed finances and anticipates continuing to do so, how is a member of the next generation to be chosen and prepared to take over when the Founder retires? This question applies whether the Financial Manager is a Founder, or second or third generation.

5. If family units are assessed shares of expenses, what happens if one unit, because of loss of job, severe illness, etc. is unable to pay their yearly share?

6. What happens if a family unit wants to be bought out of their share? (Chapter 11)

7. Who serves as Cottage Manager, overseeing maintenance and taking responsibility for seeing that minor and major repairs are completed?

8. How will an expensive repair, such as a new roof, be paid for?

9. How is "extreme sweat equity" defined and what is it worth? If you spend half of your slot painting the trim of the cottage, will you be compensated by money or time?

10. Will a log be kept of normal tasks and maintenance each family unit has done, as well as any trouble spots to keep an eye on?

11. What happens when a major appliance gives up the ghost, especially, as it usually happens, when the cottage is filled with guests? Who decides which new refrigerator or washing machine to get, and how is it to be paid for?

12. How and by whom is it to be decided when furnishings and furniture must be replaced, and with what? How will they be paid for?

13. What plans could/should be made to make the house more accessible for a family member who is disabled, either through accident or disease, or the debility of old age?

14. If the family has grown too large, and the cottage is simply too small, how could decisions be made about remodeling or expanding it? These questions include When, How, and Who Pays?

15. Should rental of the cottage be undertaken to defray costs? (See Chapter 14 for a detailed discussion of issues involved in rental.)

16. Is rental to be done by the whole family or could a family unit rent their slot? If they can do this, how is the family compensated?

17. Could a family unit make a gift of part of their slot, for example, as a wedding present or for a charity auction, to non-family members?

18. If elderly family members can no longer use the cottage alone, and must stay with younger members, will the younger family unit be compensated and if so, how?

GOVERNANCE

1. How is the cottage to be managed, directly by members or by managers? (See Chap. 12)

2. How should such roles as Financial Manager, Cottage Manager, and Scheduler be filled? Should these individuals be compensated in some way?

3. If you are a Founder and have been handling all of these roles, how will you handle selecting and preparing successors? How can you establish an orderly process of filling these roles?

4. How often should these roles be rotated among family members? Should there be a restriction against all the roles being assumed by one generation or branch of the family?

5. As the family grows into a fourth and fifth generation, should there be a Board of Trustees, including members of all generations? What should be the duties of such a Board?

6. How can shares in the LLC, and what SFC calls, "The Cottage Club" be transferred? This includes issues of step-children, surviving spouses, and new arrivals. (See Chapter 9).

7. If a member wants to be bought out of his share, how can this be handled? (see Chap. 11)

8. How can federal and state estate taxes be minimized? (See Chapter 15). This is an especially important question if you are a Founder. States vary widely in their taxation policies. Be sure you know the situation in your state.

9. Can any property, e. g. a sailboat, be reserved for one family unit and off limits for others?

10. What rules should there be regarding pets? For example, some families require members with pets to flea bomb the cottage as they leave.

11. Should use of artificial fertilizers, herbicides and insecticides be permitted?

12. Will moderate environmental practices, such as recycling, be required? What about more extreme measures, like a composting toilet?

13. If the cottage is used as a hunting lodge, will any firearms be permitted to stay on the premises? If so, what safety precautions will be taken?

14. What procedure will there be for amending your FOA and LLC?

WRITING TASK

Every family and its circumstances is unique and changing over time so I'm certain that some important issues that your family is dealing with or will inevitably face has been too lightly dealt with or completely overlooked in the scope of this workbook. Once you have retained an attorney, she may suggest other questions that are particularly pertinent in your area.

For this reason I encourage you to:

1. List any and all that you think of not already committed to paper in the course of all the work we've done so far. Do your best to categorize them as Time-Sharing, Cost-Sharing, and Governance.

CHAPTER 9

NOW WHAT?

I hope that soon you will be talking with an attorney that you have trust in, and will be working with your family to develop the Formal Operating Agreement that will be the by-laws of your family LLC.

I want to leave you with a couple of reminders and a couple of other suggestions.

First, include children and adolescents to the absolute maximum that their maturity permits. Remember that they will have to live with this LLC.

Second, recognize as valid all feelings, including negative ones, but keep family members on task.

Third, when you circulate suggested Policies and Practices, use the passive voice, e. g. "It has been suggested that we. . ." rather than the active voice, e. g. "Uncle Bob thinks we ought to. . ." That will help mitigate existing tensions and reduce charges of self-interest in terms of a suggested Policy or Practice.

Finally, as important as any concrete steps in this process will be your modeling of the kind of behavior you want everyone to demonstrate, even if you have painful and legitimate grievances against other family members. Stay calm, bite your tongue, truly listen (ideally with Ginger Madison's "love in your heart"), explain things multiple times if necessary, and retain optimism that your family can do this.

In other words, emulate St. Francis of Assisi, Mohandas Ghandi, Eleanor Roosevelt, Martin Luther King, Jr. or whoever your hero of peace and understanding may be. The scars on your tongue will be your badge of honor.

WRITING TASK

The final one! Yee ha!

1. Describe your feelings right now.

2. Identify the reasons why your family will be successful in this endeavor.

BIBLIOGRAPHY

Akasie, Jay. 1999. "1999 *Forbes* Money Guide." Forbes 163:12 (June 14).

_____. 1996. "Passing on the Summer House Is a Family Affair." *The Nantucket Inquirer and Mirror*. July 11. Al, C7.

Aldrich, Nelson W., Jr. 1991. Old Money: *The Mythology of America's Upper Class*. New York: Vintage Book.

Balfe, Judith Huggins. 1995. "The Inheritance of Summer Houses and Cultural Identity." *The American Sociologist* 26:4. 29-40.

Bengston, Vern L. and Robert A. Harootyan. 1994. *Intergenerational Linkages: Hidden Connections in American Society*. New York: Spring Publishing Company and AARP.

Bengston, Vern L. and Tonya M. Parrott. 1995. "The Problem of Equity and the Changing Contract across Generations." Annual Meeting of the American Sociological Association. Washington, DC. August.

Berger, Joseph, Cecilia L. Ridgeway, M. Hamit Fisek and Robert Z. Norman. 1998. "The Legitimation and Delegitimation of Power and Prestige Orders." *American Sociological Review* 63:3 (June).379-405.

Berger, Peter and Richard Neuhaus. 1977. 76 *To Empower People*. Washington, DC: American Enterprise Institute.

Blau, Peter and Otis Dudley Duncan. 1967. *The American Occupational Structure*. New York: Wiley.

Blaydon, Colin C. and Carol B. Stack. 1977. "Income Support Policies and the Family. *Deadalus* 109:2. 147-161.

Brams, Steven J. and Alan D. Taylor. 1996. Fair Division: From Cake-Cutting to Dispute Resolution. New York: Cambridge University Press.

Brown, Paula, Harold Brookfield and Robin Grau. 1990. "Land Tenure and Transfer in Chimbu, Papua-New Guinea: 1958-1984- A Study in Continuity and Change, Accomodation and Opportunism." Human Ecology 18:1 (March). 21-49.

Canadine, David. 1990. The Decline and Fall of the British Aristocracy. New Haven: Yale University Press.

Cheever, Susan. 1991. Treetops: A Family Memoir. New York: Bantam Books.

Clignet, Remi. 1992. *Death, Deeds and Descendants: Inheritance in Modern America*. New York: Walter de Gruyter.

_____. 1995. "Efficiency, Reciprocity and Ascriptive Equality: The Three Major Strategies Governing the Selection of Heirs in America." Social Science Quarterly 76 (June). 274-293.

_____. 1998. "Ethnicity and Inheritance." Inheritance and Wealth in America, Robert K. Miller Jr. and Stephen J. McNamee, eds. New York: Plenum Press.121-138.

Coontz, Stephanie. 1997. *The Way We Really Are: Coming to Terms with America's Changing Families*. New York: Basic Books.

Cross, Amy Willard. 1992. *The Summer House: A Tradition of Leisure*. Toronto: Harper Collins.

Curtis, Richard F. 1986. "Household and Family in Theory on Inequality." *American Sociological Review* 51 (April). 168-183.

Dagnall, Sally W. 1984. *Martha's Vineyard Camp Meeting Association 1835-1985*. Oak Bluffs, MA: Martha's Vineyard Camp Meeting Association.

Dart, Bob. 1995. "Summer House Legacy Continues." *Rochester Democrat and Chronicle*. (Cox News Service). Aug. 26. 3E.

Davis, Leverett B. 1974. "Own the Whole Island?" *Country Journal*. November. 38-41.

Diesenhouse, Susan. 1997. "Keeping Vacation Homes in the Family." *The New York Times*. October 10. 10:1, 8.

Domhoff, G. William. 1970. *The Higher Circles: The Governing Class in America*. New York: Random House.

Ellickson, Robert C. 1991. *Order Without Law: How Neighbors Settle Disputes*. Cambridge, MA: Harvard University Press.

Elster, Jon. 1992. *Local Justice: How Institutions Allocate Scarce Goods and Necessary Burdens*. Troy, NY: Russell Sage Foundation.

GeRue, Gene. 1996. *How to Find Your Ideal Country Home*, 2nd ed. Zanoni, MO: Heartwood Publications.

Goody, Jack. 1970. "Sideways or Downwards? Lateral and Vertical Succession, Inheritance and Descent in Africa and Eurasia." Man 5:4. 627-638.

Goody, Jack, Joan Thirsk and E.P. Thompson, eds. 1976. *Family and Inheritance: Rural Society in Western Europe 1200 - 1800*. New York: Cambridge University Press.

Greenhouse, Carol J. 1983. "Being and Doing: Competing Concepts of Elite Status in an American Suburb." *Elites: Ethnographic Issues,* George E. Marcus, ed. Albuquerque, NM: University of New Mexico Press. 113-140.

Greven, Philip J. Jr. 1978. "Family Structure in 17th Century Andover." *The American Family is Social-Historical Perspective* 2nd ed, Michael Gordon, ed. New York: St. Martin's Press. 20-37.

Hamnett, Chris. 1991. "A Nation of Inheritors? Housing Inheritance, Wealth and Inequality in Britain." *Journal of Social Policy* 20:4. 509-536.

Hays, William C. and Charles H. Mindel. 1973. "Extended Kinship Relations in Black and White Families." *Journal of Marriage and the Family* 35:1. 51-57.

Hershey, Robert D. Jr. 1998. "With Favorable Loans, a Generation Discovers Second Homes." *The New York Times.* July 19. 9:4.

Hill, Reuben. 1970. *Family Development in Three Generations: a Longitudinal Study of Changing Family Patterns of Planning and Achievement.* Cambridge, MA: Shenkman Publishing Co.

Howell, Cicely. 1976. "Peasant Inheritance Customs in the Midlands, 1280-1700." *Family and Inheritance: Rural Society in Western Europe 1200 - 1800.* Jack Goody et al, eds. New York: Cambridge University Press. 112-135.

Huizinga, Johan. 1955 (1938). *Homo Ludens: A Study of the Play Element in Culture.* Boston: Beacon Press.

_____. (1924). *The Waning of the Middle Ages.* Garden City, NY: Doubleday Anchor.

Irish, Donald P. 1964. "Sibling Interaction: A Neglected Aspect in Family Life Research." *Social Forces* 42:3 (March). 279-288.

Johnson, Barry W. and Martha Britton Eller. 1998. "Federal Taxation of Inheritance and Wealth Transfers." *Inheritance and Wealth in America.* Robert K. Miller, Jr. and Stephen J. McNamee, eds. New York: Plenum Press. 61-90.

Kart, Cary S. and Carol Engler. 1985. "Family Relations of Aged Colonial Jews: a Testamentary Analysis." *Ageing and Society* 5. 289-304.

Kirstein, George G. 1968. *The Rich: Are They Different?* New York: Houghton Mifflin.

Klagsbrun, Francine. 1992. *Mixed Feelings: Love, Hate, Rivalry and Reconciliation Among Brothers and Sisters.* New York: Bantam Books.

Koburn, Frances. 1978. "The Fall of Household Size and the Rise of the Primary Individual in the United States." *The American Family in Social-Historical Perspective,* 2nd ed., Michael Gordon, ed. New York: St. Martins Press. 69-81.

Kutner, Lawrence. 1992. "Parent & Child: Strife Among Grown Siblings Can Split a Family." *The New York Times.* July 16: C12.

Lamont, Michele. 1992. *Money, Morals and Manners: The Culture of the French and American Upper-Middle Class.* Chicago: University of Chicago Press.

Lebsock, Suzanne. 1984. *The Free Women of Petersburg: Status and Culture in a Southern Town.* New York: W.W. Norton.

Logan, John R. and Glenna D. Spitze. 1996. *Family Ties: Enduring Relations between Parents and Their Grown Children.* Philadelphia: Temple University Press.

Low, Setha M. 1994. "Cultural Conservation of Place." *Conserving Culture: A New Discourse on Heritage.* Mary Hufford, ed. Champagne-Urbana: University of Illinois Press. 66-77.

Marcus, George E. 1983a. "Elite Communities and Institutional Orders." *Elites: Ethnographic Issues,* George E. Marcus, ed. Albuquerque NM: University of New Mexico Press. 41-58.

Marcus, George E. 1983b. "The Fiduciary Role in American Dynasties and Their Institutional Legacy: From the Law of Trusts to Trust in the Establishment." *Elites: Ethnographic Issues.* George E. Marcus, ed. Albuquerque NM: University of New Mexico Press. 221-256.

Mark, Noah. 1998. "Beyond Individual Differences: Social Differentiation from First Principles." *American Sociological Review.* 63:3 (June). 309-330.

Matlack, Louis R. 1998. Personal communication.

McNamee, Stephen J. and Robert K. Miller, Jr. 1989. "Estate Inheritance: A Sociological Lacuna." *Sociological Inquiry* 59:1 (February). 7-29.

_____. 1998. "Inheritance and Stratification." *Inheritance and Wealth in America,* Robert K. Miller, Jr. and Stephen J. McNamee, eds. New York: Plenum Press. 193-214.

Mead, George Herbert. 1932. *The Philosophy of the Present,* Arthur E. Murphy, ed. Chicago: University of Chicago Press.

_____. 1934. Mind, Self & Society, Charles W. Morris, ed. Chicago: University of Chicago Press.

Miller, Robert K. Jr. and Stephen J. McNamee. 1998. "Inheritance and Wealth in America." *Inheritance and Wealth in America,* Robert K. Miller Jr. and Stephen J. McNamee, eds. New York: Plenum Press. 1-22.

Millman, Marcia. 1991. *Warm Hearts and Cold Cash: The Intimate Dynamics of Families. and Money.* New York: The Free Press.

Munro, Moira. 1988. "Housing Wealth and Inheritance." *Journal of Social Policy,* 17:4. 417-436.

Newman, Katherine S. 1993. *Declining Fortunes: The Withering of the American Dream*. New York: Basic Books.

Ogionwo, W. 1975. "Family Structure and Development: Cart and Horse or Chicken and Egg?" *International Journal of the Family* 5:1 (Spring). 53-65.

Otto, Herbert A. 1977. "The Family Value Fugue Incident: Initial Exploration of a Neglected Area." *The Family Coordinator.* (January). 13-17.

Ridgeway, Cecelia L, Elizabeth Heger Boyle, Kathy J. Kuipers and Dawn T. Robinson. "How Do Status Beliefs Develop? The Role of Resources and Interactional Experience." *American Sociological Review* 63:3 (June). 331-350.

Romano, Jay. 1997. "When a Summer Home is Not a Vacation." *The New York Times.* April 13. 9: 1, 6.

Rosenfeld, Jeffrey P. 1980. "Social Strain of Probate." *Journal of Marital and Family Therapy* (July). 327-334.

Rosow, Irving. 1964. "Intergenerational Relationships: Problems and Proposals." *Social Structure and the Family: Intergenerational Relations*, Ethel Shanas and Gordon F. Streib, eds. New York: Prentice-Hall. 341-378.

Saari, Jon. 1996. "Upper Peninsula Summer Camps: An Historical Look at Their Place in Our Lives and Nature." Unpublished paper. Marquette, MI: Northern Michigan University.

Satow, Roberta. 1993a. "Strangers in Paradise: Class, Status and Ethnicity in a Connecticut Town." *Research in Community Sociology*, Vol 3. Greenwich, CT: JAI Press. 113-135.

_____. 1993b. "New Yorkers in the Countryside: Status Conflict and Social Change." *Journal of Contemporary Ethnography* 22:2 (July). 227-248.

Scher, Les and Carol Scher. 1992. *Finding and Buying Your Place in the Country*, Pled. Chicago: Dearborn Financial Publishing, Inc.

Schorr, Lisbeth B. 1997. *Common Purpose: Strengthening Families and Neighborhoods to Rebuild America*. New York: Doubleday Anchor.

Segalen, Martine. 1984. "'Avoir sa part': Sibling Relations in Partible Inheritance in Brittany." *Interest and Emotion: Essays on the Study of Family and Kinship*, Hans Medick and David Warren Sabean, eds. New York: Cambridge University Press. 129-144.

Sena-Rivera, Jaime. 1979. "Extended Kinship in the United States: Competing Models and the Case of La Familia Chicana. *Journal of Marriage and Family* 41:1. 121-129.

Sennett, Richard. 1972. *The Hidden Injuries of Class*. New York: Knopf.

Shammas, Carole, Marylynn Salmon and Michel Dahlin. 1987. *Inheritance in American from Colonial Times to the Present*. New Brunswick: Rutgers University Press.

Simmel, Georg. 1955 (1904). "The Sociology of Conflict." Conflict and the Web of Group Affiliations, ed.& tr. Kurt H. Wolff. New York: The Free Press. 11-124.

_____. 1971a (1903). "The Metropolis and Mental Life" (tr. Edward A. Shils). *Georg Simmel on Individuality and Social Forms*, Donald N. Levine, ed. Chicago: University of Chicago Press. 324-339.

_____. 1971b (1910). "Sociability" (tr. Everett C. Hughes). *Georg Simmel on Individuality and Social Forms*, Donald N. Levine, ed. Chicago: University of Chicago Press. 127-140.

_____. 1971c (1918). "The Conflict in Modern Culture" (tr. K. Peter Etzkorn). Georg Simmel *On Individuality and Social Forms*, Donald N. Levine, ed. Chicago: University of Chicago Press. 375-393.

Simon, Rita, William Rau and Mary Louise Fellows. 1980. "Public Versus Statutory Choice of Heirs: A Study of Public Attitudes about Property Distribution at Death." *Social Forces* 58:4 (June). 1263-1271.

Small, Stephen J. 1992. *Preserving Family Lands: Essential Tax Strategies for the Landowner*, rev. 2nd ed. Boston, MA: Landowner Planning Center.

_____. 1997. *Preserving Family Lands: Book II: More Planning Strategies for the Future*. Boston, MA: Landowner Planning Center.

Spillerman, Seymour. 1994. "Wealth and Stratification Processes." Department of Sociology Colloquium. New York: City University of New York Graduate Center. November 11.

Spreitzer, Elmer, Robert Schoeni and K.V. Rao. 1995. "Tracing Intergenerational Relations through Reports of Transfers of Time and Money: A Comparative Study of African-Americans, Hispanics and Whites." Annual Meeting of the American Sociological Association. Washington, DC. August 21.

Stark, Oded. 1995. *Altruism and Beyond: An Economic Analysis of Transfers and Exchanges within Families and Groups*. New York: Cambridge University Press.

Stegner, Wallace. 1987. *Crossing to Safety*. New York: Penguin Books.

Sweeney, Paul. 1997. "Taking Time to Unwrap the Family Finances." *The New York Times*. December 17. 3:4.

Thompson, E.P. 1976. "The Grid of Inheritance: A Comment." *Family and Inheritance: Rural Society in Western Europe 1200 - 1800*, Jack Goody et al, eds. New York: Cambridge University Press. 328-360.

Titus, Sandra L, Paul C. Rosenblatt and Roxanne M. Anderson. 1979. "Family Conflict Over Inheritance of Property." *The Family Coordinator* (July). 337-346.

Tyson, James L. 1995. "Family Values Bolstered by Summer Homes." *The Christian Science Monitor.* September 25. 15.

Volgenau, Gerald. 1995. "There's No Place Like (a Summer) Home." *The Detroit Free Press.* September 6. El, 4.

Verdon, Michel. 1979. "The Stern Family: Toward a General Theory." *Journal of Interdisciplinary History* 10: I . 87-105.

Waller, Kim. 1991. "Thoughts of Home: A Family, an Island." *Town and Country* (September). 15-16.

Weber, Max. 1946 (1920). "Bureaucracy." From Max Weber, Hans Gerth & C. Wright Mills, ed. & tr. New York: Oxford University Press. 190-244.

_____. 1958 (1904-5). *The Protestant Ethic and the Spirit of Capitalism*, tr. Talcott Parsons. New York: Charles Scribner's Sons.

Webster, Murray, Jr. and Stuart J. Hysom. 1998. "Creating Status Characteristics." *American Sociological Review* 63:3 (June). 351-378.

Young, H. Peyton. 1994. *Equity in Theory and Practice* Princeton NJ: Princeton University Press.

Zelizer, Viviana A. 1989. "The Social Meaning of Money: 'Special Monies.'" *American Journal of Sociology* 95:2 (September). 342-377.

_____. 1990. *The Social Meaning of Money*. New York: Basic Books.

ABOUT THE AUTHORS

Judith Huggins Balfe was Professor of Sociology at the City University of New York, at two of its colleges: The College of Staten Island and the Graduate Center. Her many publications focus on the sociology of the arts and culture, in which she examines one of the primary themes of this book: the conflict between price and value, between market forces and what people find most meaningful. In analyzing the connections between these seeming polarities, she draws upon her experience as a co-owner of a summer house in Nantucket — which was the seed for this extensive study.

Judy's brother, Ken Huggins, Assistant Professor of English at Monroe Community College outside of Rochester, NY, has written *How to Pass It On: The Ownership and Use of Summer Houses,* the companion workbook to *Passing It On.* It presents two "composite" families based upon the countless interviews conducted by Judy of families struggling with the issues related to ownership, sharing, and the transmission by inheritance of summer houses and family cottages. Although fictitious, these families are all too real as they reflect many of the myriad dynamics and challenges to harmony in sharing and co-owning cherished family retreats. *How To Pass It On* includes important exercises and questions that must be explored and answered by those working to resolve difficulties in collective ownership of a summer house, family cottage, or any jointly-used/jointly-owned family property.

To reach Ken Huggins please use the contact form at our website: **www.howtopassiton.com**, where additional copies of this book can be ordered.

Made in the USA
Las Vegas, NV
25 September 2023

78134279R00142